GRAY
DAY

# GRAY DAY

My Undercover Mission to

Expose America's

First Cyber Spy

## ERIC O'NEILL

CROWN
NEW YORK

Copyright © 2019 by Eric M. O'Neill

All rights reserved.
Published in the United States by Crown, an imprint of the Crown Publishing Group, a division of Penguin Random House LLC, New York. crownpublishing.com

CROWN and the Crown colophon are registered trademarks of Penguin Random House LLC.

Library of Congress Cataloging-in-Publication Data
Names: O'Neill, Eric, author.
Title: Gray day : my undercover mission to expose America's first cyber spy / Eric O'Neill.
Description: First edition. | New York : Crown Publishers, 2019.
Identifiers: LCCN 2018038605 (print) | LCCN 2018048826 (ebook) | ISBN 9780525573548 (ebook) | ISBN 9780525573524 (hardback) | ISBN 9780525573531 (paperback)
Subjects: LCSH: Hanssen, Robert. | O'Neill, Eric. | United States. Federal Bureau of Investigation. | Cyber intelligence (Computer security) | Spies—Russia (Federation)—Biography. | Spies—United States—Biography. | Intelligence service—United States. | BISAC: POLITICAL SCIENCE / Political Freedom & Security / Intelligence. | BIOGRAPHY & AUTOBIOGRAPHY / Personal Memoirs. | COMPUTERS / Security / Viruses.
Classification: LCC UB271.R92 (ebook) | LCC UB271.R92 H37153 2019 (print) | DDC 327.1247073092 [B] —dc23
LC record available at https://lccn.loc.gov/2018038605

ISBN 978-0-525-57352-4
Ebook ISBN 978-0-525-57354-8

Printed in the United States of America

Book design: Lauren Dong
Jacket design: Evan Gaffney
Jacket photograph: Bernd Vogel/Corbis/Getty Images

10 9 8 7 6 5 4 3 2 1

First Edition

*To my mother, Vivian*
*The bravest person I've ever known*

# Contents

GRAY
DAY

# CHAPTER 1

# TIPPING POINTS

December 10, 2000—Sunday

Phones should not ring on Sunday mornings. I rolled across the bed, scooped my battered Nokia from the nightstand, and burrowed back under the covers. Our English basement apartment reminded me of winter camping trips I'd gone on as a Boy Scout. The single-pane windows trapped about as much heat as a canvas tent.

Juliana peered at me over the thick comforter. Her eyes were glazed with sleep, and her blond hair was piled around her head like windblown thistle. We'd been married four months, and each morning I woke beside her was a revelation. I checked the time—8:00 a.m. I was about to slap the phone down on the receiver when the voice on the other end made me freeze. All thoughts of a lazy morning flushed out of my mind. It was Supervisory Special Agent Gene McClelland.

"Don't bother getting dressed up," he said. "Just lace up your shoes. I'm parked out front."

As I fumbled for my pants, my mind raced through possible scenarios, all of them grim. It was unheard-of for an FBI supervisor, the man in charge of my entire squad, to show up at a private residence on a Sunday morning. To put this into perspective, imagine your boss—the president or manager of your company—arriving at your house early one weekend morning. If you are the boss, imagine the chairman of your board parked in your driveway. If you are the chairman, imagine POTUS himself dropping by, waiting for you to appear. This was worse than any of that.

FBI supervisors never come to you. They summon. Gene showing up at my apartment could only mean something was wrong. I pulled a George Washington University Law sweatshirt over my head and took a deep breath. "No idea what's going on, but Gene is parked outside." The concern on Juliana's face made me pause. "I'll be right back." Then I swallowed my hollow words and turned to leave.

I eased through the front door out onto the sparse lawn. Number 626 was only a few steps away from E Street, and a quick jog away from the US Capitol Building. Our building squatted between expensive town houses like an ugly sibling in a family portrait. The crammed one-bedroom sometimes felt like a closet, and we'd found mold behind the walls and in the lone heater, but it was all we could afford.

As the wind hit my face, I looked up. No one on the surrounding rooftops or balconies. I did a quick lateral scan and saw the red splash of a cardinal light upon a telephone wire. A runner huffed his Spandexed way down E Street, and the distant noise of traffic droned from nearby Pennsylvania Avenue like waves on a beach. Only one car I didn't recognize was parked on the street. Gene.

Each step away from the building made me wince, but no SWAT vans came crashing around the corner, sirens blazing. Instead, the window of the idling sedan rolled down. "Get in," Gene said.

I slid into the passenger seat and closed the door against the December chill.

Gene didn't bother with niceties. "Have you ever heard of Robert Hanssen?"

I hadn't. "Should I have?" I asked.

"No," Gene smiled. "That's good."

I nodded.

"That's why we chose you."

I stayed silent, trying to parse the insult from the compliment. The only certainty was that I'd been left in the dark—again. For months now, I hadn't been able to pursue any of my normal, high-priority targets for the FBI. I'd been slapped on the wrist, shuffled into the minor league. Not because I'd messed up a lead or bungled a case, but because I'd married Juliana—a German national.

No one had told me that FBI operatives with high security clearance are required to fill out a permission form *before* proposing to the love of their life. The FBI had instituted the policy after a few agents married into the mob. Meet the perfect girl, marry her, and then learn that her father is an FBI organized-crime target. Not the brightest moments for the universe's premier investigative agency.

Still, imagine my shock when I bounced into the office to let my team know that I'd proposed marriage to the most wonderful girl, and my supervisor asked after my engagement form.

Then imagine me telling the FBI brass that my new bride hailed from Brandenburg, Germany. Faces that were rarely cheerful turned to stone. "You should have reported contact with an East German national," they said.

"Don't you mean German national?" I asked. "Haven't you heard of reunification? There is no more East Germany."

"Not to us."

The FBI benched me while the FBI legat, or legal attaché office, in Germany investigated my in-laws. Think of a whale trapped on a sandy beach desperate to get back into the water. That was me. I sat in the office day after day with a suspended security clearance, working on a target-acquisition database I'd developed, until the FBI convinced itself that Juliana was not a spy. The investigation into Juliana's family occurred before I had a chance to meet them, and I'm still pretty convinced my in-laws think I'm Stasi. They aren't far off.

By this point I'd been in the FBI nearly five years working as an investigative specialist, otherwise known as an "investigator," but better known as a ghost. Not too many years before I typed up my FBI application, the agency realized that Russian targets could run circles around special agents, who focused on criminal investigations and technological and research-based counterintelligence. This was especially the case just after World War II, when a target could look over his shoulder and see a legion of buzz-cut, well-suited white males swarming him. Not exactly subtle. Without specialized surveillance and undercover investigative training, the agents were at a constant disadvantage: the Russians had more operatives and better tradecraft. The FBI was stuck solving crimes after the fact, when what it needed to do was stop the spies before they committed those crimes.

The special agents were already overburdened. So the agency decided to try something new. In the age-old tradition of American innovation, we traveled back across the pond to learn how MI5 handles surveillance in the United Kingdom through a specialized group called the Watchers. MI5's secretive group had elevated surveillance to an art form. Nothing would stand between a Watcher and his target. A story I once heard placed two Watchers in a canoe floating within a murky water tower, watching their target through a hole drilled in the tower's metal shell. There were a lot of stories like that. The FBI took everything the Watchers could do and made it better. The ghosts were born.

My training allowed me to follow a person from sunup to sundown, know what he ate for breakfast, and count how many times he tied his shoes or checked his watch. I could track each smile, know whom he met or whom he tried to avoid, log where he went and how he got there and everything in between. I'd learn his tradecraft and look like I'd practiced it longer than he had. I was a professional driver and photographer, didn't need to sleep, and could stare at a single door for hours, just waiting for him to walk through.

My dark brown hair, hazel eyes, and slightly olive complexion—a gift from my Italian mother—meant that I could easily pass for a number of ethnicities, and thanks to my father's burly genes, I could grow a beard in a matter of days. I was a master of disguise, of social engineering, of sweet-talking my way past situations. I had a badge but never used it. A target might see me a dozen times across a day's work, but he wouldn't notice me. I was trained to blend into situations, to find cover in plain sight, to look unobtrusive, uninteresting, and unremarkable. I'd call in a spy before he spied or committed an act of terrorism, then melt into the shadows while he was still wondering where all the FBI agents had suddenly come from. I knew how to be gray.

"Who's Hanssen?" I asked.

Gene shrugged. "We think he's a spy. We want you to investigate him."

It took me a moment to get the words past my teeth. "Gene. You woke me up on a Sunday morning, dragged me out of bed, scared the hell out of me by coming here, all to ask me to do my job? Couldn't this have waited until Monday?"

Gene shook his head. "We don't want you to ghost him, Eric. We want you to investigate him. Face-to-face."

I sat there, frozen.

"We need someone on the ground with him," Gene explained. "To develop a relationship, try to get some dirt. I've recommended you."

I opened and closed my mouth like a guppy gasping for oxygen. Gene had asked me to participate in what amounted to an elicitation operation—one where the undercover asset engages in conversation, memorizes details, learns facts, and draws out information. I'd been involved in high-risk cases, but I'd never been instructed to interact with a target face-to-face; my job was to play a backstage part out of sightlines. For the first time, Gene was asking me to play myself. I probably did look like a fish—one miles away from water.

"I need your answer. In or out."

There are tipping points in every life. Tiny moments in time when we're forced to make a choice: take the leap or stand by and let the opportunity pass. These are the moments that shape a future.

This was one of mine.

"What do I tell Juliana?"

Gene scratched his head. "I dunno. Tell her you got promoted. You'll be assigned to a computer job at headquarters." His eyes hardened. "I don't have to tell you to keep the rest quiet. As far as you are concerned, the only people that know about this are you and me. Juliana can't know anything."

I got it. Although Juliana knew I worked for the FBI, we had a deal never to discuss it. She once told me that she enjoyed having a husband who never spoke about work. We'd talk about other things—hopes and dreams, the drama her fellow business students got up to, our long-running debate about whether American football was better than European soccer—but never about what I did all day.

"Gene," I said. "I'm keying in on the word 'promotion.' If I really need to sell this . . ." Now I was the one smiling.

"Okay, okay, Eric." Gene's short chuckle faded into a cough. "I'll get you some extra overtime. You'll more than earn it." He put the car into drive. "In or out."

I leapt.

Target: Robert Hanssen

Suspected spy

# CHAPTER 2

# THE TYRANNY OF SECRETS

There is no such thing as a lie detector. Despite numerous advances in behavioral science and technology, a person cannot use facial expressions or verbal "tells" to sniff out a lie with a great deal of certainty. Nor can a machine measure the thoughts that speed through a person's mind.

How do crack investigators sort lies from truth when they have a suspect in the interview chair? They combine a little psychology, a little technology, and a dash of Hollywood stagecraft. The standard polygraph machine measures pulse, blood pressure, respiration, and skin conductivity while a person is asked specific questions. Today these metrics are graphed on a computer screen, but in the past the machine scratched ink across an ever-expanding roll of graph paper. In theory, a deceptive response to a particular question will spike some or all of the physiological indicators—a quickened pulse, a sweaty palm.

But the machine is not infallible, and accurate results require an expert examiner. Spies have developed many ploys and countermeasures to defeat the machine. An old story about Russian spymasters stands out: When American moles were being trained by their Russian handlers to make dead drops and other clandestine exchanges, the Russian intelligence officer in charge provided advice on how to defeat a US intelligence agency's standard polygraph. One such countermeasure, typical of Russia's often brutal espionage tactics, was to step on a tack that the spy had hidden in the toe of his shoe during the examination. The severe pain would provide a necessary physiological spike at tactical moments in order to fool the examiner.

To join the FBI as a counterintelligence investigator, I needed to receive a top-secret security clearance. And to do that, I needed to pass a polygraph.

Of course, I didn't have a tack in my shoe during my first examination. The FBI called me into a gloomy room in a nondescript office building sandwiched between a coffee shop and a shoe store. A man in shirtsleeves and a tie—security badge on a lanyard around his neck and a pile of paperwork on his lap—sat me in a chair facing the door. With practiced motions, he fit a thick band across the midpoint of my chest, right at my diaphragm, and clipped sensors onto the fingers of my right hand. A blood-pressure cuff squeezed my upper arm. Numerous wires and cables trailed from the various attachments on my body to a metal box on a side table. Nothing about the situation made me comfortable.

The questions he asked made me recall an initial step in my background investigation—half a year before I ended up strapped in the polygraph chair. One Sunday morning after I first applied to the FBI, a retired agent had shown up unannounced at the town house I shared with three roommates. I was in my early twenties, and when the doorbell rang, I was sitting on the couch with an old friend, recovering after a wild Saturday night. Christian and I had known each other since we were ten. After over a decade of friendship, he knew where I hid my skeletons.

The agent who appeared on that Sunday morning hoped to interview my roommates—a standard part of the background-check process. When he learned that my housemates were out, he pointed toward Christian and said, "Who's that?"

"My best friend of ten years," I said.

The agent smiled. "He'll do." He looked at me. "Why don't you go upstairs for a while?"

An hour later, I rejoined Christian on the couch. My old friend answered my impatience with a perplexed face.

"Strange questions," he said.

"Like what?"

" 'Have you ever known Eric to injure or torture small animals or seek their death?' "

We both had a chuckle at that one. The next question was about my relationship with money. Was I frugal or a spendthrift? Did I have a gambling problem, or take risks with money, or seem to go through large amounts of it?

No worries there either.

"The third question though . . ." He paused. " 'Has he ever been known to drink excessively, or have a problem with alcohol, or drink more than a few alcoholic drinks in any one day?' "

I pressed my palms into my eyes and pushed away the lingering headache from the party the night before.

"What did you say?"

He grinned and shrugged. Probably the same expressions he'd used with the agent. "No more than anyone else I know."

In that moment, I thought my best friend had doomed me to never make it into the FBI. I'd flunk my security clearance, get a form letter thanking me for my interest, and have to go find a desk job at some consulting firm that would suck away at my soul, hour by hour.

Instead, I passed. It probably helped that I'm an Eagle Scout, have never touched an illegal drug in my life, and come from a line of upstanding attorneys and military officers. Whatever the case, I finally found myself in a polygraph examination, the last step before securing the clearance that would start my new career, again doubting I'd pass.

"Stop whatever it is you're doing," the examiner said. "You're doing something with your breathing that will get you an inconclusive. I can't pass you with an inconclusive. I don't pass you, you don't get into the FBI."

I focused on my breath. I'd studied martial arts for the majority of my life, which meant I'd learned to control my breathing to reduce stress and promote calmness. But for the polygraph to work, the examiner needed to create stress to establish my normal patterns. I had to unlearn years of study, stat.

I also had to lie. The tester needed to catch me in an easy falsehood so that he could establish a baseline when he got to the questions that actually mattered to him. The problem for both of us was that I didn't have much to lie about. When it came to the kinds of youthful indiscretions polygraph examiners tend to ask about—stealing candy bars, smoking pot, cheating on tests—I was clean as a whistle.

Then he asked me if I'd ever lied to someone who loves me. He prefaced the question by making it clear, in no uncertain terms, that if I had, he would fail me. I pictured my mother. Over the past five years, Parkinson's disease had drawn her ready smile into a perpetual frown. A few days earlier, she'd asked me how she looked, and I'd said, "Perfect." It was the first lie I'd ever told her.

The polygraph examiner scrutinized me. "No," I answered. The needle raced across the page, the first rapid movement since the examination began. The examiner had his baseline. His next question was whether a foreign national had ever approached me to request anything, or to ask about my application to the FBI. I relaxed and answered "no." The needle ceased its furious scribbling and found the center of the page. I passed.

The intelligence community initiates new members into a tyranny of secrets. It is within this mind-set that spies and counterintelligence operatives—those who hunt the spies before they can steal, disrupt, or spread disinformation—operate. The two most important rules for a spy: don't get caught; and if compromised, lie. A counterintelligence operative follows a similar but far more difficult mandate: say nothing about your secrets. But just as in the biblical story of Adam and Eve, eating from the tree of knowledge can have unintended consequences, and a secret can corrode from within.

Some scholars claim that Tsar Ivan IV Vasilyevich, also known as Ivan the Terrible, established Russia's first spy services in the sixteenth century. But it was during the Cold War that the Soviet Union turned espionage into an art form. Russian spymasters launched massive collection campaigns to recruit American moles from within the FBI, CIA, and NSA. At the same time, they were pioneering *desinformatsiya* practices that spread disinformation and disruption in order to shape American political decisions. These active-measure (*aktivinyye meropriatia*) disinformation campaigns included media manipulation; use of front organizations (like the US affiliate of the World Peace Council, a secret Soviet affiliate) to sway public opinion; kidnappings; and provision of funds, training, and support to terrorist organizations, to name a few. In 1980, the CIA estimated that the Soviets spent a conservative $3 billion per year pursuing active measures. In his February 6, 1980, congressional testimony, John McMahon, the CIA deputy director for operations, stated that the Soviets' active-measures network was "second to none in comparison to the major world powers in its size and effectiveness."

The 1980s saw a number of audacious—and highly successful—disinformation campaigns. One involved spreading rumors of CIA and FBI involvement in President John F. Kennedy's assassination. Another seeded foreign newspapers with articles—purportedly written by American scientists—claiming that AIDS was the result of the Pentagon's experiments to develop biological weapons. During the 1984 Summer Olympics in Moscow, KGB spies in Washington, DC, sent fake letters from the KKK threatening athletes from African countries, an active measure many believe was a response to President Jimmy Carter's boycott of the 1980 Moscow Games.

Yet for all its successes abroad, the Soviet Union was suffering from serious internal tensions. In the late 1980s, massive independence protests swept across the Caucasus and the Baltic states, and soon the USSR's constituent republics began to secede. On August 18, 1991, military and government hardliners staged a coup against Mikhail Gorbachev. The coup collapsed within days, but the match continued to burn. In December 1991, Gorbachev announced the dissolution of the Soviet Union and his resignation as president. Television audiences across the former USSR watched as Boris Yeltsin lowered the hammer-and-sickle flag from atop the Kremlin for the last time and raised the tricolor flag as president of a newly independent Russian state.

During all this upheaval, former KGB spymasters—now out of a job—were raiding the agency's file cabinets. The documents they stole would serve as insurance policies for better lives elsewhere. For many, that meant the United States, which offered Levi's jeans, Diet Cokes—and what often amounted to millions of dollars in exchange for the slim files they gave to the FBI. The United States gobbled up their secrets, and the United Kingdom and other friendly intelligence services caught what we missed. The FBI and MI6 pooled the information they'd obtained, which led to a series of arrests of Russian assets within the United States. The biggest catch was Aldrich Ames, a CIA analyst turned KGB mole, whose disclosures had led to the death of many CIA and FBI assets overseas. When asked how he'd passed CIA polygraph tests during his spy career, Ames had laughed: "Confidence and a friendly rapport with the examiner." But as damaging as Ames was, his espionage couldn't account for all of the US intelligence operations that had failed without warning. Someone was continuing to corrupt the intelligence community. Someone even worse than Ames.

The intelligence community had long sought a Russian mole code-named "Gray Suit." Every ghost on the street hoped that the spy they were following might turn out to be him. He was our Billy the Kid, our Blackbeard. And so far, he'd eluded the FBI's best spy catchers. That didn't stop us from hunting.

In the meantime, FBI counterintelligence units had mountains of leads to follow thanks to the former KGB defectors. My commission as an FBI investigative specialist had come just as the agency was sorting through those leads, and months before the FBI Academy in Quantico, Virginia, had an open bunk in its National Security School. Without proper training, I couldn't be set loose in the field to hunt spies and terrorists. But the FBI could assign me to a squad of agents as part of an active espionage investigation—which is how, a little over a year after graduating from college, I ended up part of the mission to capture Earl Edwin Pitts, Russian spy and former FBI agent.

In 1995, the FBI's Washington Field Office commanded the top floors of a federal office building on the banks of the Anacostia River. The spectacularly ugly building, aptly located at Buzzard Point in Southwest Washington, DC, almost made me regret joining the FBI. But the team of agents, led by legendary spy hunter Mike Donner, quickly won me over.

A thirteen-year FBI veteran, Pitts had spied for the Soviet Union from 1987 until 1992. He first volunteered his services to the Soviet Union in July 1987 by sending a letter to a member of the Soviet Mission assigned to the United Nations in New York City. Pitts's new contact soon introduced him to Alexsandr Vasilyevich Karpov, the Soviet Line KR chief for New York, at a clandestine meet at the New York Public Library. Line KR, the counterintelligence unit of the KGB, was responsible for recruiting spies from foreign nations. The FBI learned of Pitts's treachery in 1995, when his original Soviet contact defected to the United States and became a confidential witness against him.

The accusations against Pitts created a problem for the Justice Department, which was tasked with prosecuting the case. In general, securing an espionage conviction requires the government to prove that the spy willfully handed information that was classified or related to national defense over to a foreign nation or other party seeking to harm the United States, and that he or she did so with reason to believe the information would harm the United States or help a foreign nation. It's easier to prove conspiracy to commit espionage, which requires only that the spy *intended* to provide classified information to a foreign power, and that he or she committed some act to further the espionage.

But when it came to the Pitts case, even making out the conspiracy charge was going to be a challenge. While the confidential witness had pointed an unshaking finger at Pitts, a first-year law student could see that the government's case against him was flimsy: it relied entirely on circumstantial information handed over by a defector in return for money and a new life in America. The confidential witness would disappear into Witness Protection and never testify to the evidence on the stand. A good defense attorney could easily raise enough questions about the witness's motives to secure a "not guilty" verdict. The FBI needed Pitts to confess.

In order to make that happen, the bureau created a compartmentalized squad of agents to run what's known as a "false flag" operation. In August 1995, the FBI used the confidential witness, alongside a team of FBI agents led by Donner and posing as Russian intelligence officers, to fool Pitts into believing that Russia wanted to reactivate him as a spy. The false flag operation lasted sixteen months. During that time, Pitts made twenty-two drops of classified and unclassified FBI information and documents, held two face-to-face meetings and nine phone conversations with his pretend Russian handlers, and accepted payment of $65,000 for his attempted espionage. Donner's squad had measured out plenty of rope for Pitts to hang himself.

I joined Donner's squad in the final few months of that investigation, probably because Donner heard I knew how to turn on a computer. Whatever the reason, I couldn't believe my luck. I'd joined the FBI to hunt spies and make a difference. Now, here I was, assigned to the FBI's biggest and most secretive case. I felt like a high school baseball player asked to warm up in the Oriole bullpen with a promise that the team might give me a shot at the big show. The first time I walked into the squad room, I could barely croak out a hello.

Of course, the FBI doesn't throw a twenty-two-year-old future investigator into the path of a spy. My role was to shadow the agents, learn counterintelligence from them, and organize the evidence they collected against Pitts into a computer database. But before I could even consider pressing my thumb against the biometric scanner that sheltered the Pitts squad from the rest of the FBI, I required further initiation into the tyranny of secrets.

A common misconception, even within the intelligence community, is that there are multiple levels of clearance above top secret. In reality, the top clearance is top secret/special compartmentalized intelligence, or TS/SCI. This phrase may seem cryptic, but those familiar with best practices for securing information will recognize its meaning. The idea is to section off critical information—the kind of information that could jeopardize an investigation or harm national security if it fell into the wrong hands—into "compartments," each accessible only to those who need to know that specific information in order to do their jobs. To join the squad investigating Earl Pitts, I needed to attend additional security briefings so that the FBI could grant me access to two additional compartments: Special Intelligence (SI) and Talent Keyhole (TK) intelligence. SI covers communication intercepts, such as listening in to and analyzing and decoding foreign military radio-traffic, and TK protects signals intelligence (or SIGINT), which might include target data spotted by a reconnaissance satellite. Because I would potentially have access to information derived from these compartments during the Earl Pitts investigation, the FBI had to initiate me into the relevant circles of trust.

If this sounds like a lot to handle, it is. Every investigation involves different intelligence compartments and different lists of personnel with a "need to know" the information contained in that compartment. Covert operatives quickly learn to section off secrets in their own mind in order to avoid discussing a case with someone who has an equally high security clearance but who may not have access to the particular compartments implicated in that case, or even compartmentalized information within those compartments! The result is like a Mute button on conversation. If you can't be certain that your squad mate is "read into" the case you are working on, it's always best to just say nothing.

Working with Donner's squad taught me the opposite side of the investigations I would later work as a field operative. I collected and distilled data from the field, heard about how the ghost team following Pitts each day pursued the investigation, and saw in real time how the FBI agents frowned or cheered as surveillance logs came across the wire. I discovered the camaraderie to be found among a handpicked team of agents, each working toward a common goal, and I listened carefully to Donner's frequent warnings to say nothing about the case once we left the secret squad room in Buzzard Point. Over time, I became used to carrying secrets—though I was never fully comfortable. When friends asked me about my new job, I repelled any interest by saying the Department of Justice had hired me as a geopolitical analyst. Nobody felt the need to ask follow-up questions. It made it hard to capture the interest of a date, but it kept FBI-learned information safe.

On December 18, 1996, after I'd spent a few months on the investigation, we arrested Earl Pitts at the FBI Academy, where he worked at what was then called the Behavioral Science Unit—the unit tasked with applying behavioral and social sciences to investigative techniques, including profiling serial killers, countering violent extremism, and understanding psychopathology. In June 1997, after pleading guilty to conspiracy to commit espionage, Earl Pitts was sentenced to twenty-seven years in prison. I had long since left Donner's squad to finally attend the FBI Academy at Quantico, so I wasn't around for Pitts's lengthy debrief, when he mentioned that another FBI agent made him suspicious. Pitts suspected that agent might also be a spy. At the time, the FBI dismissed Pitts's concerns and chose not to follow up with the agent he'd named: an obscure computer expert named Robert Hanssen.

# CHAPTER 3

# LAY DOWN YOUR SWORD

Gene's blue Crown Victoria prowled away toward Pennsylvania Avenue and FBI headquarters. I watched him turn the corner and then stood for a few minutes in the cold. I had agreed to take a unique case based on very little information, and I still wasn't sure whether I had volunteered or been coerced. In a case where every scrap of knowledge was kept in a locked box inside other locked boxes, it seemed I had very few keys. Gene made sure I hadn't heard of Robert Hanssen, told me the FBI would investigate him for possible espionage, and got me to agree to share an office with him. I looked at my watch. It had taken Gene less than ten minutes to recruit me.

I would begin this case mostly blind, but after five years in the field as a ghost, I understood Gene's reasoning. Hanssen was a veteran agent, schooled in the tyranny of secrets. I was a pawn. And the less I knew about the case, the fewer details I could accidently reveal.

Stomach tight and throat dry, I turned back toward my apartment. I'd come a long way since the Pitts case, I told myself. I had hunted spies and terrorists through parks and alleyways, offices and restaurants, shopping malls and nightclubs. I could manage an investigation at FBI headquarters.

I closed the door softly behind me. Before I could shrug off my coat, Juliana pressed a cup of coffee into my hands. The steaming mug warmed life into my frozen fingers. I sipped deeply, gathering my words.

Five years after my first polygraph test, I stood in front of my wife of less than a year and lied again. This would be the first lie I ever told her. It would also be far from the last.

"What did Gene want?" The slightest hint of a European accent rounded Juliana's question, made it beautiful.

"I just got promoted to a computer job at headquarters." The words came much too easily. I controlled my breath until the polygraph in my mind's eye stilled to only a straight blue line. "He said it will help me get to law school classes on time."

She brightened. "That's great! We should celebrate."

I tucked the Hanssen investigation away into a back part of my mind and compartmentalized. "Maybe my parents will have us over?"

That evening, Juliana and I were in our green Jeep Cherokee on the way to Kensington, Maryland. I tensed and bit my lip as she merged through the number four lane on the Capital Beltway to exit onto Connecticut Avenue. "Seriously, Eric!" She looked at me and rolled her eyes.

"Eyes on the road," I said. My white-knuckled grip on the dashboard matched my voice. "You'll wreck my car."

Her eyes flattened—hint of danger. "You mean *our* car."

"It won't be *our* car for long if you don't slow down."

Juliana sighed. "How do you ride with anyone at your job?"

"I'm usually the driver," I said. "Plus if someone else crashes an FBI car, I don't have to pay the bills."

"I won't crash."

Juliana knew that my aversion to riding as a passenger bordered on obsession. Much of my perhaps unhealthy conviction in my own driving ability stemmed from my FBI training. After graduating from the FBI's Tactical Emergency Vehicle

Operations course, and then refining that intense training against Russian spies on their way to drop sites, known terrorists priming their courage for an impending attack, and some of the best foreign operatives using the DC metro area as an espionage playground, I held every other driver to an impossible standard.

But Juliana had learned to drive from precise German instructors. When we first started dating, I'd asked her if she wanted to learn to drive stick. Desperate to impress her, I took her to a quiet alley and spent a good ten minutes lecturing her on using a clutch and shifting, finding the friction point with the left foot as the right slowly came off the gas, and shifting smoothly to avoid stalling the car. She listened to each explanation with the seriousness of an eager student and yielded to my multiple demonstrations of shifting into first. When I finally switched places with her, we barely had our seat belts on before she charged off like a drag racer seeing green lights. Juliana laughed away my shock and shifted from second to third so smoothly I had to watch to see it happen.

"Don't you know anything about Germany?" she said. "All the cars are stick shifts there."

Ever since that moment, Juliana has never missed an opportunity to insist she take the wheel. We could be like gasoline on fire that way sometimes. When both people want to be in control, neither can be happy until someone yields.

"I'm sorry," I said. "What's mine is yours."

"Better."

"Do you know the turn for my parents' house?"

She raised an eyebrow. "Yes, why?"

"I'm going to close my eyes and not look at the street."

I stepped out of the car onto my parents' driveway and looked up at the home where I'd spent six years before heading south in a packed Volkswagen van to attend college at Auburn University. The Victorian house had the kind of character that only comes from weathering countless families and numerous additions. But in 1987, during my freshman year of high school, it had been gutted by a fire. We had spent a year renting a tiny house a few blocks over while contractors repaired and remodeled this one. That lost year meant that the blue-painted shingles and solemn swing hanging under a decorative porch felt comfortable, but never quite like home to me.

My dad answered the front door and ushered us in with his usual bear hug. Dad grew up on a farm in Hartford County, Maryland, and built a lifetime's worth of muscle throwing hay bales into the back of tractor-pulled carts. He'd joined the Navy not only to follow a family tradition but also to escape the horrible hay fever that he'd generously passed on to me—there aren't many hay fields in submarines.

We found my mother in the kitchen, stirring a pot of pasta sauce. The smells of garden tomatoes, mushrooms, and fresh basil mingling with her secret ingredient, a cup of wine, finally made me feel at home. The kitchen had always been my mother's favorite part of the house, which may have had something to do with the house she grew up in, a split-level town house in Jamaica, Queens. When I say split-level, I mean that the family who lived upstairs walked through my mother's kitchen to leave through the front door. Mom had escaped those cramped circumstances by attending Hunter College in Manhattan and becoming a nurse. This evening, my mother's dark eyes flashed with intrigue. "Tell me about your promotion."

I frowned. The twinge in my stomach had nothing to do with my itch to grab a bowl and race to the kitchen table. I hated the thought of lying to my mother. My parents knew I worked for the FBI, but I had never told them about the ghosts.

"It's a computer job," I said, forcing the words out. "I'll be working in a new division, but they haven't told me all the details yet."

My father brandished a bottle of wine. "You don't tell us much about what you did before, so . . ." The cork came away with a pop. "Any excuse to celebrate!"

Juliana helped my mother smother bowls of pasta in sauce. "For once, Eric is being modest," she said. "His boss came by our house personally to tell him about the promotion." She paused for effect. "On a Sunday."

Dad looked up from where he filled our wineglasses. "Couldn't wait until Monday?"

I took two bowls from Juliana and avoided her eyes. I could already feel the lies piling up, so I simply shrugged. I could only think back to my first polygraph exam and how, once again, I was lying to someone who loved me.

"How is law school?" My mom changed the subject.

Speaking about my legal studies placed me on solid ground. I hadn't followed my father's footsteps into a navy career, but I had followed him into a second family tradition in the practice of law. After three years ghosting targets, I realized that if I wanted to move up within the FBI, I would need an advanced degree. I dreamed of graduating from George Washington University Law School and applying to the Special Agents Program, or trading in my disguise kit for a position at the Justice Department. I had started law school at night uncertain about where exactly it would take me, but I'd always felt drawn to the sanctuary of rules and laws. I hoped attending law school would allow me to continue to serve my country, but as the person calling the plays rather than the one in the field.

"The new job will help," I said. "I'll be working a nine-to-five desk at headquarters, so no more missed classes when I have to work nights."

We migrated to the table and took our seats. Out of the corner of my eye, I watched my mother's laborious walk from stove to table and ground my teeth as she fell more than sat into her chair. My parents had first told me about her Parkinson's disease in a tearful phone call during my third year at Auburn University. Years later, the disease had progressed enough to slur her speech and make walking more difficult. It also affected her facial expressions. My temperamental mother, who could switch from an angry shout to a beatific smile in a second, now struggled to lift her cheeks.

"Do you have a title for this new job?" Dad asked.

"Not yet." I took a sip of wine. Avoided eye contact. "They really haven't told me anything."

"Do you have time for it?" Dad refreshed half-full wineglasses. "You've got a lot on your plate."

My father's understatement sent a needless shot of adrenaline through me. A few words shouldn't kick me into fight or flight, but when your life is an arena, it's hard to lay down your sword. Each day felt more and more about surviving to the next, not living the one before me. Survival didn't mean patience with those I loved, or time for friends or family. Nor did it mean careless moments free of the pressing concerns that orbited me. I wanted to build on my new marriage, not scour law books late at night, chase spies during the day, and worry about my mother's decline during the few hours I should be sleeping. Even before the Hanssen investigation swept apart the house of cards I'd built of my life, I'd already set it on fire.

My parents exchanged a look. Finally my mother shrugged in that very Italian way that means: *Whattaya gonna do?*

Dad raised his glass. "To Eric and Juliana. New beginnings and new opportunities."

I made sure to meet Juliana's eyes as we clinked glasses— one of her few superstitions. "*Prost.*"

We said our goodbyes, and Juliana graciously let me drive home. We opened the door into our tiny combination kitchen/living room. As tight a squeeze as it was, I felt more at home there than in all my years in Maryland. Juliana and I had hung photos from our shared lives in clever spaces. The old couch we'd inherited from my uncle Ralph proudly wore a slipcover Juliana had sewed during the long, boring month she spent waiting for her student visa. A television wobbled precariously on top of a corner cabinet that we'd picked out together from IKEA and assembled, cursing playfully as we followed the complex instructions. Our short lives together so far surrounded us with promise. Better days would come.

As soon as we walked in the door, we heard an elderly voice echoing from upstairs: "Hello! Hello!"

We both glanced at the ceiling and laughed. We'd heard the Hello Lady since we moved in, night after night for about an hour. The first time we had heard the repeated greeting, we had tried to answer back. If the woman in the apartment above us heard, she gave no sign. Instead, she—or someone, anyway—would continue saying hello in a singsong voice over and over. It was the great mystery of 626 E Street.

Juliana grinned. "It has to be a bird."

"Or she's just talking to herself."

"It's a bird." Juliana pulled me into an embrace. "I just know."

I glanced at the old clock that squatted on the mantel of our non-functioning fireplace. "At least she's consistent. Every night at eight p.m. on the dot."

"Every place has a story."

I looked around us. Thought of my parents' home. "Do you ever want more than this?"

"More than what?" Juliana teased.

"It's cold and drafty. The heater barely works. We had to save for months to buy the TV. . . ."

She drew back just enough for me to see her face. Her green eyes, flecked with gold, sparkled. "My mom had a saying, something she told my dad when they were first married and moved into my grandfather's house together. Mom didn't even speak German. She had to learn my father's language before they could have a conversation." She smiled. "We will just live on love and air."

"Air doesn't pay the bills."

"Hello. Hello." Juliana breathed in my ear until I finally smiled. Then she pulled me back through another tiny hallway and through the door to our bedroom.

"Hello yourself."

## CHAPTER 4

# MOUSETRAP

December 20, 2000—Wednesday

I followed Gene through the maze of FBI headquarters. Gray hallway yielded to gray hallway, illuminated by fluorescent lights and the occasional hint of sunlight through an open office door. Multicolored strips—like hieroglyphics—on the walls hinted at directions to cryptic locations. I couldn't break the code and was soon lost, trailing Gene like a faithful hound.

Before that moment, I had only set foot in headquarters once, when I was in training at Quantico. Many of the future ghosts in my class had never toured the nation's capital and had declared me tour guide over a free weekend. After exploring monuments and museums, we had stopped in FBI HQ to raid the gift shop. Christmas was right around the corner, and my little brothers delighted in wearing official FBI gear. This visit had none of the laughter and camaraderie of my former one. Instead, I marched at a sober pace toward a meeting that could make or break my career.

"Through here," Gene said. "Be polite. Make me proud."

Gene ushered me through an office of administrative workstations. A smartly dressed woman in her thirties looked up from her monitor as Gene approached, scrutinized him, and then waved us past. She barely glanced at me before returning to her work.

I looked past Gene to the door at the far side of the room,

and my heart kicked up a notch. The placard beside the door read ASSISTANT DIRECTOR BOB DIES.

I quietly thanked Juliana. Over the New Year's holiday, she had insisted that we buy a new suit for my new job. After a few hours in Macy's, we'd emerged with a navy-blue suit, two ties, and a few trim white shirts that didn't require me to twist in front of a mirror to stuff away the excess cloth. As a ghost, you have to be able to blend into any situation, and my standard outfit of light pants with useful cargo pockets and a collared shirt fit most of them. I could walk unnoticed across a college campus; transform myself into a Washington, DC, tourist; and stroll into the majority of restaurants, bars, shops, and malls without anyone turning an eye. Sometimes I would exchange trousers for biker shorts and a backpack; in the years before the terrorist actions of September 11, bike messengers could walk into any building. Very rarely would I shrug into my only suit in order to chase a target into an elegant restaurant or stodgy office building. Before Juliana took me to Macy's, that suit was the same black one I wore to funerals.

She had also turned her nose up at my battered but highly trusted backpack. I had cut a pinhole in the front pocket to hide a small concealment camera, and if you looked closely, you could see tiny marks on the shoulder straps that allowed me to hide radio wires. Juliana argued that the backpack wasn't professional and had insisted I buy a shiny leather briefcase. We'd compromised on a black-and-gray Timberland messenger bag that now hung off my shoulder. While I didn't wear a suit and tie as effortlessly as Gene, I felt confident that I at least wouldn't embarrass myself in front of the assistant director.

I had stuffed a few items into the messenger bag: a legal pad and pen to take notes, my FBI credentials that told others in law enforcement whom I worked for and the golden badge that proved it, and a letter that Gene had handed me at the field office to make my part in the Hanssen investigation official. The letter had come from Assistant Director Dies's office and had assigned me to his office for temporary duty (TDY, in FBI-speak) of one year. I would report directly to Section Chief Richard Garcia and would be assigned to the Information Assurance/Security Team. The carefully drafted letter created my cover for the assignment to Hanssen:

> *AD Dies requested Investigative Specialist O'Neill be TDY'd to FBIHQ IRD Information Assurance/Security Team (IAST) based on O'Neill's computer expertise and familiarity with National Security Division and counterintelligence matters as they relate to computer hardware, software, and systems. AD Dies also noted his desire for a field office perspective to the envisioned work of the IAST.*

Reading the TDY letter, I could almost believe that the FBI had truly promoted me. To fool Hanssen, I'd have to sell the story to everyone, including myself.

"Speak little, nod in the right places," Gene said. Then he opened the door.

AD Dies looked up from his desk and motioned for us to take a seat. I eased into a comfortable leather chair and resisted the urge to sink backward. The assistant director had his shirt-sleeves rolled up and looked slightly frazzled behind the array of papers spread across his desk. He swiped a pair of wireframe glasses from his face and rubbed his eyes.

"Assistant Director Dies, sir." Gene's voice took on a formal tone I hadn't heard before. "This is IS O'Neill."

An open IBM ThinkPad to one side of the desk drew my envy. The model was top of the line, complete with a track pad and the little nub mouse embedded in the keyboard that everyone called an eraser. Totally out of bounds for the FBI rank and file, but entirely appropriate for a man with Dies's pedigree.

After thirty years at IBM, where he'd last served as a vice president and general manager for the company's network and personal computer division, Dies had been about to retire when FBI Director Louis Freeh convinced him to take on what he called "the toughest job in the FBI today." Dies would lead the FBI's Information Research Division (IRD) as an assistant director and member of the director's senior staff.

In the late 1990s, the newly interconnected world had left the FBI behind. IRD was responsible for drafting a modernization plan that would wake the FBI up to the new networked reality. Under Dies's leadership, IRD would upgrade computer systems and networks and invest in new hardware and software platforms that would enhance the FBI's mission. The new assistant director had a steep hill to climb.

Dies caught me staring at his laptop. "I'd like one of those on the desk of every agent," he said.

I glanced at Gene, but he kept his expression neutral. Was this a test? "They would be just as useful in the field, sir," I said.

The assistant director slid his glasses back over his eyes and looked at me over folded hands. "I heard about your computer program."

It wasn't a question. I followed Gene's instructions and kept silent despite the thrill that squared my shoulders. Dies sifted through a few sheets of paper. "Your squad has some of the latest computer systems and even a few laptops." He looked at Gene. "This is left over from a pilot program?"

"The idea was to allow specialists to upload surveillance logs directly into a database that would then coordinate the information." Gene paused. "IS O'Neill could explain this better. He wrote the program."

I had organized and led the effort to computerize our squad ahead of most of the FBI, even to the point of sending ghost teams out with laptops. Lengthy periods of downtime during molasses-paced surveillance operations leave a lot of time to type up a log. The ghost with log duty could then upload the electronic file directly into the target database on the same day as the surveillance. Prior to computerization, it might be days before a ghost would cycle out of the field for an administra-

tive day of typing up logs, training, car and equipment mainte-
nance, weightlifting, and practical jokes played on other teams.

Dies looked at me. I tried not to squirm. "I . . . sir . . . I had
the idea after following Russians. . . ." I looked at Gene. Could
I say any of this? He nodded.

"Russians usually work based on a series of points in time.
They prearrange their signals and dead drops and whatever
ahead of time so that they rarely have to communicate in person or over the phone with an asset." I wished I could use a
whiteboard, but Dies's stare made me go on. "I got the idea that
if we catalog all those dates over time, we would see a pattern."

Dies looked at Gene.

"We found a pattern, all right," Gene said.

"And you wrote this in wha?" Dies said. "C++?"

I took a breath. "Actually, Microsoft Access."

"Access!" Dies sat back.

You could cook an egg on my face. My interest in computer
systems began in 1986 when my mother bought our first Apple
IIGS out of the first proceeds from a catering company she
started. I taught myself rudimentary programming so that I
could modify video games and soon graduated to building my
own computer systems and then to challenging my newfound
knowledge by testing security as I explored the nascent World
Wide Web. I could program, but I didn't have time or funding
to create a database from scratch for the FBI. "We didn't have a
budget, and Microsoft Office was already installed on the desktop Gene assigned me. Sir, I used what I had in front of me.
Also, I'm used to using a mouse. I wanted to design something
that didn't look left over from the 1970s."

Dies laughed, but I could hear the underlying morbidity in
the mirth. I had touched on a sore spot for the FBI. After the
turn of the twenty-first century, the FBI's primary computer
program was an obsolete, mainframe-based program called the
Automated Case System. Because none of the FBI computers
had enough horsepower to run a distributed program like ACS,

the information resided on a powerful mainframe computer that the desktop in a squad office would connect to in order to access case information. To upload a single document into ACS, an agent had to traverse a dozen green screens that looked like they would fit right into the movie *War Games*. The system was incompatible with Microsoft Windows OS, which was already ubiquitous in the civilian world. And as slow and complicated as it was to use ACS, it was still ultimately just a filing system used to direct legions of assistants and clerks to hunt down paper files. In a nutshell, everyone hated it.

My system uploaded all our investigative logs into a Microsoft database that allowed the user to perform keyword searches over time and dates, either specific moments or ranges of them. It also allowed a user to instantly retrieve any surveillance log in Word format. No more hunting down old information in dusty file cabinets. You could keyword-search a Russian intelligence officer by name and see how many times ghosts had followed him over the past year to a certain telephone pole that we knew served as a Russian signal site. If the system showed that he had passed that signal site at three o'clock every second Tuesday of the month for a year, you could plan to set up ahead of him the next month and increase the odds of breaking a major case.

Of course, Dies didn't know that I didn't have entirely altruistic reasons for creating the database. I needed a way to spend more time at law school and less time out on the street missing class. I proposed the program to my supervisory special agent with the caveat that I'd code during the day on weeks when my team had overnight operations.

The idea had come to me when I'd started law school and began using Westlaw and LexisNexis, databases that served as searchable, cross-indexed law libraries. If every lawyer in the United States could call up every case related to the one they were working on with just a few mouse clicks, why couldn't the FBI do the same? The FBI should have come up with the idea of approaching major systems designers to develop a Westlaw or Lexis for the bureau. Instead they had an investigative specialist in his mid-twenties coding modules in Access during rare days in the office and on nights and weekends. But the fact that my database worked got me noticed by the powers that be.

"Don't worry, Eric," Dies said. "We are going to change everything." He reached across the desk to shake my hand. "Welcome to the team."

A smile finally ghosted Gene's face.

Once we were back out in the hall and safe from other ears, I asked Gene whether Dies knew about the Hanssen investigation. "That's need-to-know," Gene answered. "You don't have a need to know."

Gene led me back through the halls filled with the noisy chatter of FBI employees. We rode an elevator up two floors to the ninth and stepped out into a clinical hallway of white walls and drop ceilings striped with bright, cased fluorescent lights. Doors framed in dark wood stood an even-spaced sentry until the hall ended in a sharp left turn. Just to the right of the elevators, the bathrooms faced each other inside an alcove divided by a water fountain.

Gene looked over and chuckled. "What's the first rule of surveillance?"

"Never inspect a bathroom, and never pass one by."

He slapped me on the back. "Well done! Who told you that?"

"Tom Reilly. While we worked the Earl Pitts case." Tom was a counterintelligence agent, years my senior, who had taken me under his wing. One afternoon while rushing after Pitts, Tom had stopped us both by a public restroom. I'd told him to go ahead, I didn't feel the need, but he'd lectured me about opportunity. "You'll find yourself trapped in a car chasing a target though streets with no end and that's when the need will strike," Tom had said. "So when you have downtime, always hit the head. And when you're in there, don't inspect: get in, do your business, and get out quick before your target moves again."

In all my years as an undercover operative, that advice had been the most important.

"Tom's a good guy," Gene said. "Here's another."

Gene led me through an open door into an office that looked pleasantly out of place in the otherwise drab headquarters. A glass-fronted bookcase of polished wood held thick volumes related to operations and investigations. A massive executive desk dominated one side of the carpeted room. A comfortable couch that matched the voluminous desk chair relaxed along the opposite wall. The walls and shelves were decorated with baseball memorabilia, along with numerous awards and plaques in both English and Spanish.

"Eric, meet Rich Garcia."

Garcia's exuberant smile under his burly mustache and thick glasses made the corner of my mouth tick up. We shook hands. "Anything you need," Garcia said, "I'm here. Just right down the hall."

I looked at Gene.

"Rich is in the know," Gene confirmed. "As far as you are concerned, he's the only person at headquarters that knows about the investigation."

Richard Garcia's FBI career had followed a unique trajectory. He had joined the FBI out of the Dallas Police Department and had continued to serve as a Dallas FBI agent until an assignment in San Juan, Puerto Rico, landed him a spot in Miami and then a position at FBI headquarters supervising a Colombian/South American Drug Traffickers Unit. Years later he would return to Texas as assistant special agent in charge of the FBI's El Paso office before finally returning to headquarters as section chief in charge of information technology operations.

"All the cameras you see in the halls, the security systems, the phone systems, and every lock on every door. That's all out of my section," Garcia explained. "We are installing tech in the office to monitor that bastard."

"Got it," I said. But I didn't.

"I'm taking him to the room," Gene said.

Garcia glanced at the unfinished work on his desk. "Kate's there. I'll be along later."

I hiked up my shoulder bag and remembered that the letter Gene had shown me hadn't just TDY'd me to HQ; it had also technically placed me under Garcia's supervision. I realized I knew next to nothing about this assignment. Only that the FBI somehow expected me to help catch a spy.

"O'Neill." Garcia stopped me before I could follow Gene from the room. "If it ever gets too hot in there, if you need help: I'm right down the hall."

"Thank you, sir." I could tell he was speaking in earnest, but I couldn't decide whether his words comforted me or made me more apprehensive.

"The room is a few doors down," Gene said. For once we didn't have to thread a maze of featureless corridors broken only by red and blue color-coded markers. Gene led me a short way down an empty hallway toward the rolling whine of drills and dull thumps of hammers.

"The room?"

Gene escorted me through a doorway framed in black steel. A massive door hung open on heavy hinges. I spotted holes in the top and bottom rails where bolts would secure the door to its frame. A combination dial bulged above a latch that I could fit both my hands on. A lonely placard displayed the room number in red, blue, and black: 9930.

"On paper, you are TDY'd to headquarters and to Garcia's desk," Gene said. "Covertly, you're assigned to the WFO team investigating Hanssen." Gene stopped me. "This is important. As far as you are concerned, no one knows about this case. Mum's the word. Not me, not your wife or grandma. Not even Garcia. You discuss this case with only one person. Eric, meet Special Agent Kate Alleman."

Special Agent Alleman had worked in army intelligence before coming over to the civilian side, and she moved with the grace of someone familiar with the track and the weight room. Streaks of blond shot through her short brown hair. Though her smile needed little prompting to break through, I could tell there was steel within her. I didn't yet know it, but that fortitude would guide me like an evening star.

Kate shook my hand and pulled me into Room 9930. This was where I would be working one on one, side by side, with Robert Hanssen. I still had no idea who Hanssen was, what he was suspected of doing, or what kind of dirt I was expected to find, and Kate wasn't about to tell me. She dodged my questions and broadly explained the crux of the situation: after a career of rattling the wrong cages, never shy about letting his superiors know he thought them foolish or incompetent, Hanssen had been banished to an obscure desk job at the State Department. (I was also told he'd had a dispute with a subordinate that involved him screaming, and ended with her sprawled on the floor.) This was because the government rarely fires an employee, even for cause. Instead, the FBI shuffles its unwanted souls to administrative hell, where they're put out to pasture, left to boredom or advancement Siberia until they quit or retire. Which was exactly our problem: Hanssen was about to hit mandatory retirement in just a couple of months.

You might think that the FBI would wish the suspected spy good riddance, but then you wouldn't understand the spy game. The only way a spy hunter could possibly catch Hanssen in an act of espionage was to keep him working at the bureau—meaning the FBI needed to woo Hanssen back from his cushy, if boring, job at State. They needed to coax him back into the fold in a way that would mend his fractured ego, give him access to juicy information, and encourage him to spy. And they needed to do all that without tipping him off that he was walking into a mousetrap. Much like the way Donner's squad operated during the Earl Pitts case, the squad investigating Hanssen wanted to slowly build a case. A key difference was that no FBI agents would false-flag Hanssen. We wanted him to spy for the actual Russians.

To accomplish this impossible task, the powers that be decided to give Hanssen his dream job. He'd spent years complaining that the FBI's systems were vulnerable to outside hackers and inside spies, and the FBI had spent years ignoring his concerns. Now, at the twilight of his career, they were capitulating. Imagine Hanssen's surprise when the FBI told him not only that he would be returning to headquarters to start a new squad to protect the FBI from computer espionage but also that the new role included a promotion to executive service. Hanssen would make more money and get the fancy office he had spent twenty-five years dreaming about. The deal was too good to pass up—but also too good to be true.

Contractors had split Room 9930 into a main office for Hanssen and a second, larger squad room for me. Hanssen would have an executive desk and a credenza, a coatrack, and a TV stand—all standard issue for an agent in executive service—as well as a safe rated for special compartmentalized information (SCI). My office would contain a few more modest desks, a separate computer station for accessing the Internet, and a copier. The extra desks were just for show. Hanssen would only ever have a staff of one.

In the meantime, however, workers had been busy gutting the room that Kate walked me into. Wires slithered from unfinished walls pocked with holes. Uninstalled equipment waited on top of every flat surface. I couldn't identify half of it. The FBI had classified the room as a sensitive compartmented information facility (SCIF—pronounced "skiff"). This meant that within 9930, Hanssen and I could analyze and access information classified as top secret/SCI. It also meant that 9930 was in an interior office without windows, that technicians had soundproofed the walls and vents, and that they'd installed a door that belonged on an Egyptian pharaoh's tomb. There were hidden cameras and surveillance equipment all across the room.

"If you have all these cameras, what do you need me for?" I asked.

I received the first of many trademark Kate grins. Somewhere between supportive and condescending, it had a way of making you reach back inside yourself to answer a question you'd just asked.

"You never rely on technology alone," Kate said. "The most important wins come from people. Not machines. We can't see everything. That's your job. Watch and listen."

I nodded, chewing over the question that had needled me since Gene pulled me out of bed: Out of everyone in the bureau, why had the agents selected me for this role? At age twenty-six, I could dress up to play the part of a seasoned corporate professional, but I could also stroll through a high school without attracting a second glance. As a ghost, I could *21 Jump Street* across a college campus, but since meeting Juliana, I'd been shouldered into second-string cases. This feeling drove me to push the boundaries: selecting choke points ahead of targets in shadowed alleys, hanging off the edge of rooftops to find the perfect camera angle, spending nights and weekends developing a target-tracking database to make the entire squad more efficient. All these things lent me a certain reputation, but they didn't change the fact that, according to the training manuals, I was the wrong person to take on what appeared to be a high-level suspected spy. But sometimes in the spy game a perceived disadvantage can become an asset. Maybe an older, more seasoned and well-trained agent couldn't do the job that I could.

"Any tips for me?" I asked.

"Just be yourself," Kate answered.

I tried to swallow, but the sound of the ticking clock made my mouth go dry. It was January, and Hanssen's twenty-five-year retirement was coming up in April. I didn't have much in the way of information, but I did know I only had a few months to help catch a suspected spy.

# CHAPTER 5

# THE WEAKEST LINK

## January 16, 2001—Tuesday

The chilly January morning layered Washington, DC, in stark grays. Black streets cut precise paths past stone buildings and forgotten monuments, everything solid and immobile under the heavy sky. The air frosted ahead of my labored breath. I'd jogged up the many escalator steps emerging from the Archives–Navy Memorial Metro station and then walked with purpose toward the sandstone-colored temple that was the FBI Building. Now my hurry had stalled against the weight of a single moment. Kate had advised me to "be myself." How could I be myself when I felt like an actor playing my part in a movie?

It had taken the going-away party with my ghost squad for me to appreciate how strictly the FBI had compartmentalized the Hanssen investigation. Officially, only a handful of my fellow ghosts tasked with surveilling Hanssen knew why the FBI had transferred me to headquarters. The rest of the Special Surveillance Group (SSG) in WFO believed the same lie I had told Juliana: I had accepted a computer-security job. I knew that the teams shadowing Hanssen's every step would never tell. The SSG is the most highly compartmentalized group in the FBI. Ghosts learn to say nothing about the work they accomplish for fear that an errant word might reach the wrong ear. The Roman poet Juvenal wrote in his *Satires* "*Quis custodiet ipsos custodies?*" The Latin question literally means "Who will guard the guards themselves?" but is more commonly translated as "Who will watch the watchers?" Among the secret hallways of the SSG, we silently watched one another.

Our silence with respect to classified matters did not stifle the usual banter and interpersonal drama that blossoms within a close-knit team. We could care about one another while burying our secrets. And so, a few days before I stood in front of FBI headquarters on that cold January morning, the assortment of oddballs and jokers that I trusted to have my back each day we chased spies and terrorists through the DC streets celebrated my move to the Big House.

Friends circulated flyers for "Eric O'Neill's Luncheon" in our office. We descended on a buffet at Charlie Chiang's in Shirlington, Virginia, and clinked beer glasses in a toast to my future as an FBI HQ computer nerd. I smiled along, but secretly wondered how many of my fellows knew what my actual role would be and were laughing inwardly as they watched me pretend graciousness. How many would later learn that the "promotion" was a smokescreen for the FBI's grandest spy-hunting operation? Would they see the deception as another secret tucked into one of many compartments? Or would they feel that I had cheated them out of a $13 lunch?

I'd had the same sick feeling over New Year's. Juliana and I rang in the first moments of 2001 with our best friends Mike and Vivian under fireworks in Orlando, Florida. I had known Mike since we shared a desk in Ms. Fredrickson's first-grade class at the Saint Jane Frances de Chantal elementary school in Bethesda, Maryland, and I was overjoyed when his long-time girlfriend Viv started becoming close to Juliana. Juliana eventually asked Viv to be her maid of honor at our wedding. We were excited to celebrate the holiday together, and we'd planned a weekend of amusement parks, great restaurants, and maybe a little drinking to excess. But that was all before Gene had shown up in front of 626 E Street. During a New Year's Eve party, I stood and listened as my oldest friend and my very new wife applauded my new job. Maybe it was the Champagne that brought a smile to my face at my pal's flowery words. Or maybe the lies that now continually crossed my lips were starting to flow more easily. Neither possibility sat well with me.

The J. Edgar Hoover Building, named for the first director of the FBI, is a nearly 3-million-square-foot Brutalist monstrosity that squats on Pennsylvania Avenue a stone's throw from the Capitol Building. The lopsided structure is actually two buildings of different heights connected by two wings that surround an interior trapezoid-shaped courtyard. Three of its floors plus a parking garage are completely underground. It was the sort of building that might swallow a person up just for the crime of walking inside.

I adjusted my shoulder bag and turned up the collar of my new overcoat against the cold. My single act of rebellion against the stodgy dress that overwhelmed the hallowed halls of the FBI was to replace the small lapel clip on my FBI Secure Access Control System key card, known as a SACS badge, with a green Caffrey's Irish Ale lanyard I'd won at bar trivia. Small shamrocks traced the thick cord like a little luck around my neck. I wasn't a special agent, and no one would ever confuse me for James Bond, but I'd done my damnedest to look the part.

I squared my shoulders, plastered a cocky grin over my chattering teeth, and strode to the entrance off Ninth Street with the purpose of someone intent on changing the world. I showed my SACS badge to the bored FBI security officer at the security desk. He waved me by without a second glance. I belonged here. I could do this!

I was lost.

My bravado eloped with my courage and defected. I coughed back an irrational panic. The elevator topped out at the eighth floor of the sprawling FBI HQ complex. I followed the echo of my steps down a quiet hallway, looking for an upward stairwell. Any ghost with an ounce of training would find me suspicious. Tentative movements, checking my watch every few minutes, loosening my tie as my breath came hoarse and stubborn, furtive glances around corners and upward toward security cameras. I cringed at the thought of arriving late for my first day on the job. If I couldn't even find the ninth floor in my own headquarters building, when I'd already been there once before with Gene, how was I supposed to catch a spy?

I backtracked to the elevator and down to the security guard. The affable FBI police officer could have tried harder to hide his laughter as he explained the lay of the land. I'd spent my career learning to blend into every situation. Now I felt like a naked guy trying to hide behind a planter in the middle of a crowded shopping mall. I was a stupid kid in a big-person suit with a beer lanyard around my neck.

The two-tower design of FBI HQ meant that elevators on the Pennsylvania Avenue side only went up eight floors. I would have to either take the elevator back to the sixth floor and thread the labyrinth or walk around the outside of the building to the entrance on E Street.

I chose the second option and headed out the door I'd come in. Without thinking, I walked a few steps toward the Metro before wrestling my feet around. Despite my misgivings, I had a job to accomplish. I thought about what my parents would say if they saw me wandering away from my duty.

As a child, I never dreamed of joining the FBI. Although I've always loved Bond movies, my earliest ambitions aimed far away from Earth's problems. I was NASA-bound.

The logical step toward astronautics was to join the military, at least in my family. My father's father served as a navy gunnery officer in the Pacific; I grew up with childhood fantasies of him leaning back into a deck cannon and personally shooting kamikazes out of the sky. As a nurse, my mother started the first maternity ward at the naval hospital in Charleston, South Carolina. And my father was an Annapolis graduate handpicked by Admiral Rickover to serve as one of the first nuclear submarine officers in the Navy.

Dad made it back to shore a day before my birth, and thereafter traded his commission for a berth at Yale Law School. My mother worked at the hospital while my father studied. While Mom earned our family bread and put my father through law school, Dad spent quiet afternoons reading me stories in our wicker rocking chair.

After graduating at the top of his class, my father took an energy-litigation job with a DC law firm. My mother quit medicine to raise four sons, but also ran her own business between school pickups, homework, and all the various sports four kids can pursue. She never slowed down until Parkinson's disease slammed the brakes on her vitality, and even then she soldiered on as long as possible.

My family prizes achievement, duty, and hard work. An O'Neill never quits.

I poured myself into honors mathematics at Gonzaga High School, only steps from the Capitol Building, spent weekends learning to fly a Cessna 172 at Montgomery Air Field, and even spent a summer at Space Camp in Huntsville, Alabama. When the Naval Academy deferred my acceptance for a year, I chose Auburn University for its elite Aerospace Engineering curriculum instead of opting for a Navy preparatory school. I would attend Auburn, returning to my Southern roots for a year, and then start over at the Naval Academy as a midshipman, where I'd have an engineering edge on the rest of my class.

But a year in engineering and the ROTC didn't invigorate me like I thought it would. I still loved math, but I found myself drawn away from the science of numbers and toward the science of the mind. I walked onto the Auburn lacrosse team and within a year started as a face-off midfielder. I met a girl from Georgia and thought I could stop searching for happiness. Those dreams of flying for the Navy on my way to space took a backseat to new dreams and an equal set of challenges.

One quiet Sunday, perched on an uncomfortable Victorian settee in my mother's formal living room, I told my parents that I had decided to stay at Auburn and forgo our shared dreams of a Navy commission. I would leave engineering for psychology, political science, and law. I wanted to understand the motivations behind a person's decisions more than I wanted to calculate the distances between stars.

My mother cried quietly, but not out of anger. To my surprise, instead of disowning me, my father smiled away a touch of disappointment and told me that I had to follow my own path. If my decision to walk away from the Navy was not due to personal failure, but because I saw a different opportunity, my parents would support me.

I graduated from Auburn University with honors and with a new plan. My degrees in psychology and political science made me set my sights on a legal career, but I wanted at least a year of experience in the outside world before diving back into academia. I settled in as an economic consultant, organizing numbers in databases to tell litigators how much they could sue for. My life became a relentless series of Excel spreadsheets and long flights. Within a few months, I knew I'd fallen off my path.

A year to the day after I'd started, I walked into my boss's office and quit my consulting job. My Navy dreams had passed me by, but I could still serve my country. I filled out index cards and mailed them to every alphabet agency I could find in the phonebook. The FBI, NSA, Secret Service, and DEA all sent back thick applications that I fed into my old typewriter. (The CIA never responded. Their loss.)

I decided to focus my efforts on the FBI and the DEA. In the early '90s, you had to be at least twenty-five to become an FBI special agent, but my application had caught the attention of the SSG. The DEA didn't care if I was twenty-two or thirty, as long as I met its rigorous physical standards, had the mental discipline to know when to shoot, and could keep calm under fire. Both the FBI and DEA house their training academies on the US Marine base in Quantico, Virginia. I decided to choose whichever agency gave me a berth at Quantico first.

The FBI called a day before the DEA. I've never heard a person curse as colorfully as the DEA recruiter when I told him I'd already joined the FBI, but I smiled as I hung up the phone. I would serve my country. In that service, I would cast off regret and find my way back to my path. It was a big leap, but knew I'd chosen correctly.

Now, standing in front of FBI HQ, I called on that feeling of purpose again. The bureau had called me to serve. Quitting wasn't an option.

I stepped out of a different elevator onto a polished hallway I recognized. Bathrooms to my right and a stairwell to my left. I passed four offices on my left, including Rich Garcia's, and a secretary station and file room on my right, then a few steps farther to Room 9930.

The plaque to the right of the door read IA/ST (Information Assurance/Security Team), with the numbers 9930 set in white on blue, red, and black strips. Below it, a white keypad stared back at me with a single red LED, now dark. Grateful that Kate had taken me for a dry run, I ignored my shaking hands and passed my SACS badge over the red LED, bringing the eye to life. I then punched a code that Kate had made me memorize into a small keypad and examined the heavy safe combination dial. Someone had already entered the combination and unlocked the deadbolts. I fished in my pocket for a key and inserted it into the doorknob. The lock clicked, and a loud beep announced my entrance into the SCIF. The lights in the main room were already on, and I could hear shuffling coming from the office.

Hanssen didn't come out, so I crossed the room and hovered before his open office door. My new supervisor was tall and lanky in an off-the-rack navy suit over a crisp white shirt. He wore a red tie that I would come to know well; he'd change it once in two months. I placed him in his late fifties, more than twice my age.

Hanssen had left his overhead lights off. A desk lamp cast

more shadows than light across the stark space. The television on the other side of the room glowed with a real-time feed of Pennsylvania Avenue as seen from a rooftop camera.

When Hanssen stood up, I saw that he had three or four inches on me. As he came around the desk, the keys in his pocket jingled. He had a slight limp that made each step a lurch. His dour expression bore down with a physical weight, and I could see why he'd received the nicknames "Dr. Death" and "The Mortician" around the FBI.

I reached out a hand. "Bob Hanssen? Hello, I'm—"

He held up one long-fingered hand. "You can call me sir, or boss."

A bead of sweat dripped down my back. I held on to my mask and shook hands with Hanssen. "Okay, boss," I said.

"Get yourself situated at your desk. I'm busy right now. We'll talk soon."

I retreated to my brightly lit desk and blinked as my eyes adjusted back from the gloom. An old IBM desktop squatted beside an ancient monitor. I frowned at a system so obsolete the FBI couldn't donate it to charity. The system I'd built on my home workbench could run circles around this dusty monster, something I'd told the FBI on a number of occasions. How could we assure information if our data crept through machines that couldn't even run outdated security software?

The FBI's mission is to protect the American people and uphold the Constitution of the United States. The bureau traditionally accomplished this mission by investigating crime and protecting the nation against foreign and domestic spies and terrorists. In the past, FBI agents would rattle doorknobs and pound the pavement, conduct elaborate sting operations, and orchestrate raids on a bounty of paper files seized from potential criminals and spies. Trained analysts sifted through that information, essentially functioning as human data processors. They relied on decades of experience to identify the patterns and find the evidence that broke cases, assured successful prosecutions, and carved the FBI's legacy into the stone of history.

Somehow along the way, however, technology left the FBI behind. Five years before I first entered Room 9930, when I was manipulating Excel spreadsheets for the consulting company that had driven me to the bureau in the first place, the civilian world had already embraced digital data over paper. When I first joined the SSG, I was shocked to witness analysts arguing over piles of physical surveillance logs as they attempted to predict a target's next location. It boggled my mind that the FBI took days to accomplish what a simple database could manage in a search that took less than a second.

In July 2001, Assistant Director Dies would testify before Congress that the FBI was suffering from a lack of modernization. Criminals across the world were able to dodge the FBI's long arm by ensuring that their technological savvy stayed one step ahead of law enforcement. The FBI needed to up its game.

One look at the aged IBM beside my desk told me we were losing the battle. In the year 2000, more than 13,000 FBI desktops were four to eight years old and couldn't run the most basic software that American teenagers had been enjoying for years. FBI agents spent hours tapping through screens of information using complex keystrokes. Few of them would know what to do with a mouse even if you could install one.

Civilian businesses and most neighborhoods had graduated to DSL connectivity, but smaller FBI offices and field sites connected to the FBI's internal network at speeds equivalent to a 56KB modem. The minimalist FBI databases couldn't store detailed investigative information like photographs or graphical and tabular data. Forget calling up a video of a crime scene—or of a spy setting a signal or approaching a drop site. Dies testified that "fundamentally, at the dawn of the twenty-first century, the FBI is asking its agents and support personnel to do their jobs without the tools other companies use or that you may use at home on your system."

Email was the FBI's other Achilles' heel. While the world transitioned from paid AOL accounts to free Hotmail accounts, making email ubiquitous, the FBI continued to print memos and route them in interoffice envelopes. For this, at least, there were good reasons. The transition from paper to digital introduced new vulnerabilities that, frankly, terrified the FBI. Before email replaced conference calls and in-person meets—before instant messaging, texting, and tweeting—the FBI had locked information in guarded vaults and gave only a few people the keys. Internet connectivity changed the way we conduct business, how we communicate, and how we gather information. It shrank the earth to the size of a data point and created shared communities between people who previously could never know each other's stories. But it also became the spy's closest companion—and the security expert's nightmare. The FBI and the majority of the intelligence community implemented extraordinary controls that mitigated the dangers posed by an open and accessible Internet. The most classified information remained behind servers that didn't touch the anarchy that we call the World Wide Web.

In the year 2000, though, email had revolutionized world communication, and the FBI had caught the buzz. It was either jump on board or become obsolete. But we still hadn't figured out how email could be integrated into a secure system without compromising that security. The FBI's initial solution was to continue to keep the two separate. Each squad had a single team computer that was exclusively used for the purposes of email. Which meant that everyone used two computers: one internally connected computer to deal with sensitive government work, and a separate, external computer to access the Internet.

Email gained traction as the preferred method of communication, and employees cried for change. The single squad Internet computer created the same problems that any big family living in a smallish house manages every morning: everyone wants to use the bathroom at the same time.

We were all behind the curve, which is why Room 9930 had two computers, both of which had clearly been recycled several times over. I knew that the covert purpose of IA/ST was to catch a spy, but the FBI could have at least given better tech to the team ostensibly tasked with securing the FBI's data.

My chair squeaked beneath my weight. The FBI could have also given us better furniture. I leaned back and forth, making noise the way one might worry a painful tooth. While the dinosaur on my desk booted to an already-outdated version of Windows, I picked up my executive office phone and called Kate.

"I'm here."

"Good. How's it going?"

I shouldered the phone and typed my username and password into the FBI NET prompt. "Fine. I'm just not sure what I'm supposed to be doing here."

A low voice, almost a whisper, made me lose my grip on the phone. "Who are you talking to?" I looked up to see Hanssen looming over me. In the first ten minutes he had already thrown me off my game.

"Sorry, honey, I have to go," I told Kate. "My, ah, new boss just walked into the room." I hung up before she could answer.

"That was my wife, Juliana," I said. Hanssen could dissect a frog without a scalpel. His eyes cut right through me. "First day on the new job, you know."

"It's good that you're married," Hanssen said, and walked out of the office. His feet barely made a whisper of noise on the blue industrial carpet. I couldn't remember the last time someone had snuck up on me.

Hanssen's only other words that day were to tell me he was going out around lunchtime. I dutifully called Kate to let her know the boss had left the SCIF and then counted to ten before leaving myself to shadow him. Within two turns I knew I'd never try to follow him inside FBI HQ again. He knew his way around the building like a man who walks a church labyrinth for an hour's meditation every morning. Numerous employees, mostly on the older side, welcomed Hanssen with friendly waves and the sort of greetings that hid an undertone of *How did you get promoted before me?* If they saw me next and disclosed that fact to anyone, I could compromise the investigation. Not to mention the risk of getting lost again each time he took a blind turn I couldn't follow.

My first day as a crack spy hunter fizzled and died without anything of note to write in my surveillance log. After Hanssen left for the evening with a goodbye dripping with manufactured politeness, I locked up and met Kate a few blocks away.

Our first debrief had a single positive note. I hadn't screwed up. Hanssen had come to the office, met his new staff member, and hadn't yet detected that we'd built an extraordinary mousetrap. Mission accomplished, but I'd have to do better.

Kate drove me to law school, listening silently as I detailed each of my few interactions with Hanssen. As I grabbed my books and stepped out of the car, she said, "Great job, kiddo. Put it all in your log."

Kate wanted written surveillance every day. That meant memorizing everything Hanssen said and did so I could type it out later. As soon as I settled into the last row of my Corporations class, I turned to the back of my notebook and scribbled down everything I could remember. What Hanssen said, whom he met with, what he ate, how he dressed, where we went, and what meetings we set up. Anything he mentioned about computers, or old cases. All his hopes and dreams and past indiscretions. At least the ones I could pry out of him—which, at the moment, numbered zero.

If Professor Wilmarth happened to glance toward the back of his lecture hall, he might have thought I was riveted by his lecture on corporate transactions. I wrote furiously in a black-

and-white composition notebook, but not one word was about piercing the corporate shield or forming subsidiaries. I lost myself in the minutiae of my day, dumping my carefully hoarded memories onto the college-ruled pages before time could steal them. I prayed that Wilmarth didn't call on me.

Turley's Criminal Law class followed a short break spent exchanging a few pleasantries with fellow students at an enterprising coffee shop that stayed open late for the future lawyers. When finally the clock stuck nine and Turley rested his case for the evening, I trudged to the Metro to catch Juliana before she turned in for the night.

I would sometimes find Juliana studying at my desk. She would spread out her books in a small clearing of computer parts and floppy disks. As an evening student, I had time for two classes a semester. Juliana was taking six classes across town at American University with an eye on a business degree. She had rounded out courses in reading and writing with Macroeconomics, Psychology 101, and Russian Studies. Knowing law classes would keep me out late, she also continued her lifetime study of the piano with a private instructor.

"Russian?" I leaned over her shoulder and glanced at the textbook cracked open in a pool of lamplight.

"*Da,*" she said.

"Almost done?"

"Maybe enough for tonight." She craned her neck for a kiss. "I'd love a bath."

"I'll heat up some water."

"*Spasibo balshoye.*"

Juliana yawned and left for the tiny bathroom. I filled our biggest pot with water and put it on our two-burner stove. By the time I changed out of my suit into comfortable clothes, the water had boiled.

"Scootch back."

Juliana moved to the back of the tub and shivered in the lukewarm water. The building's pathetic boiler never had enough hot water. Showers required speed and dexterity before the water turned to ice, and warm baths demanded multiple trips to the stove.

Juliana sighed as I poured boiling water at her feet. She stretched into the now-steaming bath and purred her thanks. "How was work?"

I set the heavy pot out in the hall and peeled oven mitts from my hands. "Okay. I met my new boss."

She turned to look at me. "Was he nice?"

"Not exactly."

"How do you mean?"

"We barely spoke two words. I'm not even sure what I'm expected to do."

"Ask him about the Redskins." She laughed. "All you American men love talking football."

"Maybe I will." I picked up the pot.

"Honey," Juliana said, stopping me. "You'll be fine. You always are."

"Thanks," I said.

She pretended to shiver and made big eyes at me. "Maybe another?"

I laughed. "Anything for you."

"Good boy," she said.

I closed the door behind me and quickly set another pot of water to boil. While I waited, I unlocked a drawer in my work desk and removed a laptop the FBI had issued me. I set the blocky netbook on Juliana's Russian textbook and fired up the boot sequence. Before the ancient machine could finish booting, the water boiled.

I donned oven mitts, made another trip to rescue Juliana from hypothermia, and promised her another pot. While the third pot heated up, I snatched my composition notebook out of my shoulder bag and turned to my work. The following evening, I would need to provide a surveillance log to Kate, and I couldn't very well write it and print it out with Hanssen looking over my shoulder.

I slotted a 3.5-inch floppy disk labeled LAW SCHOOL NOTES into the laptop, opened up a Word document, and started writing.

"Eric!"

Juliana's shout nearly made me fall out of my chair. I slammed the laptop shut and spun around in time to catch her dash past me in a dripping bathrobe toward the kitchen. The forgotten pot bubbled scalding water over the stove and onto the floor.

Juliana reached for the pot and then cursed. She glared at me and then at the oven mitts in my hand before thrusting her hand into a stream of cold water from the kitchen sink.

I spared a moment to slip my composition book back into my shoulder bag before rushing the three steps it took to reach the kitchen. The oven mitts hung useless from one hand. As little and late as my apology.

"I'll be fine," Juliana said. "What were you doing over there? Playing video games?"

"I wish," I said honestly. "I wanted to type up some law school notes."

She pushed past me to the freezer and cracked an ice cube from its tray. "On that laptop? When did you get that? We can't afford . . ."

I took the ice cube from her and wrapped it in a paper towel, then took her hand gently and examined the red burn across her palm. "The FBI issued it to me. I'm only supposed to use it for FBI memos, but didn't think anyone would care if I wrote a law school paper on it."

I held the ice against her hand as I told my lie. She leaned her head against my chest. Her wet hair chilled my skin where it soaked through my hoodie.

"I'm going to go get my pajamas on," she said. "Tuck me in."

She left wet footprints in her wake as she retreated to the bedroom. I hid the laptop under the couch and followed more slowly. When I got into the room, Juliana had curled up into a ball under the comforter. I quietly slid in beside her and lent my warmth to hers.

When she relaxed into the measured breathing and tiny movements that told me honest sleep had come, I slipped out of bed and took all four steps to the living room and the laptop under the couch. I typed up my notes, encrypted them, and saved them to the small floppy disk. The following night, I would hand the disk to Kate on the way to law school and she would give me back another one, blank. Each night this would become my routine.

My father used to say that sleep was a weapon. For me, sleep was an adversary.

## CHAPTER 6

# THE WORST POSSIBLE PLACE

January 17, 2001—Wednesday

**W**ake up. It's a new day."

Thoughts of murder fled before the smell of freshly brewed coffee. I cracked my eyes to find Juliana smiling at me over my favorite mug. Tendrils of steam curled lazily above a golden FBI seal. I'd bought the mug for myself from the FBI gift shop after receiving my badge and credentials. The fact that a highly classified undercover operative sipped his morning coffee from an official FBI mug was a joke I shared with myself.

Juliana was already dressed in jeans and a startling red blouse. She woke with the sun. I preferred that the sun be in its proper place in the sky before I fell out of bed.

"How is your hand?"

She wiggled her fingers. "Better this morning. Nothing serious."

"I'm sorry."

She smiled. "Get dressed. Breakfast is ready."

We didn't have a table, so we ate on our couch with plates perched on laps. Juliana had woken me up an hour early so that we'd have time together. I couldn't tell her that I'd slept less than four hours. By the time I got my surveillance log finished and skimmed the cases I'd need to know for class, midnight had come and gone.

"The Hello Lady was at it again last night," Juliana said.

I took a bite of my scrambled egg on toast. "She's completely crazy."

"It's a bird. I'm sure of it." Juliana's smug grin made me laugh. "Wanna bet?"

"How can we ever know?"

"Aren't you some sort of FBI investigator?"

I set my empty plate on our tiny coffee table. "The FBI didn't train me to spy on our neighbor!"

"But aren't you curious? You got onto the roof."

I shushed her. I'd picked the lock on the padlock leading up to the roof so we could install a satellite dish and watch more than five TV channels. As far as we knew, no one in the complex knew that I'd dropped a cable over the side of the building and in through one of our windows.

"I only use my powers for good."

She snorted. "Good like fifty-five TV channels we never have time to watch."

"I won't be in law school forever."

She glanced at our clock. "You'll be late for your second day at work. I'll drop you off at the Metro."

A beautiful blonde had woken me up with a cup of coffee, I didn't get lost on the way to 9930, and I'd beat my boss to the office. Not a bad start to the morning. It could only go downhill from here.

The combination lock confounded my first few tries. I hated those locks. So did most FBI personnel. It wasn't uncommon to see a whole squad standing out in the hallway in the morning, waiting for the one guy who knew how to open the thing to arrive. I was not that guy.

"Need help?" Garcia grinned under his thick mustache. As he reached for the combination dial, his blazer gaped, and I saw a holstered gun at his hip. Most veteran agents locked their guns in desks when they arrived at HQ. You could always spot the newbies because they walked around heeled. Garcia was anything but a newbie. It was clear the investigation had us all on edge.

"Open Sesame," he said. The lock clicked and I heard the deadbolts slide home. "You can do the rest. The last number is sticky."

I thanked him and completed the security sequence to enter the SCIF. I felt like the dumb teenager who returns to the haunted house while the audience is screaming for him to run.

"I'm right down the hall," Garcia said, and walked away.

I left everything unlocked and paced the Spartan room. Blank walls and boring furniture. Thin carpet that would set your hair on end if you walked around in socks. Zero windows, one door, baffles on the vents to prevent noise from escaping. Harsh overhead lights beat down relentlessly. A massive whiteboard dominated the wall that Hanssen's office door shared. On a whim, I picked up a black marker and wrote "Information Assurance Security Team" in big letters at the top. Then I underlined it.

The door beeped. *Here we go.*

Hanssen plowed into the room clutching a small cardboard box with one arm and dragging an exercise contraption behind him with the other. He paused and peered past me at the whiteboard.

"Do you want help with the, um, exercise machine, boss?"

"It's a rowing machine," Hanssen said. "I row."

I didn't know what to say to that, so I took a page from Hanssen's book and said nothing. Hanssen set the machine down and strode past me to the whiteboard. He thrust the box at my chest, snatched an eraser from the whiteboard tray, and attacked my markings. He then wrote "Section" after the remaining words.

"Information Assurance Section," I read, and immediately regretted opening my mouth. "Boss, aren't we a security team under Garcia's operations section?"

His withering glance nearly made me drop the box. "We are deciding who we are and what this section will accomplish. Not those paper pushers out there."

"Understood."

"We'll see. Your first task is to define 'Information Assurance.' We need to know what we are doing before we start doing it."

"I'll get right on that."

He peered at me just long enough to push me from uncomfortable to concerned, then took the box from me. "My office." He paused. "Bring the rowing machine."

I followed Hanssen from the bright halogen lights of the main pit area of the SCIF into his gloomy cave. He paused before slumping into the executive chair to pull a thick gray device from his back pocket. My eyes tracked his hand.

"It's a Palm Pilot." He froze, watching me watching him.

I stared at the thick digital assistant and caught the label on the back. A Palm IIIx. "I have a pager," I said through a mouth dried out by my pathetic joke.

He slipped the Palm into the blue canvas bag beside his desk. "And that's why you'll always be a worthless clerk."

The desk lamp illuminated half his face and left the rest of the room adrift in shadows. The analytical part of me wondered if the technical team had tested the hidden camera under low-light conditions. The rest of me stood like a chastised student before a very angry principal.

Two leather seats waited before my new supervisor's desk. Without asking, I sank into one as a long, uncomfortable silence stretched between us, interrupted only by the machine-gun click of Hanssen's ballpoint pen.

I could see the suspicion on his face. Go find your nearest friend from the military, police, or rescue squad—or anyone doing intelligence, special ops, or high-stakes investigative work. Any of them will agree that their work requires them to balance on the razor's edge that separates suspicion from paranoia. Suspicion is healthy. It guards your back, keeps your eyes up and open and alert to signs of danger. Paranoia is suspicion's ugly younger brother. Paranoia paralyzes decision-making, invents threats out of thin air, and crushes all confidence beneath a heavy boot. Right now, Hanssen was suspicious. But any mistake I made—an errant word, a stray slip of paper, a phone call, a feather's touch—could push him over the edge. If this guy really was a spy, he would, at best, cut and run. At worst, he might shoot me on his way out the door.

"So what do you think of the Redskins?" I asked.

There are many ways to unnerve someone. Long periods of uncomfortable silence will often prompt random forays into conversation. I didn't want to talk about the weather, so I took Juliana's advice from the night before and chose my favorite football team. In 2000 the Redskins had fired their coach after winning six of their first eight games. Everyone was still talking about it.

Not Hanssen.

"Football is a gladiator sport," he said with a wave of his pen. "Only idiots and brutes play. You'd have to be just as much of an idiot to watch it."

I hunched back in my chair. My first attempt at conversation had flamed out as spectacularly as the Redskins' season. Hanssen clicked his pen and glared at me.

"Tell me about your wife," he said.

Saying something unexpected in a conversation can also unnerve someone. I didn't want to speak about my personal life with someone who'd done something to get on the wrong side of the FBI. But alone in the room with Hanssen, I didn't have a choice.

"She's from Germany," I said. "We were married in August." I forced a smile. "It's all very new."

"Where in Germany?" His voice sounded less robotic, more pleasant.

"The far east. You wouldn't know her hometown. I couldn't even find it on a map."

"You'd be surprised what I know." Hanssen sat back. "Does she speak Russian?"

"Yes." I wanted to lie, but how much did he already know?

"Interesting," Hanssen said, leaning back, his stare unmoving.

Before the fall of the Berlin Wall, the Allied Forces controlled the west side of Germany and built it into a country of peace, democracy, and prosperity; Russia, however, controlled the east. The machine-gun turrets on the east side of the Berlin Wall had faced inward, toward their own population. Russian socialization began as early as possible, and every child learned Russian as a second language. Juliana's English schoolbook was filled with anti-Western propaganda. Although churches speckled the countryside, the Socialist Party frowned upon religion and reached the barest accommodation with the dominant Protestant faith. Each house in Juliana's village was a compound. High walls and wooden shutters blocked neighbors who might report to the local Stasi. The government stole acres of land from Juliana's grandfather, and neighbors hesitated to accept her half-Polish mother.

When the Berlin Wall finally came crashing down in 1989, and David Hasselhoff united the east and west in song, Juliana had just turned twelve. By 1994, under the "Two Plus Four" Treaty signed by East and West Germany and the four Allied Forces, all foreign troops had to depart the now-unified country. Russia shuffled more than 485,000 soldiers and dependents, along with thousands of tanks, armored personnel carriers, artillery pieces, planes, and helicopters, back across the Russian border. Germany's two halves might have reunited, but the east suffered a recession that sparked a migration of young professionals to the west. Juliana left her small village the moment she could. Her first job was in Aachen, Germany—over 800 kilometers directly west from the town of her birth. A year later, she found a program that would take her to the United States, farther west than anyone in her village had ever traveled.

Hanssen clicked his pen, his pupils as round as bullet heads in the dim light. "Do you know what we are doing here?"

"Protecting information?" I ventured.

Hanssen sighed with disgust. "Where on earth did they find you?"

My mask slipped, and I could feel microexpressions colonize my face. "I'm an investigator," I said, forcing myself back to neutral. "Years on a terrorism squad ghosting targets. Two years ago when I started law school, I transferred to computer analytical work." I thought it best to leave out the years I spent tracking spies.

Hanssen scooped up his pen and wrote a single word on a yellow legal pad: "Investigator."

"We are protecting every data system in the FBI—FBI NET, ACS, Trusted Guard, our data center—all of it." The pen whirled and clicked. "Take the Automated Case System, for example. Complete garbage. All it would take is one bad bureau person to invalidate the security. ACS works as long as someone is not a spy."

As of 2018, the FBI has jurisdiction over violations of more than 200 categories of federal crimes; employs 35,000 people; and staffs 56 field offices throughout the United States, more than 400 resident agencies in smaller cities and towns, and more than 60 international offices called "legal attachés" in US embassies worldwide. In other words, the FBI is massive, and it does a lot of things. The FBI relied on ACS to share immediate information between squads. It sought to solve the problem of FBI SWAT agents kicking in the front door of a drug-cooking operation while, unbeknownst to them, an FBI organized crime task force stormed the back door. Worst-case scenario? Top FBI marksmen fire at each other while the bad guys cower in the middle of the raid site with their hands over their heads.

To add to the complications, the FBI is not the only agency that conducts counterintelligence and counterterrorism operations, or chases spies, or deals with corruption, crime, and kidnapping. Tens of thousands of civilian law-enforcement personnel across the DEA, CIA, NSA, Secret Service, ATF, and others all have a stake in the game of defending the United States from domestic and external threats. For this reason, the FBI shares certain case information with other agencies as well.

Hanssen made a good point. Sharing information works only as long as no one gives access to a spy. He clicked the pen. The noise had grown past a distraction. Each press of his thumb drove a nail into the side of my head.

"I heard you attend George Washington Law School," he said, a switchback turn. "I have a nephew who graduated from there. My son is in law school at Notre Dame."

I grabbed the lifeline and pulled my way back into the normal rhythm of conversation. We learned that our mothers share the same name—Vivian. Both of our fathers served in the Navy when we were born. Hanssen's father had then become a Chicago police officer. My grandfather walked the beat in Queens, New York. Commonality. The more I could find in common with the guy, the better I could do my job and chip away at him. I sat forward and fought against the smile that tickled the edge of my lips. Maybe I could do this. Hanssen was known to be discreet, to keep to himself. He rarely spoke to people, and he made those who spoke to him feel inferior, turning them off from further conversation. If he went to a party, no one remembered him. If he walked up to a craps table, the next throw would seven out. He was the ultimate cooler. He had the perfect demeanor for a spy.

The detail-oriented, analytical FBI had chosen me over countless senior agents with decades of experience in making people talk. I had no idea why, but maybe they'd put me in this chair across from Hanssen's desk because they knew I had something that the undercover superstars didn't. Maybe *I* was the superstar.

Hanssen shoved the legal pad across his broad executive desk. I caught it before it could slide off onto the floor.

"I'd like you to write your full FBI name, your address, Social Security number, and birthdate. Under that I'd like your wife's name. Juliana, was it? And her Social Security number. Then jot down your parents' names and address."

I froze. Every scrap of confidence retreated. It took all my self-control not to look back at the spot where I knew a hidden camera probably couldn't see a thing in this gloom. Radios, cell phones, and sometimes hand signals dialed us in to constant contact in the field. When I was a ghost, a team member always had my back, and I could consult my team leader in real time for orders. But Hanssen's face murdered all thoughts of excusing myself to a forgotten appointment or to the bathroom. There would be no opportunity to call to Kate to ask how I should proceed. I was alone in the wind. Undercover as myself.

"Why do you need this?" I tried to keep my voice from squeaking.

Hanssen waved away my concerns. "Protocol. I'm your supervisor."

I picked up a pen and wrote. Each letter, every number invested me deeper into the case. Since antiquity, the oldest stories have shared a common trope: knowing a person's true name gives you power over them. Criminals use what we now call personally identifiable information (PII) to steal someone's identity. Spies can use it to compromise a target. If information is the most valuable commodity on earth, personal information is the Holy Grail.

I finished writing my parents' names and address and hesitated before pushing the pad back to Hanssen. In my mind, I tore the page away and ate it, or set it on fire as I ran from the room. In reality I shrugged. No big deal.

Yeah, right.

Hanssen pursed his lips like a schoolteacher grading an exam. One thumb moved along the paper almost intimately. I would have to change my shirt when I escaped his office or I'd spend the day smelling like sweat.

Two seconds before I succumbed to nerves, he spun the pad around so I could see my writing. Hanssen's next words burned into my brain.

"Did they ever teach you about Hanssen's law?"

My wife's name, written in blue, caught my eye. I wet my dry lips and asked the obvious question. "What is Hanssen's law?"

"The spy is always in the worst possible place."

Hanssen's opening salvo punched me in the gut. "We didn't learn that in Quantico," I said, each word measured and tested against the baseline. I recalled the polygraph examination chair, tight belly bands strapping me in. "What does it mean?"

Hanssen held up a finger. "One, the Russians are constantly targeting the most damaging information at the most damaging places. That is where you'll find the spy." He held up a second finger. "Two, the spy has the knowledge to take that information and sell it where he can make the most money and do the most damage."

Hanssen clicked his pen, his eyes never leaving mine. To this day I don't know whether he was challenging me to catch him or toying with me like a cat batting around a cornered mouse. In the moment, I could only stare back, not trusting my voice.

"We are here to catch the spies, Eric," he said. "Think you can do that?"

I raised my chin. "I'm going to try."

Kate's FBI car pulled up on the corner of 11th and E, which would become our usual nightly meeting spot. I'd spend my day locked away with Hanssen and wait patiently until he left. I would call Kate, who would inform a team of ghosts that their target was approaching. Then I'd rush down nine floors and two blocks to meet her.

"You'll never believe what Hanssen told me today!" I slid into the passenger seat. Kate started the car and pulled into traffic. "Did you hear the recording?"

She glanced at me. "Sorry, kiddo. We can't hear anything. Something is wrong with the audio in the room."

"He whispers." I frowned. If they couldn't hear audio, my job just became a lot harder. "He's a low talker."

"You'll have to do a better job memorizing," Kate said. "Do you have yesterday's notes?"

I handed her my "law school notes" disk. "On there. Not much, but today's will be better."

"Do tell."

I told her about Hanssen's law, about his theories about the ACS and the holes in our security. I told her about how he interrogated me about Juliana, and the business with the legal pad and my personal information. I talked until we pulled up outside the GW Law Building and then for five minutes more. I was late for class, but also giddy with excitement over all I'd accomplished.

"Great start," Kate said when I took a breath. "A few notes . . ." She drew up a knee so she could turn to face me. Kate had a way of giving you her full attention when sharing a conversation. She never looked away or fidgeted—microexpressions of boredom and escape. She knew how to build rapport and trust.

"First, never call him Hanssen. Not in our conversations or in your logs. From now until you write a book someday, he's Gray Day—or GD if you prefer." She winked. "Second, good work. It might seem like he was trying to intimidate you. GD probably was—but you got him talking. Keep it up. Third, we want you to steal his keys. If you get an opportunity to nab them without him knowing, you're authorized."

I turned to leave and then turned back. "Gray Day. The

name reminds me of another guy we followed. A CIA guy named Brian Kelley. He had a similar code name. We called him GD too."

Kate's look gave me chills. "Forget Kelley. Gray Deceiver is old news. Hanssen changes everything. If the mole was in the FBI this whole time . . ."

We both stared at the passing traffic on Twentieth Street. Kate's sobering words brought home the gravity of the Gray Day case. It would scoop the intelligence community into its orbit and forever change the business of counterespionage. But sitting in Kate's car on a lonely January night on the second day of the investigation, we knew only one terrifying fact: the FBI had a trusted insider problem.

"I thought we never spoke his name," I said.

Kate snorted. "Speak of the devil."

I opened the passenger door. The noise of Washington, DC, drove away the haunted moment. "I'm the one that has to speak *to* him."

"You'll do fine."

# CHAPTER 7

# TRUST BUT VERIFY

On February 28, 2007, Hanjuan Jin lined up with other passengers before a jet bridge at Chicago O'Hare Airport. Jin's cropped black hair and petite frame lent her a disarming pixie quality that few would ever consider a security threat. Born in China, Jin accepted a position with Motorola's global headquarters in the Chicago suburbs in the late '90s and worked for the communications giant for nearly a decade. Her degree in physics from the University of Science and Technology of China and master's degree in physics from the University of Notre Dame gave her the perfect background to work on Motorola's Digital Enhanced Network (iDEN) program. Over the course of her employment with Motorola, Jin received eight merit increases in her salary, two hierarchy promotions, and a special adjustment. She was a star employee working on one of Motorola's critical cellular telecommunications technologies. She had become a naturalized citizen of the United States just a few days earlier.

Jin shuffled through the line. Three people ahead of her showed their boarding pass and passport to the gate attendant and passed US Customs and Border Protection officers behind a small table. When Jin showed her documents to the attendant, a small beep ruined her life.

Officer Nicolas Zamora called Jin over and asked her to place her carry-on bags on the table. She had been randomly selected for an examination. Jin handed over her travel documents and Zamora noticed something odd about Jin's ticket to Beijing: it was one-way.

"Are you traveling with more than $10,000?" Zamora asked. "If so, you are required to declare the currency."

Jin fought for composure. "I have $10,000."

Zamora hadn't expected Jin to answer so frankly. He gave Jin a form that explained the currency reporting requirements. She asked for one in Chinese and he produced it. It didn't take a crack investigator to spot that something was off with this passenger.

After reading the form, Jin amended her currency declaration to $11,000. She drew two bank envelopes from her laptop bag, each stuffed with $5,000 in cash. Then, after a moment, she fished another $1,250 out of her purse. The other passengers streamed by Jin on their way down the jet bridge toward the massive plane that would carry them to China. Each rubbernecked out of the corner of their eye, relieved that customs hadn't singled them out. How embarrassing.

"Is this all you have?" Zamora asked.

Jin nodded. "Yes."

"I'll have to examine your bags."

Jin watched the last person pass and board the plane. If only she had lined up one person earlier or perhaps later—

"Ma'am."

Jin nodded.

Zamora found four additional bank envelopes, each containing $5,000, for a total of $31,252. He also found Motorola documents marked as "confidential and proprietary information," a laptop, a hard drive, several thumb drives, and other documents in Chinese.

"You'll have to come with us."

Zamora and his CBP colleagues escorted Jin to their office. They read Jin her Miranda rights, parked her in a nondescript holding room, and called the FBI. Two FBI agents interviewed her for nearly five hours. Jin missed her flight.

In February 2012, a judge convicted Jin of three counts of theft of trade secrets. According to the evidence from Jin's laptop and numerous FBI interviews, Jin took a medical leave of absence from Motorola in February 2006. While on sick leave, she traveled to China and pursued employment with Sun Kaisens, a Chinese telecommunications company that among other things developed products for the Chinese military. From November 2006 until February 2007, Jin worked directly for Sun Kaisens on military projects for the People's Republic of China. Sun Kaisens even gave her classified Chinese military documents to review in order to better assist with her work.

On February 15, 2007, Jin returned to the United States, in part to become a naturalized citizen five days later, but also to steal secrets. She purchased her one-way ticket to China on February 22 and the next day told her boss at Motorola that she wanted to end her medical leave and return to work. On February 26, Motorola put Jin back on the full-time payroll and reactivated her building access card.

Jin got right to work, just not for Motorola. On her first day back, Jin accessed more than two hundred technical documents belonging to Motorola on its secure internal computer network. After calling it a day, she waited until the building emptied and then returned at nine p.m. to download additional documents. A review of Motorola security cameras showed Jin twice leaving a Motorola building with hard-copy documents and other materials after midnight.

The next day Jin sent an email to her supervisor, Bob Bach, saying that her physical condition would prevent her from further work, and that she'd like to volunteer for a layoff. "I'm afraid that I have to disappoint you," she wrote. Bob had no idea that the real disappointment was yet to come. Or that the entire company would regret trusting Jin with proprietary secrets. To add insult to injury, once Bob and her other colleagues left for the day, Jin returned to the office for the second night in a row to download additional documents and snag a laptop bag to carry them.

By stumbling onto a search moments before Jin disappeared to China, the CBP and FBI seized more than a thousand electronic and paper Motorola documents from Jin. Many of the documents detailed Motorola's iDEN technology, which combined a cellular phone, two-way radio, alphanumeric pager, and data/fax modem in a single network. When Jin stole the technology, Motorola still had about 20 million iDEN customers spread over twenty-two countries. She had handed iDEN to Motorola's competitor. Some estimates have valued Jin's stolen documents at $600 million.

Hanjuan Jin was a trusted insider. According to federal prosecutors, she abused Motorola's trust and compromised carefully guarded information in order to benefit herself, a Chinese competitor, and ultimately the Chinese government. Jin was charged with theft of trade secrets and economic espionage under the Economic Espionage Act. At a bench trial, she was convicted on the theft of trade secrets charge and sentenced to prison for forty-eight months and an additional three years of court supervision. The system denied her appeal but ultimately reduced her court supervision sentence by two years, setting her free in March 2018. Many would find that sentence lenient.

Trusted insiders are not the only security threat governmental agencies and private companies face, but as Jin's case showed, they can do significant damage. A trusted insider can be an employee, a business partner, a contractor—anyone who, by virtue of their position, has authorized access to critical systems as a part of their daily duties but uses that access to steal, disrupt, or destroy. They know internal information and the secrets of the organization and are granted access to both physical locations and computer networks. They have access to and relationships with personnel at all levels and know exactly what keeps the organization afloat—and, therefore, how to cripple it. They are the "spy in the worst possible place." In the world of espionage, we have a different term for the trusted insider. Spies like Gray Day are called moles.

There are many reasons people choose to spy. The basic motives are money, ego, ideology, coercion, blackmail, and divided loyalties. Most spies are motivated by more than one of these factors. Espionage also requires an opportunity to betray, a reason to commit the crime, and sometimes a stressful trigger event to set things in motion. People who spy tend to share certain character weaknesses, too: greed, impulsivity, narcissism, feelings of entitlement, a belief that the rules only apply to others, vindictiveness, alienation, paranoia, naïveté, and thrill seeking. If Hanssen's grim image just popped into your head, you're right on the money. But serious personal problems alone don't necessarily lead a person to turn traitor. It's when these factors come together and play off one another that a spy chooses to betray their company, or their country.

How does one catch a trusted insider? The same way you catch a spy, starting with a focus on security and controlling access. Motorola had layers of dedicated security, including limited access to only certain necessary doorways for employees, mandatory bag checks as personnel departed the building, and a fleet of security guards and constant monitoring from strategically placed cameras. Despite these layers of protection, Jin managed to access critical information while on sick leave, entered the building multiple times late at night, and dodged bag checks that might have revealed stolen documents. I suspect that Motorola security may have suffered from a common Achilles' heel. When we focus our efforts outward, we may forget the old Russian proverb about diligence: *Doveryai, no proveryai*—"Trust but verify." Sometimes the greatest threat sits in the office next door.

Diligence is the key to security. When it comes to your personal space, diligence can provide the seconds you need to avoid an attack, save your wallet from a pickpocket, or keep you from bumping into someone who is too busy texting to look around. Diligence helps you spot trouble in your surroundings before it can reach you, makes you aware of escape routes, and provides you with a catalog of facts and observations necessary to later deconstruct an emergency. FBI ghosts frequently drive at high speeds through traffic and rarely get into accidents. We move safely through dangerous alleys in bad parts of town and pass through rooms without anyone taking notice. The FBI trains a hyperawareness of surroundings into the ghosts. We are diligent to the point of being human early-alert systems. Look around you every once in a while. You might spot a spy.

The NSA could have done a better job of heeding that old Russian proverb made famous by President Ronald Reagan. In 2013 a contractor and former CIA employee walked out of the NSA with thumb drives loaded with (according to the NSA) an estimated 1.7 million classified files. Edward Snowden has personally admitted to stealing hundreds of thousands of highly classified files detailing US intelligence-collection programs by the NSA. (The actual number is likely somewhere in the middle.)

According to the director of national intelligence, Snowden's information leak has compromised critical foreign intelligence collection sources and may be one of the most damaging in US history. To add insult to injury, after stealing the documents, Snowden fled to Hong Kong and then for all intents and purposes defected to Russia, where he has since remained under the watchful eye of Russian intelligence in exchange for asylum. Operationally, the US intelligence community must now assume that all information stolen by Snowden has been collected by the Chinese and Russians—and not just the information that has been published. Many of us in the intelligence community would enjoy personally escorting Snowden to stand trial for theft of US government property and espionage. Some of us would enjoy a one-on-one cage fight.

Snowden has argued that he acted because of an ideological stance that the NSA's collection practices went above and beyond what was required to protect the interests of US citizens. As a trusted insider, Snowden had the capability to both collect information with his own access and to use social engineering (or trickery) to convince others to provide him their access. He likely knew that providing the stolen information to the *Guardian* and the *Washington Post* would enable maximum exposure of the NSA's activities in order to damage the ability of the NSA to continue those practices into the future. Let's apply Hanssen's law. Snowden had a high level of access to critical information in the center of the National Security Agency. He had the knowledge to extract that information without immediately setting off alarm bells and a plan to distribute it as widely as possible. Snowden was a spy in the worst possible place.

While Hanjuan Jin's theft from Motorola and Snowden's NSA leaks are perfect examples of the severe damage a trusted insider can inflict, an old campfire story may explain it best. After a long, trying evening, a babysitter has finally gotten the children to sleep upstairs in their rooms. She settles into the comfortable living-room sofa, pillow on her lap and remote in hand, to watch TV for the next hour until the parents return and she can go home. Before she can touch the Power button with her thumb, her cell phone rings on the coffee table in front of her. She doesn't recognize the number, but answers anyway.

"Hello?" she asks in a hesitant voice.

Breathing on the other end. Then a man's voice: "Do you know if the kids are all right?"

The caller continues to call and ask after the children in a breathy voice until the babysitter calls the police, who promise to trace the call.

No sooner has she hung up than he calls again. "Do you know if the kids are all right?"

This time she draws out the call, trying to keep the caller

on the line so the police can trace it. As soon as they do, they call the babysitter and tell her to run: "The call is coming from inside the house."

That old campfire tale first came to mind while I sat across from Hanssen in Room 9930. If the children were FBI secrets, then I was the babysitter. The spy was already inside the house.

## January 18, 2001—Thursday

I spent Thursday morning attempting to define "information assurance" while Hanssen cloistered himself in his office. When I'd dared to listen at his door, I heard the unmistakable sounds of a movie. I'd slave over my keyboard while the boss hung around until he could make a few edits to my memo and then replace my name with his own. Middle management at the FBI was no different from anywhere else.

Whether Hanssen was trying to test me or had just assigned normal grunt work, I couldn't say, but my real boss—the covert one—wanted me in Hanssen's good graces. Kate had also asked me to steal his keys. I idly tapped at my keyboard to see what the FBI's databases had to say on the matter of information assurance while most of my brain wondered how I'd get Hanssen's keys. On the few occasions he ceased clicking his pen, one hand would jiggle the keys in his right pants pocket. The man was a fidgeter.

The secure databases my desktop computer could access through the sluggish intranet scarcely mentioned information assurance. This shouldn't have surprised me, but a chill that had nothing to do with the nonstop air-conditioning that Hanssen blasted into our SCIF forced me to my feet. I think better on my feet, and best when moving. Five steps from my desk to the door. Another three to the opposite side of the room from Hanssen's office, where a separate Internet computer station waited. Eight steps in reverse to reach the closed door behind which I could hear the cinematic blades of *The Mask of Zorro* beat against each other. I was a fidgeter too. Another thing I had in common with the spy.

I'd start at the beginning. I uncapped a red dry-erase marker and wrote "Information Security" in big letters on the massive whiteboard between my desk and the door to Hanssen's office, just under the black words spelling out "Information Assurance Section." The antiseptic smell of the red ink lingered. I stared at the phrase to pull it forward into my mind.

Assurance is not the same as security. We assure that information will be available, authentic, and confidential. We secure that same information by defending it from attack. Eventually, the term "cybersecurity" would come to encompass both of these poles. But at the time, most technology experts talked about information assurance and information security (INFO-SEC) as mutually exclusive practices.

I picked up a green pen and finished the full title of our small office in Room 9930. *Information Assurance/Security Team.* All that Hanssen had told me about the flaws in the ACS and Hanssen's law flooded forward in my mind until I imagined the answer swimming just behind my eyes. Our task was protecting information from outside attack and assuring that the FBI could trust and manage confidential information stored in ancient databases. Hanssen had told me that *ACS works only as long as someone isn't a spy.* We needed to protect information from attackers inside the FBI as well.

As I considered Hanssen's words, the room blurred and I stumbled back to my seat. Had we just put possibly the most damaging spy in US history in charge of cybersecurity for the FBI?

I yanked my keyboard into my lap and logged onto the Automated Case System. A black 3270 terminal emulation window popped onto my desktop. Nothing happened when I shook my mouse. "You've got to be kidding me," I said.

The FBI had dropped a thick ACS manual on my desk that I hadn't bothered to open before now. The highly technical manual required dozens of actions just to upload a single document. No wonder most agents preferred to work with paper.

I eventually figured out how to type my own name and address into the system. ACS returned no records. I wasn't under investigation. Was Hanssen?

Before I could hit the H key, his door opened. Not for the first time I wondered if Hanssen had a camera on me. He had an uncanny ability to surprise me at the most inopportune moments.

"What are you looking at there?" Hanssen strode past my desk and came to stand behind me so he could see my screen. He leaned forward over the back of my chair and put his hands on my shoulders.

I froze. The tensed muscles under my white dress shirt must have felt like stones in Hanssen's hands. I wished I hadn't left my suit jacket on the chair opposite my desk. An additional layer of cloth would help ward off the spikes of adrenaline that turned my stomach. The knot of Hanssen's tie pressed into my hair as he moved closer to the screen. My torts class spun into my mind. Assault: an imminent harmful or offensive contact. Battery: an unconsented-to touching. The FBI employee manual might call what was happening sexual harassment, but I couldn't exactly go to HR.

"You searched yourself," he said.

"Boss . . ." I scooted forward in my seat at the same time I pushed the chair back.

Hanssen chuckled but took his hands off my shoulders.

"I've been testing security in ACS," Hanssen said, scooping up my ACS manual as he passed my desk. "I still have my old access from the State Department that gives me full clearance through a full-text search. The account they gave us here doesn't have full access." He dropped the manual into my trash can. "An oversight I am certain they will correct."

I glanced from my boss to the trash can and tried not to roll the tension out of my shoulders. Hanssen followed my eyes.

"ACS is a joke. We are going to propose something better."

"Maybe add a mouse?"

That cracked a small smile. "ACS is flawed and the FBI hasn't a clue. I've been typing in names and addresses and searching through cases with my full access and then performing the same searches with my limited account. Want to know what I found?"

I fought past the question that dominated my thoughts— why had Hanssen come behind my desk?—and focused on my boss's words. Anything Hanssen thought about ACS would help Kate and her team.

Hanssen rolled his eyes and continued before I could stammer a response. "If you search with the limited account, you get the same records, but with the data replaced by $x$'s." He stood excitedly and picked up a dry-erase pen. Then he wrote a series of numbers on the board:

$$65A\text{-}WF\text{-}123456$$

"A typical file number for a suspected spy," Hanssen explained.

I had seen hundreds of these file numbers over the years and knew that the 65A stood for an espionage case, the WF for Washington Field, and the number a sequence that identified the specific case. So what Hanssen had written would translate to Case 123456, an espionage investigation out of the Washington Field Office. There was a similarly numbered case assigned to Hanssen: 65A-WF-220648. I hoped that the FBI hadn't screwed up and added it to ACS.

"If you search with full access, you see the entire number, plus the name and address and other information of the person suspected of espionage." Hanssen used his palm to strike everything after the 65A; then he replaced it with $x$'s. "This is what you see if you don't have access."

$$65A\text{-}XX\text{-}XXXXXX$$

"So you don't know anything about the record," I said. "But if you type in a name and you get a 65 case file back, you know the file is related to the person—"

"And the person is under investigation for espionage." Hanssen slammed the pen into the tray beneath the whiteboard. "All the Russians have to do is recruit someone at the FBI with ACS access, feed him a name, and have the mole conduct full-text searches." He jammed a finger against the 65A, smearing it across the whiteboard. "All that comes back is a 65A and a bucketload of $x$'s, but that is enough." He picked up the eraser. "Our mole now knows that the person he searched is compromised."

How many times had Hanssen searched his own name? "And I suppose he sells that information back to the Russians?"

"Exactly." Hanssen hefted the eraser and struck out my addition. "If *information security* is the best definition you can come up with, the future of the FBI is doomed."

I sucked down my exasperation. "It's not my definition of information assurance. I'm working through the problem."

Hanssen tossed the eraser on my desk. "Try harder." He looked at his watch. "I'm meeting my wife for the Right to Life March and won't be back for a few hours. Think you can manage things while I'm gone?"

I swallowed my laughter when I saw he wasn't joking. What did we have to manage? "You can count on me."

"I doubt that." He scooped up his coat and settled it on his shoulders. "But you are what I have to work with."

## CHAPTER 8

# DILIGENCE IS THE MOTHER OF GOOD LUCK

Thursday, January 18

After Hanssen left the office and the door closed behind him, I counted to a hundred and then walked around to look back at my desk from Hanssen's perspective. Two additional desks presented the illusion that the FBI would assign more staff to Hanssen's tiny section. I had chosen my desk over the other two because it sat in a camera blind spot. The thought of analysts watching my every move throughout the day had given me the shivers: I was used to being on the opposite end of the camera. After Hanssen's hands-on-my-shoulder trick, I regretted that decision.

Ghosts are trained to live in the shadows, to not get familiar with our targets. A ghost lives a covert professional life, relying on telephoto lenses, disguises, quick-change outfits, and the ability to disappear into a crowd. We think fast on our feet, are always ready with multiple excuses and explanations, and only show our golden FBI shield when all other options have been extinguished. Breaking cover equals failure.

I had to remind myself that I was still undercover now. Even though Hanssen knew my true name, I still had a role to play. Still, working undercover as Eric O'Neill lacked all the gravitas of my former alias: Werewolf. As a ghost, I hadn't associated with many agents after my time with Donner's squad; I'd stayed buried where they couldn't learn my name. This is because names are power, and because every now and then an agent went rogue, like Earl Pitts had, and the FBI needed unknown operatives to tail the traitors.

Code names are typically two syllables because at the FBI, the greatest investigative agency in the world, we have issues with field radio transmission. Remember your childhood games with walkie-talkies? Super-expensive FBI field radios weren't much better in the year 2000. Only one person could transmit at a time, so you needed to count one second before transmitting and one second after you finished in order to make sure everything you sent made it to the other radios. This delay in transmission and reception birthed radio codes to simplify the whole process, along with the practice of saying "over" when you finished speaking. We say "10–7" instead of "I'm taking a break" and "10–8" when we come back into the surveillance. We use two-syllable names, like Werewolf, to identify ourselves. This way if someone reaches out on the radio and either cuts themselves off early or gets "stepped on" by someone else keying in, the "were" or the "wolf" would still come through.

So why Werewolf? Code names are given, not chosen. Early in our training, my academy class had stumbled into the Boardroom and instantly fallen in love. There are many secrets for the intrepid explorer to discover in the FBI Academy at Quantico: a library, a screening room, a store, a weight room, a martial-arts dojo and boxing floor, a computer lab, a forensics lab, a devilish obstacle course called the Yellow Brick Road, and Hogan's Alley, a movie-set town the FBI commissioned Hollywood to build in order to train agents. But none of those places had beer.

The Boardroom was the FBI Academy's bar. It had a military break-room feel, with American flags hung on the wall, and it dished up bland pizza, spicy wings, and beers from half a dozen taps. Patches from the many national and international police students who attended the FBI National Academy police training school ringed the walls. Like something out of a science-fiction movie, the FBI Academy students wore identical blue polo shirts and tan Royal Robbins tactical pants. Fourteen wooden boards that looked pulled from a fence hung on the wall, and each had a different letter carved in the center and painted in gold: THE BOARDROOM.

When my new squad stumbled into the Boardroom, we found a second home. After we had sampled all the beers on tap, someone looked out the tall windows and mentioned that the weak fluorescent lights couldn't dim the majesty of the full moon. Before I could stop myself, I climbed up on a table, threw back my head, and howled. I'd carry the name Werewolf for the next five years.

Code names also protect ghosts from intercepted radio transmissions or eavesdropping. And just as we mask ourselves, we hide the names of our targets. Hanssen became Gray Day. Investigators never used his true name when referring to the case in order to protect from prying ears, or those who might hear the name by accident. Even in the halls of the FBI, diligence meant holding your trust close to the vest.

Hanssen posed an enormous problem to the FBI. We couldn't rely solely on surveillance to catch him. He had evaded dedicated spy hunters who had flipped countless stones throughout the intelligence community to examine what crawled out. He knew the FBI's blind spots and had only needed five minutes and a whiteboard to demonstrate the ACS's flaws. In the big-game-hunter world of espionage, Hanssen was a lion.

I knew from my days on the street that ghost teams following Hanssen would groan and delight in equal measure. The Gray Day case could make a career, but Hanssen's suspicious nature would make the ghosts earn every success. Ghosts are not infallible. Sometimes targets take that single turn that a ghost can't follow. Sometimes a traffic accident on a lonely street stymies the pack's pursuit. Sometimes a black cat crosses your path as you walk under a ladder, beneath a full moon through a circle of mushrooms, and the target disappears. Sometimes catching a spy requires an act of God.

On an early October evening in 1998, I stood outside the Dulles International Airport in Virginia and watched people stream out of the airport doors toward ground transportation. The sunny autumn day had turned gray, but cold couldn't penetrate the nervous energy that shifted my feet and spun my head like a roving security camera. Our surveillance had fallen apart around us, and a flow of negative statements assaulted my right ear. I adjusted the volume of my field radio and kept searching.

I'd met my team hours before in a Circuit City parking lot around the corner from a shopping mall. Our team leader, code-named "Rugby," handed out grainy photographs of a nondescript middle-aged man in his late forties. Slightly overweight and doughy, with hair turned partly gray, our target stared back with the barest of smiles. I flipped the picture over. A carefully printed label read: DAVID SHELDON BOONE.

"This photo looks old," I said.

"Best we have, Werewolf," said my team leader. "Keep your eyes open and you'll do fine."

I pocketed the photo and checked the battery level of my field radio and earpiece while Rugby handed out assignments. Boone had boarded a flight from Munich, Germany, that arrived in a few hours. We would identify him at the airport and ghost him to his hotel. Another team would relieve us around midnight.

I frowned at my position. If our operation were an NFL game, my role was free safety. I'd wait out at ground transportation to sweep up the spy if he managed to get past an entire team of veteran ghosts. I readied myself for six hours of boredom.

"Who is this guy?" one of the ghosts asked, tucking her radio in her handbag and adjusting the wires.

"David Sheldon Boone." Rugby peered through his glasses at a briefing folder. "Former army sergeant that sold out to the Soviets in 1988 while he was with the NSA. He's been living in Germany since then. Even married a German woman. We tricked him into coming back here so the shooters can arrest him." By "shooters" he meant the FBI agents. Most ghosts are unarmed.

Rugby dropped the file on the hood of his car and took off his reading glasses. "Our job is to keep him in pocket until they do."

No one would call David Boone a master spy. Indeed, Boone's erratic decisions and collapsing personal life should have led to an early investigation and arrest. In 1988, while finishing his tour of duty as a cryptanalyst with the NSA, Boone walked into the Soviet embassy on Sixteenth Street in Washington, DC. He handed his Ft. Meade and army identification badges to an embassy employee and then waited anxiously until three Soviet intelligence officers came to interview him. He established his bona fides by handing over a classified NSA document based on foreign communications that the NSA had intercepted and decrypted. The Soviets paid Boone $300, gave him a wig and mustache to wear to their second meeting, and bundled him into the back of a van so surveillance wouldn't see him leave the embassy.

Boone put on his disguise and met with his Soviet handlers a second time. They led him down to the tunnels beneath the embassy and interrogated him for hours. The spy proved his value again by handing over additional documents that he had smuggled out of the NSA by folding dozens of pages at a time under the half liner of his army windbreaker. When later asked why he spied for the Soviets, Boone said, "I needed money. Plus, well, plus I was extremely angry."

When he walked into the Russian embassy the first time, Boone's life had fallen apart. In the three years he worked for the NSA, Boone's wife divorced him and won custody of his two children. He lost most of his finances to court fees, and the court garnished the rest to support his former family. The army would deposit Boone's monthly paycheck into his ex-wife's account. She would then pay him $250, barely enough to keep him in beer. Boone's anger made him an easy mark for the KGB.

In late 1988, the army reassigned Boone to a cryptanalyst role in the US Army Field Station in Augsburg, Germany. He left his family behind and met a German woman. Six months later, he moved in with her, but he didn't report his foreign relationship until June 1990, during his security-clearance background reinvestigation. One of Boone's army supervisors told Defense Investigative Services investigators that Boone's finances had fallen so sharply that he owed money to creditors, and that Boone's estranged ex-wife had complained to his commander that Boone's paychecks had stopped coming. Boone would later tell investigators that he had deliberately allowed his debts to accumulate so creditors would garnish his military pay, leaving none for his ex.

While Boone courted his second wife, fended off his creditors, and responded to his background reinvestigation, he secretly continued to spy. In June 1990, Boone lost access to classified information because his financial woes demonstrated a lack of personal and professional responsibility. The army reassigned him to sergeant of the guard in an Augsburg military hospital. From late 1988 until he retired in 1991, Boone met with his Russian handler, "Igor," four times a year in shady spots along the Rhine River. At each meeting, Boone gave Igor classified documents in exchange for money, and the two would then set up the next meeting. On one occasion, Boone left documents at a drop site for Igor to pick up later. Often, Igor would task Boone to steal specific documents. One such top-secret document was titled United States Signals Intelligence Directive (USSID) 514. It detailed the targeting of US nuclear weapons against Soviet targets.

When Boone's spying came to light in 1998, the FBI decided to launch a false-flag operation against him. An FBI asset posing as a Russian intelligence officer called Boone, still living in Germany, and asked him to come to London for a meeting. During the meeting, an FBI asset introduced himself as Igor's successor with the new Russian intelligence service and paid Boone $9,000. Over a four-hour breakfast in September 1998, Boone told the undercover FBI asset all about his previous adventures in espionage, from wearing wigs and mustaches to smuggling top-secret documents and lying to his background examiners. The FBI asset noted that Boone carried a black canvas laptop bag slung over his shoulder.

The FBI now had everything they needed to arrest Boone, but first they needed to get him on US soil. The fake Russian intelligence operative set up a second meeting with Boone at the Marriott Hotel on Airport Road, a short drive from Dulles Airport in Virginia. Boone promised to board a plane heading from Munich to Dulles, and the FBI drafted an affidavit of arrest. FBI agents had staged an arrest plan for Boone's hotel, a quieter and more controlled location than the crowded airport mezzanine. But before they could knock on his door and read him his rights, my ghost team needed to tuck him into bed.

I rolled my head to ease the tension in my shoulders and watched sidelong through sunglasses at each person who left the bustling doors to Dulles Airport's baggage claim. This was before 9/11, so anyone could walk through the entire airport and right to a gate. We should have spotted Boone lumbering off the plane, but the two ghosts stationed there had missed him.

No one spotted Boone along the hallway to the shuttles that transport tired travelers from their flights to the main terminal. We also missed him at the shuttle docking points and at Customs. One of America's more inept spies had just dodged an entire ghost team without even trying. Bad luck.

Rugby spoke in my ear. "Werewolf, do you have anything?"

I pushed past a guy in a three-piece suit dragging a rolling bag and dodged a mother pushing her crying three-year-old in a battered stroller. "Werewolf, negative," I said. I didn't have to pull out the picture to refresh my recollection. Stress had burned it into my mind. No one matching that description had come past me.

The rest of the team was spinning anxiously. Ghosts were dashing across the breadth of the airport, looking for places he might have gone. The radio clicked and chirped. Had Boone ducked into a coffee shop or stopped for an early dinner? Did you check all the bathrooms? Could he have missed the flight? No, Rugby had already called Munich. The team there had put him on the flight.

We were rapidly losing our grace under pressure.

"Excuse me," a quiet voice asked. "Do you know where the Hertz Gold bus stops?"

I froze. The slight European accent struck me like a lightning bolt. I chased the surprise from my face and answered, consciously turning my right ear out of his sightline. The man who had approached me wore a thin smile and dark clothes. His hair looked grayer and he'd put on more weight, but face-to-face, I couldn't argue the resemblance to the photo in my pocket. He'd changed his clothes somewhere en route, defying the description the Munich team had handed over. But the black canvas laptop case on his shoulder gave him away.

*Hello, Mr. Boone.*

I pretended to stretch and turned down the volume on the field radio hidden in my coat. The tiny earpiece doesn't make much sound, but worried chatter was coming across in angry bursts and Boone stood very close. European close. "Turns out I'm heading there too," I said with my most cordial smile. "We can wait together."

"I appreciate that." He followed me down the ground transportation concourse to the Hertz sign, chatting all the way.

"Long flight?" I asked.

"From Germany," he said. "You?"

Bingo. "Not so far as that." I thought fast. "New York. I'm in for the weekend to visit my brother."

"That's nice," he said.

As we shared a congenially banal conversation, I furiously mashed the Talk button on my radio, sending static and clicks to my team. After a moment, Rugby's voice silenced everyone else. "Team check in," he commanded before calling out our code names. When he reached mine, I clicked twice.

"Do you have the target?" Rugby asked.

One click. YES.

"Can you talk?"

Two clicks. NO.

"Is the target outside the airport?"

One click.

Relief flooded Rugby's voice, but his answer stayed professional. "Werewolf, keep the target in pocket until you can give us a twenty. The rest of you mount up. Once Wolf gives us that location we'll need to scramble."

"You have no bags?" Boone surprised me.

Crap. I thought fast. "Hertz Gold," I said. "You can have your bags checked through to the car." I shrugged. "Probably not for international flights, though."

"Ah, good to know," he said in a way that sought to disengage from the conversation. I was saved from answering by the golden Hertz bus that lurched to a stop.

"Enjoy your visit," I said.

He nodded. "Thank you for the help."

I let him climb aboard first. He took a seat near the driver and I made my way directly to the back. Once there I called out to my team sotto voce to let them know to come to the Hertz Gold car-rental lot.

I exited the van, watched Boone rent a car, and then called out the make, model, color, and license plate once he drove off. In seconds, one of my teammates was on the road after him. I jumped in the backseat of another car and knew my day was over. I couldn't approach Boone again, or even get close to him. In operational terms, I was burned. That didn't matter to me in the least. Ghosts rarely come out of the shadows to share the light with the spies they hunt. I was happy to disappear into the background again.

We were lucky to catch Boone that day. But as Benjamin Franklin wrote, "Diligence is the mother of good luck." There are two kinds of lucky people: those for whom luck strikes like lightning in a storm—buying the winning lottery ticket or walking away from a six-car pileup—and there are those who make their own luck by placing themselves in the optimal position to succeed. It was fortune that made Boone approach me in that parking lot, but without my years of FBI training, I'd never have been able to talk him back into our net of surveillance. If I wanted to break the Hanssen case, I needed to get to work. It was time to take advantage of my time alone in the neophyte Information Assurance Section. Talking had worked with Boone. It wouldn't be enough to snare Hanssen.

I thought back to the mission Kate had given me: steal Hanssen's keys. I assumed that the agents wanted to get into his car or home, and this was the easiest way for them to get in and out quickly, undetected. Maybe the Right to Life March was my lucky break.

I slipped into Hanssen's office, leaving the door open so that a long rectangle of light cut through the darkness. As my eyes adjusted to the gloom, I tiptoed through the silent room with my hands shoved into my pockets. Hanssen didn't need his keys to get back into the office; his SACS badge was his golden ticket to headquarters. He didn't need his keys to drive to the march, either; it began right around the corner. Hoping against hope that Hanssen had left his key ring behind, I eyed the space.

A small team was waiting three floors down. In the unlikely event that I found my quarry and snuck it away, the crew would need to copy the stack of keys before Hanssen returned and realized they were gone.

I scanned Hanssen's bookshelf. No keys. The lone credenza in the far corner of the office was shut tight. My eyes traveled to the floor; the blue shoulder bag he kept by his desk was gone. And on his desk, the green ledger books he usually left open were shut. No keys anywhere. I traced a ledger with a finger, anxious to see what was inside, but ultimately left it alone. My training didn't extend to forensic searches. Hanssen might have left the books out in the open just to catch me rifling through them. I couldn't trust the convenient invitation. With nothing left to do, I retreated to my desk.

Hanssen returned from the Right to Life March with the lumpy wad of keys in his pants pocket. He hadn't found his wife and had spent the last few hours stomping around the march looking for her. He asked what I'd accomplished during his time away, and I made up a research project by stringing together technical jargon. It was good enough, and boring enough, to ward off further questioning, and Hanssen retreated into his office.

Later that afternoon I escaped down to the FBI weight room, which resembled the kind of old gym you'd find tucked away in a corner of the Bronx. The worn leather weight benches dated from the J. Edgar Hoover era. Few FBI agents worked the old iron at that hour, and I was glad. I needed the quiet. I hadn't been able to get Hanssen's keys; I didn't know what I was doing, or even what I was trying to dig up. I picked up a barbell, screaming in my head the same way a person might scream at the bottom of a pool. I thought about something Henry Rollins, the former Black Flag front man and now all-around Renaissance man, had written: "The Iron never lies to you. You can walk outside and listen to all kinds of talk, get told that you're a god or a total bastard. The Iron will always kick you the real deal."

I stacked too much weight on the bar and punished myself with each lift. I may have been spending my days lying to Hanssen and my nights deceiving my wife, but at least the iron always told the truth.

# CHAPTER 9

# TRUTH IS A SPLENDID WILD STALLION

January 19, 2001—Friday

When I agreed to meet with Kate over lunch, I didn't expect her to point her car south over the Fourteenth Street Bridge. We drove into Virginia and parked in an underground lot beneath a Crystal City office building that looked as stark and lonely as all its neighbors. Kate grinned as an elevator took us to the top floor. "It's worth it," she said.

Broad windows displayed Washington, DC, in all its glory sprawled along the banks of the Potomac River. I gawked for a moment before Kate nudged me. We joined what seemed like all the contractors and office workers in Crystal City in the small, noisy eatery.

Kate wouldn't let me pay after we made our way through the busy line. We took our trays to an isolated corner table.

"Told ya," she said. I followed her gaze and spotted the Washington and Jefferson Memorials under a crystal January sky.

"You weren't kidding." I made a mental note to take Juliana here when I had a few moments between Hanssen and law classes and debriefings and office searches with Kate and her team.

Usually Kate and I met in her car, or halfway down an unused HQ stairwell or some empty office. In my experience, when routine bent for the unusual, bad things happened.

"Is this your usual lunch spot?" I picked at my salad.

"More like my favorite," Kate said. "The food is inexpensive, place is loud enough to have a quiet conversation, and you can't beat the view."

I realized I didn't know much about Kate. But we sat in a tiny cafeteria overlooking the National Harbor, ghosts had Hanssen in pocket and didn't expect him back anytime soon, and Kate hadn't said anything yet—perfect time to dig.

"What other cases have you worked?"

Kate raised an eyebrow. "That's a baited question. Which ones can I tell you about?"

We both chuckled and shrugged. The tyranny of secrets iced my icebreaker.

"We have one thing in common, though." Kate waved a fork imperiously. "*Sprichst du Deutsch?*"

My eyebrows shot up and I racked my brain for the tiny bit of German Juliana had hammered into my head. "*Ich spreche nur ein bisschen Deutsch.*" I held up a hand to forestall her response. "That's about all I know other than '*Hol mir ein Bier, bitte.*' "

Kate laughed. " 'Get me a beer, please'? Where did you learn that?"

"Juliana's dad. We can't speak to each other, but we could power through bottles of German beer at their kitchen table. Each time we reached empty, Gerhardt would have Juliana's little brother Hagen fetch two more from the basement—the *keller.*"

"Sounds fun." Kate sat back from her empty plate. "But you should learn German."

I raised an eyebrow. "Did Juliana put you up to that?"

"I'll never tell." Kate glanced at her watch. "On to business?"

I sat back and crossed my arms.

She ran a hand through her short hair. "We'd like you to make him angry."

I looked up. "Come again? You know he's armed and I'm not. He wears a revolver in an ankle holster and keeps an automatic in his desk."

Kate took a sip of her coffee to hide her smile.

"Fine," I said. "Make him angry. Anything else while we're at it? Should I get him to confess?"

Kate gave me a look. "It would have been great if you had gotten those keys."

I bit my tongue; the case left no room for pleasantries with either of the German-speaking women in my life. Hours earlier, I'd exchanged angry words with Juliana over an argument manufactured by too little sleep and less time. She had wanted me to review a report she had written for class, and I couldn't find the bandwidth to pull my face out of a frantic read of ancient case law. Any chance at morning conversation had spiraled past a pissing match over who had the more important homework assignment into which of us was more present in the relationship. My last shouted words chased Juliana's rigid back before the door slammed behind her.

After a cold walk to the Metro, I'd walked into the office to find Hanssen at my desk, on my phone, animated. He'd looked up and laughed, and then put the phone back down on the receiver with a single word: "Juliana." My breath caught. Juliana and I hadn't laughed together for days. The case was sending me into a free fall, and my self-flagellation didn't end with business hours.

Watching Hanssen laugh at some secret joke with Juliana had taken away what was left of my decimated confidence. Hanssen was playing me better than I was playing him; I had nothing while he had tendrils snaking toward the person I wanted to protect the most.

Juliana and I had met two summers before. At the time I was living in a group house in Adams Morgan, so close to the National Zoo that I woke to the sound of monkeys screeching and lions roaring to shut them up. I was living there with another guy and two girls, all of us convinced that our brownstone, with its four bedrooms, large living room, and dining room, meant that we'd made it. It even had garage space for my bureau-issued car.

During the summer, Patrick, one of my three housemates,

moonlighted as a bartender at Capitol City Blues Café, which became a frequent meeting spot where we could count on great music and the occasional free beer. I arrived there late one Thursday night after a hot and lengthy shift chasing a terrorism target around Old Town, Alexandria. As I opened the door to the café, the cool air and strumming blues washed over me, but everything stopped when I spotted Juliana. Tall and beautiful, willowy in tight jeans and a short top, she had long blond hair that fell behind her as she threw back her head and laughed at some joke. I don't know how long I was standing there staring, but eventually I realized I was blocking traffic, and one leg was still on the steps to the street outside.

I pried my eyes away and walked over to my friends, who'd seen the whole thing. Patrick laughed. "Out of your league, man! But I have a beer for you."

A group of the guys had just returned from a backpacking trip in Germany, and they were holding court. "You don't even need to speak German in Germany," one of them joked. "You only need to know one phrase. *Das ist wunderbar!* That's wonderful!"

We tried the new words out over our beers, raising our pints and yelling over the music. "*Das ist wunderbar!*" Two knocks on the table. I turned. It was my crush of ten minutes ago, standing at the table next to me, fist poised. She knocked again and said, "*Guten Abend.*"

The table fell silent for a long moment. And then, as though choreographed, we all yelled again. "*Das ist wunderbar!*"

Her face flushed. She turned to run, realizing she had greeted not a group of countrymen, but a gaggle of drunk Americans. Of course, I stopped her.

The months that followed were a kaleidoscope of color and light. I proposed to her on a quiet beach in Mazatlán, Mexico, under a full moon. We had been dating less than a year at that time, but Juliana's professional exchange ended in two weeks.

We came from separate worlds. I wanted her to take a part of me back to Germany.

After a yearlong engagement spent apart, we married in an ancient church one village over from the place she grew up. My parents and brothers, my aunt Mary and uncle Don, and my best pal, Christian, made the long trip to attend a wedding held in German, English, and Polish—all the languages of our shared family. The hard work began after we returned to the United States.

Juliana's government-funded exchange placed a restriction on her visa that would not allow her to immigrate to the United States for two years. We had spent one apart and had another to go. We desperately sought the counsel of lawyers at my father's law firm, wrote our Maryland representatives and senators, requested waivers from both governments, and filed volumes of pages of documentation with the US State Department. We took up our swords to be together.

Eventually the waivers came through and we passed our green-card interview. Juliana became a permanent resident of the United States, and we could lay down our swords. But sometimes the battle becomes the thing that keeps you together. Now that we'd won the war, we had to replace our shared struggle with something grander.

Life together made our dank apartment seem brighter. We still missed the sprawling brownstone high above Adams Mill Road, and a stone's throw away from the clubs and restaurants of Adams Morgan, but we had made this home together. Our cold, rent-controlled apartment was a palace as long as we shared it—at least until I was tasked to the Hanssen case. Now we were spending far too much time fighting, and had raised those swords against each other.

I muttered into my steaming mug.

"It's tough stuff, kiddo," Kate said. If anyone else had called me that, I would have blown my top. But Kate was becoming more like an older sister than a handler. She was, after all, the only person I could talk to about the case.

After giving me a minute to drown my sorrows with caffeine, Kate went on to tell me that since Hanssen was such a low talker, she could barely hear anything through the audio feed. She instructed me to work harder on remembering things for my logs.

"What's wrong with the logs?" I asked.

Kate handed me a sheet of paper. "I keep this framed on my wall. I took it down and copied it for you. Give it a read."

I turned the page over and looked at a large-font quote attributed to Charlie Donlan, an FBI instructor:

> There will be times when the answer will lie at the end of a maze so complicated by the law and circumstances that if we try to guess the next turn, we will simply be lost forever. No. We simply report what we have seen, clearly, honestly, without regard for the consequence. We are *witnesses of the truth*. It is our foremost priority. Truth is a splendid wild stallion whose presence will give us unparalleled strength. If we try to saddle it with our own purpose, its power and satisfaction will never ride our way again.
>
> CHARLIE DONLAN
> FBI AGENT
> LEGAL INSTRUCTOR

When I looked up from the page, Kate was smiling. "You got it, kiddo?" I did. My role was to observe, record, and investigate without inserting my personal opinions and thoughts. I thought back to my previous logs and kicked myself. How often had I drawn a conclusion based on limited knowledge, or thrown in some irrelevant thought drummed up at two a.m. while sleep deprived and shivering in my pajamas? Fact versus opinion—it was a crucial distinction I needed to make if I wanted the case to succeed.

The FBI needed agents like Kate, willing to follow the facts where they led without jumping to conclusions or twisting facts with their own preconceptions. I'd learned in psychology classes that observation requires distance from emotions. Ideas that come from outside a controlled study corrupt the results. It's the reason that jurors are sometimes sequestered to lonely hotel rooms without access to newspapers or television during high-profile cases. Outside influences can distort facts and thread bias through what the jury observes in the courtroom.

Kate's Donlan quote reminded me that my FBI Academy instructors had thumped the objective observations of facts into me until my surveillance logs read like a robot had drafted them. That was by design. When investigators draw subjective conclusions, they miss clues that can break cases. A few more people with Kate's investigative sensibilities in senior management might have meant catching Hanssen more than a decade earlier.

The year 1985 was a terrible one for US intelligence. During the "Year of the Spy," the FBI identified and arrested more than eight highly placed moles in the US government who were passing secrets to foreign intelligence services. In the same year, the KGB identified and eliminated as many as eleven Soviet double agents who were providing information to US intelligence. Three of the top Soviet spies for the CIA disappeared within the same year. Boris Yuzhin had spied for the United States from the Soviet consulate general in San Francisco. The KGB arrested him one afternoon in Moscow without warning, and Soviet courts sentenced him to twelve years in prison. Valery Martynov, an intelligence officer charged with stealing Western technology who was also working as a double agent for the US government, and Sergei Motorin, a mole spying for the United States out of the Soviet embassy in Washington, DC, were coaxed back to Moscow and executed. Between 1985 and 1991, Soviet human assets continued to disappear without warning or explanation, and technical operations unexpectedly fizzled and died.

Soviet counterintelligence in Moscow was good, but it wasn't that good. The only way so many espionage efforts could have fallen apart without warning was if a mole was betraying the US intelligence community from within.

Between 1987 and 1991, the FBI launched two studies to identify the mole they code-named Gray Suit. The first study analyzed historical allegations of a possible mole in the FBI. By late 1988, the team had chronologically reached the 1960s. In the summer of 1989, they issued an interim report and abandoned the study.

The second study focused on more than fifty operations compromised since 1986. Although the final report detailed problems with the FBI's Soviet operations, it refused to entertain the possibility of an FBI mole and instead concluded that the KGB had recruited a spy from within the CIA who began his espionage in 1985.

Things turned around in the 1990s. The FBI and CIA hugged it out and formed a joint investigation to find the mole, and senior management got out to the field to supervise. In 1991, the FBI worked with the CIA's Special Intelligence Unit to prepare a list of suspects that could account for the staggering intelligence losses caused by Gray Suit. None of the suspects on the list were FBI agents.

After arresting Aldrich Ames in February 1994, the FBI cranked all counterintelligence efforts up to eleven and turned its powerful searchlights fully onto the CIA. Despite finding a number of clues to the contrary, the FBI continued to believe that the mole festered within the CIA and pursued a suspected spy named Brian Kelley. The bureau code-named Kelley "Gray Deceiver" and dogged his heels long past the time when we should have turned our attention elsewhere.

Part of a 2003 DOJ Inspector General Report reviewed the FBI's pursuit of Gray Deceiver. The IG found that in the 1970s and 1980s the FBI suffered from a lack of cooperation with the CIA and from inattention on the part of senior management. In 1985 and 1986, the CIA and FBI lost nearly every significant human asset then operating against the Soviet Union. Despite these unprecedented losses, senior FBI management failed to thoroughly investigate whether an FBI mole had caused the deaths of our sources. The DOJ inspector general wrote:

*The FBI should have seriously questioned its conclusion that the CIA suspect was a KGB spy and considered opening different lines of investigation. The squad responsible for the case, however, was so committed to the belief that the CIA suspect was a mole that it lost a measure of objectivity and failed to give adequate consideration to other possibilities.*

The FBI had allowed bias to color the investigation. Instead of witnessing the truth, FBI agents had saddled it with their own purpose. The FBI's refusal to abandon the Gray Deceiver investigation and look elsewhere blinded us to the possibility that the spy might be one of our own.

"I've made edits to your logs and highlighted in blue areas where you added your own thoughts to the observation." Kate handed me a folder. "Remember, you observe everything. Write down just the facts. Save all your thoughts and impressions for debriefs with me."

"It's not like anyone but you sees my logs," I grumbled.

"Yeah, not anyone." Kate laughed. "Just the director."

I set down my coffee mug before I could drop it. "The director?"

"He sees your logs every day."

"You've got to be shitting me."

Kate's smile slipped off her face. "Eric, Director Freeh is running the case personally. What you're doing is more important than you know." She paused. "Than you're allowed to know."

I flipped through the slim folder. Blue highlights crossed each page like slender rivers bisecting a map. I could do better. "What about searching his office? I went in there to look for his keys, but didn't see anything."

Kate sat back in her chair. "Marching orders?"

"Sure."

"Don't. You don't search his office or go in there unless we tell you to." Her eyes crinkled at hard edges. "This guy . . . he's unlike other spies we've gone after."

"You can say that again!"

"He's careful. He's . . ."

"Crafty."

She smiled. Some of the tension fled from her face. "Bingo! Crafty. Leave the search to the search teams. That is, unless I tell you to."

"Copy that."

"Good." She checked her watch. "Looks like lunch is over."

# CHAPTER 10

# STRAIGHT LINES

January 22, 2001—Monday

Can you inject coffee directly into a vein? I considered the thought as Juliana's words washed against and past me like a river around an obstinate rock. We were sitting beside each other on the couch, but my mind had already turned to the case. I'd spent the night reworking my surveillance logs on my secret laptop and researching a definition of information assurance for the boss. The Donlan quote that Kate had given me hung on the wall over my computer desk. Truth might be a splendid, wild stallion, but what I needed was sleep.

"Are you here?" Juliana said.

I opened my eyes and eyed my cup of coffee the way a drunk checks whether his beer has spilled after a momentary lapse of consciousness. Focus. I bit the inside of my cheek.

"I'm here." Liar.

Juliana had her schoolbooks spread across our small coffee table. I vaguely remembered she had macroeconomics in the morning over at American University. A spike of adrenaline roused me into a panic. Corporations! I had spent so much time working through Kate's highlighted lines, I'd forgotten to study for law school.

"Hey, you with the nose in your face." Juliana touched her voice with the soothing quality you use with a wild animal, or a recalcitrant husband. "Are you okay?"

I smiled at the old joke between us. She had once translated the old saying *plain as the nose on your face* to *plain as the nose* in *your face*, which I'd found hilarious. Now it was our private joke, the kind of small connection that glues a couple together. Except these days, I felt like I was becoming unglued.

"I'm just tired," I said. "There's a lot going on at work."

She placed her pencil into the seam of her open book and spent a moment tucking her long hair behind her ears before turning to lock eyes with me. Each small, delicate movement reinforced my love for her. "Look at me." It may have been a quirk, or the fact that English is not her first language, but Juliana believed that all conversations require complete attention.

"I'm here."

"Are you?" She took my coffee and replaced the mug with her hands. Her long fingers, the same ones that coaxed magic out of any piano, gently held mine. "You haven't been for days."

There's always a storm before a flood. A moment of warning before the water sweeps everything away. A hurricane surged in my wife's eyes, green and gold and held at bay by a gentle touch. We could sandbag the flood together or let it sweep us apart. The choice was mine.

"I'm not stupid," she said. "You have a nine-to-five computer job at headquarters, but you're working more than you ever did when you worked all those crazy shifts." Her hands squeezed mine. Holding on. "I thought the idea was to work less and go to law school more."

Guilt has a funny way of turning to anger, especially when stress and lack of sleep are added in. The rational part of my brain spun up presentations and diagrams proving that Juliana was seeking to comfort me. But I couldn't get past all the demands. Law school classes I hadn't studied for, bills I needed to pay, mounting debt from paying for my law school and Juliana's undergrad degree on a GS salary, Parkinson's disease stealing my mother's voice and balance, a spy to catch . . . a wife to love and lie to. It was too much. I let go of her hands. Let the fucking storm come.

Juliana froze and then dropped her hands in her lap. She turned to collect her books. I could feel the tension vibrating against my skin.

"You talked to him."

She sat upright. "What?"

Now I turned toward her. "My boss. Mr. Hanssen. You talked to him."

She looked at me like someone waiting for a punch line to a stupid joke. "And . . ."

"He's creepy, right?"

Her shoulders fell from her ears and she slumped into the couch. "Yeah. You could say that."

"What did he want?"

She shrugged. "He asked a lot of weird questions. About Germany and growing up behind the Wall. Personal things."

"So you called and he just picked up the phone?"

She shivered. "Yes. I called you and he answered, *Eric's line.*"

I relaxed hands that had clenched into fists. I'd learned that with Hanssen, nothing was innocent. He'd crossed a line in the sand, redrawn it, and then kicked it in my face.

"He speaks Russian, you know," Juliana said. She scooped her books into her backpack. "Not well, but he asked me whether I had ever been to Russia."

Lightning rode my back and exploded behind my eyes. Now I was fully awake. "What did you say?"

She frowned. "What could I say? Of course I've been to Russia. I have family in Russia. You know that." She stood and grabbed her heavy backpack. "Was I supposed to lie to him?"

"No," I said. "Of course not."

"Wait . . ." She narrowed her eyes. I could feel the connections forming in her brain. "Is this a case?"

I crossed my arms before I could stop myself. "No!" I answered too quickly. "I mean, of course not. It's a promotion to—"

"A computer job. I get that, but . . ."

"But nothing." My eyes hardened. "It's not a case."

Juliana held my eyes for a long moment. Neither of us blinked. "See you tonight."

She left without kissing me goodbye.

Rain battered my umbrella on the way to the Metro and hounded my long slog to headquarters. I reached Room 9930 rumpled and grumpy, hoping to get a few minutes to skim case law before the boss stormed in. I found the lights off and the office empty, and smiled for the first time that morning.

Juliana's picture stood on my desk. Her father had snapped the photo a week before she first left for America. Juliana's smile, full of youth and promise, curls to the side as though she holds the secret of a great adventure. During the long months of our separation and engagement, I would stare at that picture and take comfort that I was the adventure she crossed the sea to find. Now her picture filled me with guilt for failing her expectations.

Beside it, my office phone blinked with the angry light of an unheard message. I couldn't have Hanssen speaking to Juliana. I'd begged off phone calls with Kate in front of Hanssen by pretending the conversation was with my wife. If he picked up my phone and asked Juliana about one of those calls . . .

I decided to make it difficult to come behind my desk. Instead of studying, I arranged the three unused office desk chairs around my workstation so they made a phalanx. I pulled my FBI NET workstation around to the side of my desk and left only a narrow space between the two to pass. Hanssen would have to work through my defenses to answer my phone or massage my shoulders.

Pleased with my work, I cracked my thick Corporations book and flipped through to the cases for the evening's lecture. Before I could read a word, Hanssen barged through the door into the SCIF and slumped into one of my defensive chairs. "Buzzwords are bullshit," he grumbled.

I looked up from my law book and tried to surreptitiously slide it off my desk and into my lap. Hanssen either didn't notice or didn't care. His shoulders slumped and a few extra lines traced his face, making him look older. " 'Information assurance' is a buzzword that agencies are real hot on right now. Everyone thinks they need to create an office for it, and no one knows what it is."

I felt as defeated as Hanssen looked. "Are you saying we're wasting our time?"

"No, idiot, I'm saying that the FBI is wasting everyone's time. This place is so filled with incompetents it's no wonder Russia outthinks us."

Hanssen retrieved his pen from his pocket. That pen. The moment he clicked it, I forgot the investigation. Everything fled from my mind except for the crazy urge to dive across the table and stab him with the thing. Instead, I plastered a smile on my face.

"John Boyd," Hanssen said.

"Boyd?"

"Am I not making myself clear?" Hanssen leaned back in his professorial pose—slouched in the chair, legs wide, one hand clicking that accursed pen—and began the lesson.

During the Korean War, Boyd studied why the F-86 Sabre was so successful in shooting down the Russian MiG-15 of that generation. Boyd discovered that the US planes, while inferior to the Russian MiG in terms of speed, range, and altitude, were more maneuverable and therefore able to act faster than the MiG could react. Boyd saw in the Sabre's ability to turn in rapid response to the more cumbersome MiG a blueprint for succeeding by thinking and reacting ahead of the enemy. He used that insight to devise a system: gather all the facts, observe the way the target reacted, process all the information, and then make lightning decisions. He called this an OODA loop, a rapid process of observation, orientation, decision, and then action. The decision maker who moved through this process faster than an opponent prevailed because, by acting first, he changed the situation for the adversary.

The idea is to make a better, faster decision than your opponent using the information directly at hand. In military terms this meant distilling information from the often chaotic combat environment into the essential facts needed to make choices that outplayed the enemy. In other words, in a confusing and jumbled situation, the soldier who adapts to what is happening around him and shoots first wins.

The example Boyd gave, in a thought-experiment presentation titled *Strategic Game of ? and ?,* required his students to imagine a few scenarios: carving the snow on a ski slope, towing water-skiers behind a motorboat, riding a bicycle during a spring day, and showing your child a toy tank with rubber caterpillar treads in a department store. He then challenged students to remove the skis, outboard motor, handlebars, and rubber treads from each scenario and asked what you created when you combined them.

If you guessed a snowmobile, congratulations! You just accomplished the most important aspect of the OODA loop: orienting effectively in the face of uncertainty. The first student to orient the scenario to an active decision that you have a snowmobile won.

It may sound simple, but as Boyd pointed out, most of us view the world around us as we insist it should be rather than shifting our perspective and incorporating new circumstances as they arise. And in the world of espionage, circumstances, allegiances, even truth change on every day that ends in a *y.* Those who are not flexible in their thinking are destined to lose.

"The FBI is terrible at thinking and reacting to the Russians." Hanssen gestured at the room around us. "Look at this place. The Information Assurance Section is an example of the FBI's difficulty upgrading technology, working outside the system, and conducting counterespionage." He slammed one hand down on my desk. "This place is a joke. You'd have to be a moron to expect the FBI to modernize."

I clenched my jaw to bite back my words. Hanssen liked to intersperse "idiot," "moron," and "dummy" into his conversations the way a politician might sprinkle applause points in a campaign speech, and I had little choice other than to just take the abuse. It's not like I could report Hanssen to HR or commiserate with a buddy over drinks. But this time, I had to admit Hanssen had a point. The Russians have an edge on US intelligence agencies, primarily in the number of people that they deploy. Russian intelligence officers in Washington assume that no one is following them—and they're usually right. Meanwhile, our spies in Moscow know they're being tailed by a legion of Russian surveillance operatives on any given day, requiring them to operate by deploying misdirection, subterfuge, and sleight of hand. We are more skilled, and they have more people. The result is an overall balance in the great game of spy versus spy. But the Russians continually swap the playing board and rarely follow the rules.

Even as a new Russian government stumbled from the crumbled stone façade of the Soviet Union, and we rounded up Cold War moles who had long since retired, Russian intelligence officers continued to punch their time cards. While the old guard raided file cabinets for future meal tickets, a new generation of Russian spies built castles within a new espionage sandbox. The FBI called it Moonlight Maze.

The decades-old case remains one of the most cryptic and secretive espionage investigations in the FBI's history. Sometime between 1997 and 1998 (many details remain classified), the US intelligence community learned that intruders had compromised numerous unclassified computer systems belonging to US military and government networks across the United

States. The attackers had cleverly compromised various servers belonging to universities, businesses, and even libraries in different countries and had used those computers to launch attacks against critical US agencies. The old-school hacking technique functioned like a modern-day VPN. By launching attacks from middleman computer systems, the spies could mask their origin. The complex network of attacks resembled a maze.

FBI investigators discovered that for over a year, the attackers had stolen information from air force bases, NASA, the Naval Sea Systems Command, the Army Research Lab, and the Department of Energy's nuclear weapons research lab, to name a few. The stolen unclassified records included military logistical plans, procurements, personnel records, email messages, and research information. The attackers had also left behind backdoors in each of the networks they compromised so that they could reconnect and continue stealing whenever they wished.

FBI computer forensics traced the IP addresses through cut-out servers to Russia. Agents also examined the pattern of attacks and noted that they all happened during weekdays between eight a.m. and five p.m. Greenwich Mean Time +3—that is, Moscow time. They also never occurred on a Russian holiday. The Russian spies apparently worked bankers' hours and took holidays off as they compromised US systems from afar. Moonlight Maze made the US intelligence community wake up to the new reality of Internet espionage.

The Russians integrated the OODA loop into their approach to spying. While the FBI conducted studies and pointed fingers at the CIA, the newly formed Russian Federation was preparing for a second Cold War fought in cyberspace. The Moonlight Maze of servers and compromised computer systems was a Russian OODA snowmobile. Russian spies observed the way that the Internet created new pathways to information. They oriented to the new conditions by observing how hackers in the 1980s and '90s compromised computer systems and building these practices into their espionage plans. And these new Russian cyber spies wasted no time in deciding to act.

"Boyd got things done and still bucked the system," Hanssen said. "Sometimes he worked outside of the system." The boss pointed his pen at me and gave it a click. "You should try it sometime."

I was getting four hours of sleep on a good night. I didn't have the energy to buck anything right then.

"Boyd was brought up on court-martial proceedings three separate times." Hanssen sat back. "They couldn't defeat him. He applied his theory to his life and stayed one step ahead."

I suppressed a yawn. It wasn't every day a guy's supervisor told him to rebel. I listened as Hanssen went on to criticize the FBI's behemoth way of maneuvering—politics, turf wars, silos—contrasting it with the Russians' straight line. I listened closely, mentally clocking every word for my logs. Hanssen, too, thought in straight lines—in simple, elegant approaches that worked. The ultimate OODA loop.

"The FBI can't adapt," Hanssen concluded.

"What's the solution?" I asked.

"My method," he said, and clicked his pen. "We can solve all of our computer and technical problems. A direct approach. One that outthinks the opponent." He tapped the side of my monitor. "We use a secure Linux operating system on a central HQ server network that calls to the field offices for information and uses a protocol to mask the IP address so outside hackers can't see the connection." He shrugged. "It's an evolution of the Hoover filing system. Hoover revolutionized the FBI decades ago with a simple, direct system."

J. Edgar Hoover was the legendary FBI director who served eight presidents beginning in 1924. In addition to creating the FBI, Hoover developed a filing system that incorporated extensive cross-referencing between cases. He had started his career cataloging books in the Library of Congress, and he

understood the importance of concise organization of information. As a Justice Department attorney, Hoover knew that researching case law required an index to show where courts had
amended, dismissed, or upheld past decisions. These indexed
citations tell an attorney whether law quoted from an old case
in a brief or argument remains good law.

Law enforcement works the same way. Cases often build
on each other, and without a way to index and cross-reference
cases, FBI agents would spin their wheels over already-covered
ground. Hoover brought an efficiency to the FBI's system that
was monumental in its day.

Today we would describe this as adding metadata or tag-
ging files to create groups and quickly identify files that refer
to a particular issue or idea. We do this today in our iTunes
and photo libraries to allow us to sort by album or artist, or see
every picture with Grandma's face in it or from the vacation
a few years ago in Hawaii. The FBI has called Hoover's filing
system "crucial to the success of Hoover's Bureau as it grew and
adapted to its expanding mission."

I shrugged. "Let's propose it."

He lurched forward, red-faced and tightfisted. "We shouldn't
have to propose it, dummy! If the FBI is serious about solving
these problems, *my section* should have control of all FBI technology. We're nothing but glorified advisers."

I sat back, trusting my phalanx of chairs to protect me. "Is
this a bad time to hand in my definition of Information Assurance?"

That calmed him. "Let's see it."

I dragged a sheet of paper I'd printed at home from my bag
and handed it to him. He scrutinized it and then read aloud:
"Information operations that protect and defend information
and information systems by ensuring their availability, integrity, authentication, confidentiality, and non-repudiation. This
includes providing for restoration of information systems by incorporating protection, detection, and reaction capabilities."

He dropped the page and scrutinized me. "Very good. Precise. Where'd you get it?"

"From the National Information Systems Security Glossary," I said, and stifled a yawn. "I found it last night."

He huffed. "INFOSEC. Good initiative, but these aren't our words." He tossed the paper back at me and dragged himself to his feet. "If you use someone else's work, give them credit. Otherwise you're stealing."

Talk about the pot calling the kettle black. He dismissed me and left for his office. Hanssen had beat me at another aspect of the OODA loop. Whoever progressed through the process fastest not only defeated his adversary but also sent the opponent back to square one by resetting the loop. But Hanssen had unwittingly given me a potential key to victory. All I had to do was train myself to orient and decide faster than the spy. Like a child hoping to beat a chess grandmaster, I slid back in my chair and carefully itemized my failures, hoping one of them might light my path to victory.

That evening, as Kate drove me to the George Washington Law School campus, I repeated every diminishing detail of the day. After our one conversation, Hanssen had cloistered himself in his office, so I didn't even get a chance to make him angry; and I still hadn't been able to get his keys. As I prepared to draft my notes in the back of my law book, Kate briefed me on the next steps. The FBI needed to get into Hanssen's car. I couldn't get the keys, so we needed another plan.

"We've set up the meeting Hanssen wants with the DIA. While you're there talking about computers we'll take apart his car and search it. You'll have to make sure he doesn't drive. Reserve an FBI vehicle."

"Got it."

She looked as tired as I felt. "Something big is going to happen, kiddo. We aren't sure what, but there's chatter from overseas sources." I grabbed my bag and she touched my arm. "Kiddo, this is the biggest case we've ever run."

# CHAPTER 11

# PUNCH IN THE MOUTH

January 23, 2001—Tuesday

Garcia paced his office with balled fists. He strode past the sports memorabilia and the numerous awards senior executives on the fast track to somewhere accumulate, toward his open office door, where I stood perplexed. "That bastard," he growled.

I had rolled out of bed to find Juliana already gone and the coffee pot cold. Spared our morning breakfast ritual, I leapt into my clothes and rushed to work for some extra studying time before the boss stormed in. The square of light falling out of Rich Garcia's office had turned me away from the 9930 vault, and I decided to pay the section chief a visit.

"I'm not happy about it either," I said. "Operationally, if he's answering my phone—"

"None of that!" Garcia waved off what I might have said. "Let's stick with what you told me. Your supervisor, who technically reports to me, although you'd never know it, is answering your phone and talking to your wife."

I shrugged. "Now that you put it that way, it doesn't sound so bad."

The piss and vinegar fell away from him. "No. Technically not. But it's still a problem because of . . . that other thing."

Compartments in compartments. We both knew the secret, but Garcia was an old operator. He knew I was only supposed to be speaking about the investigation with Kate. Garcia's role on the Gray Day task force was only to facilitate. I'd probably stepped in something by involving him, but when you're out on a limb, you grab for branches.

"Let's go take a look at your phone." Garcia shrugged into his sport coat. "Maybe there's a technical solution."

It took Garcia a minute to get through the SCIF door. We flicked on the light and looked at my workstation.

"Interesting furniture arrangement."

I dropped my bag on an empty desk and hung my coat on a wooden coatrack that belonged in an old private eye film. "He likes to come around my desk and stand behind me."

Garcia shook his head. "I don't envy you, kid."

I moved aside my obstacle course of chairs so Garcia could get to my phone. "Did you ever work undercover in counter-intelligence?"

"Nah, drugs and crime. The gritty stuff." He picked up my phone and turned it over. "Dallas, San Juan, Miami. I supervised squads going after Colombian drug traffickers and ran a drug intelligence squad for the mid-Atlantic." He put down my phone. "Did you know there is a beach not too far from Cartagena where they make the best fish stew on earth? You walk through this little casa, past kids playing in their living room out the back where the family set up an outdoor *cocina*. They all do it along this beach." He set my phone down and leaned a hip against my desk. The way Garcia talked with his hands made me smile. "You get a bowl of this amazing stew, sit out on picnic tables, and watch the cigarette boats pass by, one after the other. Each boat filled with cocaine. Up and down. Nothing we could do about it." He winked. "Great fish stew though."

"How did you go from fish stew and drug traffickers to running operations for FBI HQ?"

Garcia grinned and raised his arms wide. "Putting in my time in the big house. Once you make it to executive service, you put your time in here, see how things run, and then if they like you, they give you a division."

"Makes sense."

"Don't worry, kid," Garcia said. "You're a smart one. You'll get there someday."

I smiled. "I have to get through this case first."

That sobered him. "Right. On that. I can put a cutout into your phone. You can turn it off when you leave and back on when you get in."

I thought for a moment. "No. Better not. I don't want to change anything that might make him suspicious."

Garcia raised an eyebrow. "Kid, you surrounded your desk with chairs."

"That's survival."

Garcia laughed. "Whatever." He put a hand on my shoulder. "But if anything happens, I'm right down the hall."

I nodded to keep any emotion from my face. Garcia had offered the backup I'd wished for and hoped to never need. "There is one thing," I said. "I need you to reserve me a car."


"Ever heard of Felix Bloch?" Hanssen loomed in his office doorway.

I knew lots about the case. Bloch was a State Department employee who had supposedly handed secrets over to the Russians, though the FBI had never been able to collect enough evidence to charge him with a crime. We'd studied Bloch at the FBI Academy, but I was too exhausted for another round of call and response.

I settled for ambiguity. "Not really," I said.

"He was a spy," Hanssen began. "We had him dead to rights about to make a drop in Paris until the FBI and the State Department royally screwed up the case. Bloch stayed ahead of the FBI because the FBI could not apply Boyd's principle to catch him."

"He sounds like a pretty good spy."

"He was an incompetent buffoon. He was also a homosexual that was recruited by a Russian illegal that compromised him because of his homosexuality."

"Not that there's anything wrong with that—"

"Don't be an imbecile! Homosexuality is a disease of the mind. Anyone with that mental illness could easily be recruited."

I'd heard Hanssen make offensive remarks about all kinds of people, but gays were a favorite target. In this case, his disdain for homosexuality had eclipsed the facts: Felix Bloch wasn't gay. In fact, it was his relationship with a female prostitute that had brought him low. But I couldn't reveal that now. I bit my tongue as Hanssen continued his lecture on Bloch. He set the scene with a click of his pen. Bloch's handler called him to go to Europe. He brought duffel bags of classified information with him to pass to Russian intelligence. The FBI knew what he was up to—even had him confessing on a wiretap to his wife. But they couldn't put the wife on the stand due to the spousal right not to testify; and they couldn't use the wiretaps as evidence, because the phones weren't legally tapped. According to the tale Hanssen spun, all the proof was there. The FBI just had to scoop him up, and Bloch was done. But then the FBI botched the operation.

"They followed him around for months and filmed him meeting with a Soviet agent in Paris, but froze." Hanssen's face made me worry about his blood pressure. "Observe, orient, decide, act." He accompanied each word with a knock on his desk. "The FBI observed Bloch exchanging a bag with a Soviet spy masquerading as a Frenchman named Reino Gikman of all things. The FBI couldn't orient fast enough to decide to act. They just stood there with their pants down while Bloch got up and walked away!" Bloch, a stamp collector, later claimed the bag had contained only stamps, and the FBI was never able to prove otherwise.

Hanssen leapt to his feet and paced. He stopped clicking the pen and jiggled the keys he kept in his right pocket. I wondered for the hundredth time how I'd get those away from him. "As for Bloch, last I heard he took a job as a grocery bagger in North Carolina. So no. He was not a good spy. Pathetic, actually. Amateur."

Hanssen leaned in and lowered his already low voice. "The FBI didn't even get the case right. When they briefed the State Department, the FBI made an error and said Bloch passed a briefcase. It was a duffel bag."

I'd known some of the details from the FBI Academy, but this I hadn't heard before. I filed the information away for later and glanced at the clock.

"Boss, we have the DIA meeting. I reserved a car," I said. "Garcia's Tahoe."

Hanssen stared me in the eye. "I'll get my coat."

If you've ever worked in special operations, emergency services, military, or law enforcement you may have cursed a guy named Murphy. While no one knows Murphy's original identity, or the origin of the adage, Murphy's law routinely sours the best-laid plans. Simply: Anything that can go wrong, will go wrong.

The best operators plan for Murphy. On surveillance ops we would scrutinize maps to discover the best choke points to trap a target who slipped out of pocket. We would establish picket lines—static positions along a target's intended route—to call the target past and minimize any chance of being discovered. FBI training reinforced the importance of having backup plans for your backup plans.

But in the sage words of champion boxer Mike Tyson, "Everyone has a plan till they get punched in the mouth." Even the best operational strategy sometimes goes wrong. And in the world of special operations, when things go wrong, they do so spectacularly. The best operatives roll with the punches.

The FBI parking garages under headquarters were sinister.

Dim light chased shadows away from the parking spaces, some of them reserved by name for the brass, others by section or squad. As Hanssen and I descended lower and lower into the building's dark underbelly, we passed the FBI weight gym and the FBI's indoor gun range. Hanssen knew this floor well. He loved his guns—which was unnerving, but not suspicious for an FBI agent.

We walked through the dim garage on the sublevel where Garcia told me he'd left the Tahoe, Hanssen lurched each time his left foot hit the ground. I didn't know whether he had an injury or simply shuffled his feet like a recalcitrant child. Whatever the reason, he'd occasionally bump his shoulder into mine and swing his blue canvas briefcase into my hip. I gritted my teeth and withstood the abuse. I wanted to curse at him and shove him away, but the idea of even making a polite request to stop made my stomach churn. I couldn't decide which best served the case, so I did nothing. Somewhere John Boyd rolled his eyes at me.

Finally, we stopped, and I found myself staring at an empty parking space. Panic squirmed its way up my stomach and toward my ears. As the chief staff member to the Information Assurance Section, my overt job was to get my section chief to the Defense Intelligence Agency so that he could coordinate the FBI's cybersecurity efforts with them. My covert mission was to use this meeting as a pretext to remove Hanssen from headquarters long enough for a search team to drive his car into a hidden garage and comb it for clues.

I had planned it all out perfectly. The trip would take us twenty minutes in light traffic. The tour I had scheduled at the DIA and the fact-finding meeting to follow would take at least two hours, maybe more if we stopped for lunch. That gave the tech team just under three hours to accomplish their work. But everything relied on finding Richard Garcia's Chevy Tahoe.

"We'll just take my car," Hanssen said, turning on his heel.

*Thank you, Murphy.*

My panic drowned out the piercing squeal of tires as FBI employees took sharp turns out of the garage. I ignored the distant slam of car doors and the echoes of footsteps from somewhere in the distance. Sound carried everywhere down here, but none of it reached my ears. All I could hear was Kate telling me to make sure he didn't drive.

"I must have gotten the level wrong, boss." I willed him to listen. "Let's take those stairs one level down, find Garcia's Tahoe, and we can get out of here."

Hanssen agreed, but his glare could have sent the first flowers of spring back into the ground. When we exited the stairwell, my eyes were unwilling to focus on the empty parking space. Murphy had it out for me today.

"Imbecile."

"Boss, I—"

"Moron."

"Seriously, just one more level, it has to be—"

"Do you think I have time to slog around a garage when the DIA is waiting for me?"

I'm a little above average height. But Hanssen towered over me. I could feel his breath on the top of my head, and I forced myself to look up at him. And then something changed. Instead of demolishing me with a few choice words, Hanssen drew a thick keychain from his pocket and pointed across the lot. "No use worrying about it. We'll take my car, and that's final." Hanssen implemented Boyd's OODA loop—observation, orientation, decision, and then action—and in a flash, pivoted from rage to conciliation. Just like that, he took control of the situation, confused me, and forced me to start my OODA loop over. In simple terms, Hanssen knew how to act instead of react.

Once again, I'd failed in my operation for the day, and the standby team wouldn't be able to search Hanssen's car. I was about to give up entirely when I recalled that Kate had given me another task: make Hanssen angry. With nothing left to lose, I oriented and planted my feet.

"Hey, boss," I said in a tone of voice Hanssen hadn't heard from me before. "I said we're going to take the FBI car, and that's what we're going to do."

He rounded on me and almost dropped his briefcase. "What did you say?"

I raised my chin and met his eyes, puffed out my chest, and stood with my feet shoulder-width apart. Classic animal aggression. "I said, no way we are taking your beat-up, boring, outdated old Ford Taurus to the DIA."

You know how some things seem cool in your mind, but then you do them and wonder what the hell you were thinking? This was one of those times. Hanssen moved quickly for an older guy with a noticeable limp who spent most of his day in a slouch. Before I could blink, he had the lapels of my sport coat twisted in his fists and curled me up to eye level, leaving my toes tapping for balance on the floor. Blood rushed to his face. One eye twitched. "Why is it so important to take Garcia's car?"

I blinked away his stale coffee breath and kick-started my scrambled brain. Observe. I'd made Hanssen angry. Too angry. Orient. In my earnest pursuit of the case, I might have pushed Hanssen over the line from suspicion to paranoia—just a smidge. Decision. What the hell should I do next? *Osotogari?* I discarded that thought—a judo major outer reaping throw—and focused on my breath. When Grandmaster Mills had awarded me my black belt, he insisted I search for peaceful resolutions to conflicts. Only if that failed would I have license to destroy my opponent.

Action. "Sorry about that, boss." I dropped my weight back onto my heels, forcing Hanssen to lean forward, off balance. Raising my hands in supplication, I said, "I didn't mean to speak out of turn. It's just . . . we need to roll into the DIA in style, in that big black FBI SUV. You deserve that. Can't have those army people thinking less of us."

Hanssen relaxed his grip, but didn't quite let go. I could hear footsteps coming around the corner and didn't want Kate, or anyone else on my team, to intervene.

"Garcia promised the car would be there. But it's like you always say. We can't rely on the FBI."

Hanssen looked at me one way and then another. Analyzing, searching out the lie I refused to show him. "We'll take my car," he said, releasing my jacket and then smoothing the crumpled parts. "They know who I am."

I followed Hanssen to his car, completely helpless. I replayed the last twenty minutes in my head. The boss had a temper, yes. He acted in unpredictable ways, sure. But over the last several weeks, he hadn't done a single thing that suggested he was a spy. Suspicion was merited when there was due cause, no? The more I thought, the more I realized that Hanssen was completely right to question me; that didn't prove his guilt, it proved he was a solid FBI agent. The real question wasn't why he was suspicious of us, but why we were suspicious of him.

He stopped with keys in hand and turned. "Do you find all this stressful, Eric?"

Honesty: "Sometimes."

He nodded. "Do you believe in God?"

My religion lived in my heart and wasn't something I'd ever felt the need to share or preach. I've always believed that God speaks to us in our most quiet places. I shouldn't have to prove my faith to Hanssen. "Boss, my mother is Italian and my father is Irish, both big Catholic families. I went to Saint Jane de Chantal for grade school and then Gonzaga High School. Jesuits run Gonzaga. My grandfather was a deacon. You don't get more Catholic than me. Of course I believe!"

He gave me an appraising look, slightly different from any look he'd given me before. Then he turned away. "Pray more."

Target: Robert Hanssen

Suspected spy
Quick-tempered
Verbally abusive
Tendency toward physical reactions
No evidence of espionage
Knows too much about Bloch case

# CHAPTER 12

# OPEN YOUR EYES

January 24, 2001—Wednesday

I woke to the sound of Rachmaninoff flooding from our living room. I made my sleepy way around the short corner to find Juliana sitting at my desk, eyes closed, swaying to the music. Her fingers tapped the grainy wood in front of her, playing imaginary keys. She was stunning in a pale blouse and her favorite jeans, slippers on her feet.

I watched her play in her mind the piano piece she had studied and wished we could afford a piano—not that we would have had anywhere to put it. Our apartment scarcely fit two people and a television set. If we bought a piano, we'd have to lose the couch.

A smile ghosted Juliana's face as the song ended. I half thought she might stand up and practice her bow. Instead, she leapt to her feet and turned to stop the CD before the next song began. When she saw me, she stumbled.

"Good morning," I said.

"Hey," she said. A touch of color flushed her cheeks and neck.

"You sounded just like Rachmaninoff."

She smiled at that. "At least you finally got the name right. That's a first."

"Give me classic rock any day." I stepped toward her, still in my pajamas, with hair sticking up all over. Prince Charming in a bathrobe.

She stiffened, but then relaxed into my embrace. I pressed my face into her long hair and breathed. The world fell away.

We'd been sharing too few moments like these. Each day I woke up far too early after far too little sleep. Juliana and I drank our coffee together, and sometimes shared breakfast. We'd compare schedules, or I'd hear about her classmates and tell her about mine before I had to run the few blocks to the Metro stop that would eventually take me to FBI HQ. Sometimes she would drive me on her way to school. By the time I got home at night, she was often already in bed.

The endless loop of our lives paused only for fights. So far we had avoided an explosion, but I knew we couldn't keep it up forever. Juliana despised confrontation. I embraced it. Eventually these opposing forces would ignite.

I couldn't help but compare my marriage to the model I'd grown up with. My father cared for my mother throughout her slow decline. Even as they fought the rampages of a disease that ultimately stole my mother's speech, confined her to a wheelchair, stripped the dexterity from her hands and made it impossible for her to breathe, they continued to go on vacation, had family parties, held Christmas gatherings, flew around the world, and saw every Broadway show. They took up swords together and fought Parkinson's in a way that brought them closer when so many couples might have fractured and fallen apart. Would Juliana and I find such strength in our marriage? My parents founded their relationship on love and honesty, which they poured into raising four sons. Had they passed this magic on to me?

"What is it, Eric?" Juliana asked.

She tried to pull back so we could lock eyes, but I held her there. My sensible wife knew that an *it* existed, but she couldn't pinpoint what it was, and I couldn't tell her. "*It* is a little of everything," I said. Half-truth. "School and Mom and the new job at HQ. I'm up late at night studying for law class and in early to manage the FBI's computers." Some lies, some truth. "I miss you."

"You're stressed," Juliana said. "I read a study about stress. Did you know it suppresses the immune system? You'll get sick if you don't find time to relax."

I tensed. Did she seriously just tell me to relax? "Honey," I said through gritted teeth, "when am I supposed to relax? We have bills to pay. Two school tuitions! My law school average is slipping. That's a cue to work harder, not relax. You relax! All you have to do is go to school."

She pushed herself away. "I'd get a job if I could! I barely got my school permit in time to make classes at American, and even then none of my German credits transferred. No one told me it would take so long to get a green card."

I reached for her. "Jule, I . . ."

She took a step back and crossed her arms. "It's my turn to talk. I came here for you. Not to become an American or chase some silly version of the American Dream in a tiny little apartment. We can move to Germany whenever you're ready."

I'm good with words. Words have a long history in my family, from my politician great-grandfather to my auctioneer grandfather and litigator father. Juliana left me speechless. Each of those men had something else in common, too, which I'd also inherited: a stubborn refusal to admit fault. But Juliana was right.

I bit my lip hard and squared my shoulders. "I'm sorry."

Her raised eyebrow softened the sharp way she glared at me. "For what?"

When a man says he's sorry, one of two things has just happened. Either he has already processed the entire argument, analyzed both sides, and concluded that in the final balance, he's the asshole, or he's apologizing because he doesn't want to fight. Women want to know which.

"I know you sacrificed to come here," I said. "I know it's hard for you." I looked around our apartment. "If I could buy you a piano, I'd have one here this afternoon."

She held my eyes for a few painful heartbeats before stepping forward and touching her forehead to mine. We shared a silent moment of exhaustion, leaning on each other.

"I don't need a piano. Don't get me wrong, I want a piano, but I don't need one. I need you."

"I'm right here." But I wasn't, not really. My mind had already shifted from the compartment where it kept Juliana to worries about what Hanssen had in store for me and whether I'd embarrass myself in front of my law school class when the professor called me to task.

"I have my piano recital tonight."

"You'll do great," I said. "I'm not supposed to say good luck, right?"

She shook her head. "We say break a leg."

I kissed her instead.


Hanssen slouched in the chair across from my desk. He'd come in late and for once appeared almost cheerful, smiling like a college kid who'd finally gotten lucky after months of dates. It was an unsettling look on him. "I once organized a Beach Boys concert here in FBI headquarters," he bragged.

I couldn't pretend to believe that one. "No chance that's true."

"No, really," he said. I mastered my surprise. Usually he screamed at people who challenged him.

"The Hoover Building wasn't always a fortress. A decade ago anyone could just walk right through." Hanssen spread his arms. "You could walk straight across the courtyard from Pennsylvania Avenue to E Street."

"So what happened?"

His lip curled in a sneer. "Islamic terrorists. Those disgusting scumbags tried to blow up the World Trade Center in 1993. They failed to bring down the tower, but every federal building became a fortress." He looked at me. "You know all about this. Didn't you work on a counterterror squad before coming here?"

I'd told Hanssen that half-truth to trick him away from my counterespionage background, but I hadn't lied. The FBI had hired me under President Bill Clinton's counterterrorism directive, which lifted an FBI hiring freeze and staffed up squads of ghosts to conduct the fieldwork necessary for catching bombers. I received my FBI credentials and swore to support and defend the Constitution three years after the first World Trade Center attack killed six people and injured thousands. Two years after jihadists had tried to topple one World Trade Center building into the other, anti–US government extremists Timothy McVeigh and Terry Nichols parked a Ryder truck full of explosives under a day care in the Alfred P. Murrah Federal Building in downtown Oklahoma City. The bombing killed 168 people and injured more than 680 others. A year after that, Eric Robert Rudolph left a green US military field pack containing three pipe bombs surrounded by masonry nails near a concert at Centennial Olympic Park during the 1996 Atlanta Olympic Games. Rudolph killed 2 people and injured over 100 more. When I received my FBI badge, Rudolph was still on the run; he wouldn't be caught for another five years. These tragedies made terrorist targets an FBI priority, and my job, at least in theory, was to help stop them.

"Sure I know about counterterror," I said. "But how did you get the Beach Boys to play here?"

"The FBI had a concert series," Hanssen said. "One of the clerks I supervised had a friend who knew a friend. We were able to make contact."

I half believed him. The thought that the Beach Boys played "Help Me, Rhonda" next to the Fidelity, Bravery, Integrity statue in the central HQ courtyard was a truth-is-stranger-than-fiction moment. "Pretty cool, boss," I said.

He preened. "I had a lot of great ideas. Another was a robot spider that I developed that could crawl under buildings and listen in to conversations."

On that one, I called bullshit. "C'mon, boss!"

He held his hand out, palm up. "I built it in my garage. So small it could fit into your palm. I used a small radio control to—"

An alarm beeped. Hanssen dragged his Palm Pilot out of his back pocket. He checked it and smiled. "Ah, the Novena."

"The what?"

He frowned. "I thought you were Catholic? Didn't those Jesuits at Gonzaga teach you to pray?"

"More like Sister Rose at de Chantal, but yeah."

Hanssen stood up. "Then you should know that *novena* is Latin for 'nine.' Nine days of prayer. I pray to Mary every day at one p.m." He snapped his Palm Pilot shut and returned it to his left back pocket. "Come with me."

The gloom of his office made kneeling down before a small triptych feel oddly like being in church. Hanssen unfolded the triptych on his desk to reveal Mary holding a baby Jesus flanked by two angels on the surrounding panels. He gripped a rosary in one hand and started to pray.

I matched him at first, letting the old prayer to Mary soothe me into a meditative mindfulness of God. "*Hail Mary, full of Grace, the Lord is with you . . .*"

With each word, unease grew in my chest until the unbearable weight of it threatened to topple me to the floor. I stood quietly and walked back to my desk, surprised to find my hands balled into fists. I had poured everything into this investigation, into the last five years of investigations. I'd given the FBI my nights and weekends, sacrificed relationships and rest. I'd given them a promise to keep all the secrets they stacked onto my shoulders. I wouldn't use my faith to break a case.

Hanssen finished his prayers and didn't mention my abrupt departure. His face told me everything his words did not. My mind spun with excuses and rationales for why I hadn't finished the prayer, but the stubbornness of my convictions stilled my tongue. Kneeling beside Hanssen on his thin blue office carpet to pray the rosary was wrong in a way that didn't merit explanation. I refused to let even a splotch of guilt into my face.

Hanssen might have said something, but a firearms qualification appointment he had at Quantico for the remainder of the afternoon saved me from evangelization or proselytization. He paused on his way out, coat on his shoulders and scarf tight around his neck. He gripped his bag in one gloved fist. "Do you shoot?"

"I hold my own," I said.

He pushed the door open. "I'll take you shooting one of these times."

I couldn't decide whether he felt the need to fill the awkwardness with words, or if his offer was sincere. With Hanssen, you could never tell. "That would be cool."

"We'll see if you have what it takes to make agent."

Before I could think of a retort, the door shut behind him.

I called Kate and let her know I wouldn't need a ride to law school. Unless she wanted to hear about the Beach Boys and robot spiders, I didn't have much to report. I'd include it in my log for tomorrow. Next, I called a friend and asked her to take notes for me in Corporations. Juliana's piano recital at American University was starting in a few hours. I decided to skip class and go see her play. If I hurried, I could change trains and walk the final few blocks before she began. I considered commandeering Garcia's Tahoe so I could roll up in style, but reconsidered. Hanssen had encouraged me to take more risks, but getting fired seemed a little overboard.

I puffed into the concert hall and couldn't miss my wife, seated in front of the piano in a stunning red dress. She raised her hands and began. Juliana moved with the music, lithe on the edge of the polished bench, her golden hair a bright contrast against the jet-black grand piano. When you truly love someone, you fall in love again and again. As Rachmaninoff's

Piano Concerto No. 2 filled the auditorium, I forgot the investigation, buried thoughts of an upcoming law school exam, and returned from my self-imposed isolation.

After the last notes echoed into silence, the stress of life rushed to fill the void. *What was I doing chasing a dead lead instead of spending time with my wife?* Hanssen was a suspected spy—but why? He believed in God and hated the Russians. What if I was throwing everything away for the wrong guy?

"You came!"

Before I understood what was happening, my wife grabbed my hand and pulled me away from the auditorium. I woodenly followed her through the empty halls of the music school, trying to find my way amid a tempest of thoughts.

Juliana led me through a heavy door into a small, windowless room with an upright piano, a padded chair, and an end table. She sank into the chair and smiled.

"It's a practice room," she said. "The doors are soundproofed."

I glanced around, thinking that it reminded me of a SCIF. "Do you need to practice more?"

She stared at me like she'd only just met me and didn't like what she saw. My eyes lingered on her outline beneath the red dress and the way her stockinged knees made shadows around her crossed legs. The single light highlighted the waves in her blond hair and cast mysterious shadows around her eyes. I froze when I should have acted.

Juliana stood and smoothed her dress. "Forget it."

"Forget what?"

"You just . . ." She shook her head and stood up. "Forget it." Glancing at her watchless wrist, she walked out the door. "Let's go. It's late."

We drove home in silence and back to our routine.

When we arrived at our apartment, I poured two glasses of wine. My sleep-deprived brain thought we'd celebrate her successful piano jury. She'd played the complicated piece perfectly.

I honestly couldn't tell—I have no ear for music—but the judges had clapped when she finished. Although Juliana had no harsher critic than herself, when she had taken her short bow, a smile had crinkled the corners of her eyes and flushed her cheeks.

Juliana frowned at the glass of wine I offered her and turned away. I chased her into our bedroom and stood sentry while she changed out of the red dress.

She scowled at me. "A little privacy?"

"We're married!"

"That doesn't mean I need you next to me every moment we're home."

The wiser, older me would have simply nodded and walked out of the room, gently closing the door behind me. The younger, stressed-out me blurted out the one word probably responsible for the majority of fights across history.

"What?"

She speared a leg into her pajama bottoms and threw me a look that could melt ice.

"What?" I said again. A little louder.

Juliana's head popped up through her pajama top and the look on her face should have sent me scurrying from the room. Instead, I stood my ground. I was dimly aware of what a ridiculous contrast we made: she with her flowered cotton pajamas, and me in my suit and tie, with a goblet of red wine sloshing in one angry fist.

"How about you tell *me* what?" Juliana said, and advanced on me. "You're working harder at your desk job then you ever worked when you were in the field." She poked me in the chest. It hurt; all that piano practice had turned her fingers into weapons. "You're right around the corner, but I can't visit for lunch. You go in early and barely make it out before your law class. You worry more about this job than anything you've done in the past. Don't think I can't see it."

"So?"

"You're not telling me something. What is it?"

Only one thing feels worse than repeatedly lying: getting caught in a lie. Juliana had the moral high ground, but instead of backing down, I charged. "Maybe if you didn't nag so much about every little thing, I wouldn't be so stressed. I'm doing everything around here, and you're just playing piano."

The words sounded stupid to me even as I said them. I drew in a breath to take them back . . .

"You idiot," she said. "That's the dumbest thing that's ever crossed your lips."

All manner of insulting and scandalous words are written across the pages of the *Urban Dictionary*. Juliana and I kept a copy on our bookshelf as a joke. When she needed a bad word in English, as we all do from time to time, she only had to crack its dark spine and pick one at random. Any of those words would have been better than the one she'd just thrown at me.

I spent my days hearing Hanssen calling me an idiot and my nights running from the word in increasingly chaotic dreams. I could stomach the word from the target of an espionage investigation. Juliana saying it turned everything into a red rage.

"You're cleaning that up!" she yelled.

I looked from her scandalized face to the red stain spreading across the far wall. I couldn't remember throwing my wineglass across the bedroom. I took deep breaths and had almost managed to calm myself when the Hello Lady started her nightly ritual.

"Hello? Hello?" The soft voice drifted downward. Normally, Juliana and I would have both laughed and let the odd moment cut through the tension. Tonight wasn't normal.

"Shut up!" I hollered. "Just shut up, you crazy old nut job!"

"Get out." Juliana pushed me back out of the room. "Just get out."

She turned without closing the door. I thought she might

have relented until my pillow hit me in the face. I caught it reflexively and stumbled back. The door missed my nose by an inch.

I lay on the lumpy couch and replayed the night in my mind. The way Juliana moved on the piano, how we'd rushed out of the auditorium, the soundproof room, the way she sat on the padded chair. Waiting. Juliana had dangled the winning lottery ticket in front of me and I hadn't opened my eyes to see it. Instead I had dragged us into a fight that might take days to repair. Everything was falling apart, and what would I have to show for it?

The Hello Lady never performed her nightly serenade again after my outburst. Days after our tempers cooled and we found mutual civility, we waited one night for the noticeably absent "Hello? Hello?" to fall toward us. It never came. In a moment of anger I had robbed an elderly woman of her routine and had struck away one of the best parts of mine.

Idiot.

# CHAPTER 13

# JERSEY WALLS AND AIRPLANES

January 25, 2001—Thursday

I heard voices in Hanssen's office when I returned from lunch. The boss rarely went to lunch. He either ran off to church services or sat in his office behind a closed door. Hanssen might enjoy his self-imposed fast, but I needed to eat, and sitting around the office during my lunch break would look odd. Normal people ate around noon. The most important way to keep Hanssen's heavy suspicion from turning to paranoia was to treat this job like any other.

"Good to see you, Gene." Hanssen's voice had never lost the toughness that came from growing up in Chicago. "We'll get lunch one of these days."

"Thanks, Bob. Welcome back to HQ." The door opened and a tallish man stepped out ahead of Hanssen. He saw me and extended a hand. "Assistant Director Gene O'Leary."

My smile was genuine. Gene O'Leary had an affable, no-nonsense manner that set you immediately at ease. "Investigative Specialist Eric O'Neill. Nice to meet another Irishman."

Gene laughed and shook my hand. His grip was vigorous, but it didn't become the crushing test of strength that so many agents insisted on. "You'll find a lot of us here, Eric. Irish took over the bureau years ago."

Hanssen dropped a hand on O'Leary's shoulder and steered him toward the door. "Nice to catch up, Gene, but we have a lot of work to do, so . . ."

O'Leary raised apologetic hands. "I won't keep you, Bob. It's good to have you here. No one knows computer systems the way you do."

"Thank you for that." Hanssen saw O'Leary out and shut the door behind him. I expected my boss to say something modest or self-deprecating in response to the praise. Instead, he could scarcely control the rage written across his face.

"Everything okay, boss?" I asked.

"Do you have that definition of 'information assurance' yet?"

I had a perfectly workable definition, just not the one he apparently wanted. "Not yet."

"Then everything is not okay."

I hated to poke the bear, but Kate would want a report. "Who is Assistant Director O'Leary?"

Hanssen paused at his office door, his shoulders up in the hypermasculine pose my little brother Danny calls invisible lat syndrome. I readied myself for a tongue-lashing. Instead he deflated.

"He's a *Deputy* AD for IRD." Hanssen collapsed into a chair in front of my desk. "We've worked together in the past."

I used the Robert Hanssen lexicon that I'd written in my head and translated. A deputy assistant director outranked Hanssen, and I'd come to know that my boss reflexively despised anyone above him in the chain of command. I knew that the Information Assurance Section fell within the IRD hierarchy. That made O'Leary one of Hanssen's bosses.

"I've been down to his office," Hanssen said. I detected a crabby quality to his voice that he rarely allowed to surface. "Huge window. Looks out over Pennsylvania Avenue. If you turn your head just right, you can see the Capitol."

"So you two are old friends?"

"With that paper pusher?" Hanssen scoffed, and raised a pinky. "This finger knows more about computer security than he ever will. He probably has a secretary print out his emails for him." Hanssen produced his pen and clicked through his angst. "He's on the promotion track, so they bring him to head-quarters and staff him in an office overseeing the people who do the real work. Garcia's another one."

"How so?"

"He spent his career in crime squads. What the hell does he know about information security or operations?"

I scoffed. "Criminal operations are all about security—"

"Open your eyes, Eric! The FBI is chasing left-wing, nut-job diversity." His mouth turned down like he'd tasted something sour. "We've long been criticized for promoting too many people named O'Leary, so the FBI starts promoting Garcias."

That statement certainly opened my eyes, but not in the way Hanssen expected. Did the FBI even have a Human Resources Division? I honestly didn't know, which was problematic. But if they did, I had an arsenal of information about my boss to take to them. Not like I ever would. The only person who mattered in terms of the evidence I collected was Kate. And apparently the director. The thought of Freeh personally reading my logs still gave me the shivers.

I decided to change the subject. "It would be nice to have a window. These walls are pretty blank."

Hanssen smiled—not the sort of smile that makes a baby coo, the other kind. "We can do something about that." He pocketed his pen and paced the room. One hand jingled his keys. Each chime reminded me that I hadn't stolen them yet.

"He keeps some paintings in a conference room on the sixth floor." The jingling stopped. "I want you to get them for me."

"You want me to ask him for his artwork?"

"No, you moron," Hanssen said. "I want you to take them."

"You mean steal them."

"Don't be such a Boy Scout, Eric." Hanssen strode to his office. "Boy Scouts finish last."

His door shut with a bang.

Hanssen had plenty of trigger words. Each time he called me an idiot or a moron, I lost control of the part of myself that measured and cut information. The investigation demanded that I keep my emotions tightly under wraps. But it was only by imagining what Kate would say that I was able to stop myself from punching him in the mouth.

I swiveled my chair to the FBI NET computer and logged into ACS. I used the full-text search to enter a few names of targets I had ghosted into the system. ACS covered most of the information with $x$'s—but not everything.

Hanssen's words from a few days ago replayed in my mind. *ACS is flawed and the FBI hasn't a clue.* I hadn't listened then because his hands on my shoulders had distracted me, but now I made the connection. *All the Russians have to do is recruit someone at the FBI with ACS access, feed him a name, and have the mole conduct full-text searches.* Why would a spy reveal such an enormous flaw?

I conducted a few additional searches and then sat back with my hands steepled over my mouth. I stared at the screen and wondered if this is how a person became a spy.

It would be so easy. I knew the names of intelligence officers working for the Russian government. I knew their routines and where they slept at night. I even knew which of them dropped their kids off at the Russian school in the morning. If I approached them quietly, promising secrets, they'd lead me to dead drops and signal sites. No one would suspect me. I could even pin most of it on Hanssen if I wanted.

Juliana could have her piano. I could pay off law school and her classes at American University. We could move to a better apartment. Not too much better, but big enough that we wouldn't feel like two cats thrown into a steel box.

I powered down my computer.

Kate pulled up outside the University Yard quad off H Street in Foggy Bottom, and I gave her a sobering report. Hanssen didn't drink. He didn't tell dirty jokes or mention women other than his wife. He was plenty weird, invaded my personal space at every opportunity, clicked his pen to drive me crazy, and got off on bullying; but nothing suggested he was a spy.

"The weirdest thing he's done was play a Monty Python CD in the middle of the SCIF," I said. "He even told us how a spy could exploit ACS to steal information. What kind of traitor tells us how to patch code?"

"I can't speak to his choice in music," Kate said. "But there is more to this than you know."

I scoffed. "There always is." I looked past her at the redbrick buildings of George Washington Law School. The day students streamed out of a set of wide wooden doors to huddle around a keg. One student worked the tap and filled his classmates' eager hands with red Solo cups. Night students passed by with wistful looks on their way to evening lectures. Day students had all the advantages.

"I'm behind in my studies," I said, "Juliana and I fight more than we smile, and Hanssen tests me more than my law professors." I closed my eyes. "It's constant. I have to watch every word."

"Welcome to undercover work." I opened my eyes to catch Kate's smile. "I hear you, kiddo," Kate said. "No one said this would be easy. But we're close."

"Close to what? He loves his kids and grandkids, goes to church every day, and hates the Soviet Union more than Nazi Germany. He'd like to beat the pulp out of me, but—"

"We don't just think he's a spy, Eric," Kate said. "We think he's *the* spy."

I kept my mouth shut and waited for her to continue. Hanssen's favorite trick.

"We believe he sold out to the Russians decades ago. The code name we gave him—Gray Day—it's a play off the code name Gray Suit. We believe Hanssen is Gray Suit, the mole the

FBI has looked for since we found out that someone was leaking major national security secrets in the '80s. Quitting's not an option, kiddo."

I slumped into the oversized seat and listened to the car idle. The quad had filled with day students warmed by beer and collegiality that defied the early January chill. My torts class would begin soon, but even Turley's best lecture couldn't compare to the bombshell Kate had dropped.

"You mean he's suspected—"

"It's him. It's got to be him and you helped button that up. The analysts reviewed your notes on Felix Bloch. No way could he have known those details about the briefcase unless he was the mole that called the Russians to warn Bloch off."

"Remember how you told me he seemed so giddy in the office the other day? Your old ghost team has been watching him." Kate touched my arm. "He's been shining a flashlight at a sign in a little park."

I made my frozen tongue move. "He's looking for signals."

"Told ya you're a natural at this," Kate said. "Signals from the Russians. We think a drop could happen any day now. Step up your game. We need to be ahead of him."

I understood. Bad guys beat surveillance when they force us to catch up to them. The best ghosts predict the target's path and get in front of them instead of always following one step behind—which happens more often than not with US intelligence. In 1973, a Palestinian militant group named Black September attempted to detonate three car bombs in New York City during a visit by the Israeli prime minister, and in 1993 terrorists drove a truck filled with more than 1,000 pounds of explosives into the parking garage of the World Trade Center North Tower. Five years later, suicide bombers drove trucks filled with explosives into US embassies in Dar es Salaam, Tanzania, and Nairobi, Kenya. The attacks killed more than 200 people and put Osama bin Laden on the map as America's public enemy number one.

We seemed to have a truck-bombing problem. In response, the FBI, police, and other law-enforcement and security professionals devised a system to prevent the careful parking of trucks beside or under buildings: we placed jersey walls and other clever barriers at a distance that would offset any blast. The FBI surrounded its headquarters on Pennsylvania Avenue with massive planters. It began planting flowers along one city block between Ninth and Tenth Streets, but then either money ran out or the FBI tired of watering flowers. It filled the rest of the planters with gravel.

But while the FBI poured gravel into oversized planters along DC sidewalks, the terrorists were far ahead of us. They'd failed to bring down World Trade Center towers with a truck in 1993, but they eventually changed the world when they hijacked planes on September 11, 2001.

We suffer from a similar problem in the world of espionage. While the United States is used to playing defense, the Russians are going on the offense. The Russian sleeper-agent program (which US intelligence calls the *illegal* program) is a prime example of Russia's willingness to fully commit the lives of their operatives to intelligence gathering. In this program, Russian spies working for the Russian Foreign Intelligence Service (SVR) immigrate to the United States using fake business pretenses, identities robbed from dead people, or, in some cases, completely false cover stories. The Russian government spends large amounts of money and invests years of training into operatives who will become Americans so that they can infiltrate our society.

In June 2010, the FBI concluded Operation Ghost Stories by arresting ten "illegal" Russian spies working for the SVR. Each of the operatives worked under false names and identities on US soil, and none of them had diplomatic protection.

The most famous of the ten were Anna Chapman, Donald Heathfield, and Tracey Foley. Chapman, born Anna Vasil'yevna Kushchyenko, a fiery-haired twentysomething socialite, had married a UK citizen to obscure her Russian identity before working her way into the Wall Street elite. The real Donald Heathfield and Tracey Foley had died in Canada years before Andrei Bezrukov and Elena Vavilova, KGB-trained spies, assumed their identities and immigrated to America. Their two children, born in Canada but raised in the United States, did not learn of their parents' true identity until the FBI kicked in the door to their Cambridge, Massachusetts, home to arrest Mom and Dad.

The Heathfield-Foleys and Chapman blindsided the FBI by embracing new spy technology to communicate with Moscow. Anna would sit in a coffeehouse in the middle of the day like so many other young professionals, clicking through her laptop over a latte. Donald and Tracey would upload pictures of their beautiful family and white-picket-fenced home to a file-sharing site. Covertly, as Anna sat in the coffeehouse, her laptop would directly pair with the laptop of a Russian intelligence officer parked nearby. A different intelligence officer in Moscow would download and decrypt the Cambridge couple's pictures, revealing through digital steganography the secrets hidden within. As the US government defunded its peacetime counterintelligence programs, the careful and methodical spies had infiltrated our business, politics, and communities.

Russia versus the United States is a story of action versus reaction. The FBI needed to flip the script and get out in front of Hanssen. Apparently the Felix Bloch reveal had put everything into perspective. It was key evidence that made the team confident that they weren't wasting their time. But it wasn't enough. Now we needed to find the smoking gun before Hanssen could reload.

"How much time do we have?"

Kate's resolve flickered. "Could be tomorrow, could be next week, could be a month. You never know with these things."

The drop was about to happen. Which meant that everything was now time sensitive. More likely than not, Hanssen would see the finish line and keep his head down until he got there. I had to keep him feeling safe; I had to keep acting like the Information Assurance Section was real. In other words, I had to make sure Hanssen didn't sway from suspicion to paranoia, I'd have to keep returning to 9930 so he could play lord of his castle. But I also, somehow, had to get him to make a mistake.

"Do you know Eugene O'Leary?"

Kate raised an eyebrow. "Yeah, nice guy. Assistant director."

"Deputy AD, but yeah. Hanssen wants me to steal his artwork."

"We'll have to tell the AD."

I thought a moment. "Don't."

Kate crossed her arms. "Any reason we shouldn't tell an assistant director that his artwork is about to be stolen?"

"I want to see his face when he walks into the SCIF."

She opened her mouth, then closed it and finally laughed. "When will you do it?"

"I'll put it into my report." I dragged my bag onto my lap and pushed open the door. Kate stopped me.

"Eric," she said. "Be safe. That thing in the garage . . ."

I raised an eyebrow. "You wanted me to make him angry."

"I was there, you know," she said.

"I know. I heard you."

"You don't miss anything, do you?" Kate smiled.

"Neither does Hanssen."

```
          Target: Robert Hanssen

             GRAY DAY SUIT
      Compromised national security
      Planning a drop to the Russians
```

# CHAPTER 14

# THE ART OF THIEVERY

## January 25, 2001—Thursday Night

The gold FBI shield and identifying credentials are not get-out-of-jail-free cards. Ghosts only identify themselves as a last resort, which means the successful ones are tremendous improvisational actors. When you can't throw down a badge at the first sign of trouble, you learn to always have a story ready.

Early in my career at the FBI, I set up at a choke point in a suburban neighborhood. The life of a ghost isn't all ducking into shadows and driving fast on the Beltway. Most of the work happens in glacial moments anchored to one spot with the task to wait and watch. Hours might drift by before a target moves. We'd often say that in a ten-hour surveillance shift, we lived for fifteen minutes of go time.

Suburban neighborhoods are complicated for surveillance. I preferred deserted alleys in dangerous parts of town where minding one's business means survival, or busy parking lots where one car blends into legions of others. Suburban streets are flush with nosy neighbors, kids riding by on bicycles, dog walkers, neighborhood-watch programs, and the occasional roving police cruiser. In other words, civilian countersurveillance. Nine times out of ten, when I parked on a neighborhood street someone would finally brave their way across a lawn and knock on my window. I had a whole bag of excuses:

"I'm an Arlington County traffic-control surveyor, ma'am.

We've had some complaints of speeding on this street, so I'm counting traffic. . . ."

"I work for the gas company, sir. Our meter trucks will be through shortly and I'm a review supervisor to make sure they are polite and friendly. . . ."

"Hi, kids! I'm a location scout for a local production company. My job is to check out streets that we might want to use to shoot a movie. No, I can't tell you about the movie. Super-secret, but between you and me, Tom Cruise might run down your street one day. . . ."

I could spin a story as easy as breathing. These social-engineering techniques, while technically lies, put normal people at ease. No one wanted to see an FBI badge and hear the truth that a spy lived a few blocks away, or that a known terrorist sympathizer's kids went to the local school.

Sometimes the badge is necessary. A local police officer once knocked on my window and wound his hand in the *roll it down* motion. I was parked in a depressed neighborhood in rural Virginia. My target had entered a shabby house up the street for a potential meet, and I had eyes on the brightly lit kitchen window. I couldn't afford for the target to glance out and see a patrol car parked behind my undercover car. The cop had to move.

I showed my badge and didn't waste precious moments dissembling. "I'm FBI on a national security investigation. My target is close by, so I would very much appreciate you leaving the area before your patrol car spooks him."

The officer examined my credentials and looked like he might test my gold shield with his teeth, but he eventually handed them back. "Are you armed?" he asked.

Police officers always want to know this. I gave an honest answer. "No, sir. I'm unarmed and undercover."

"Damn, son!" He threw up his hands. "That sounds dangerous."

The officer then walked back to his car and returned with

a shotgun. I had no idea what to say until he tried to hand it through my window.

"Take this," he said. "Anything else you need, just let me know."

I politely begged off the firearm and bade the well-meaning cop to clear the area. I told him he had excellent initiative and agreed that he'd make a fine FBI agent someday. He'd already submitted his application.

I thought of that eager police officer on that rural neighborhood street as I walked out of my Criminal Law class and headed back toward FBI headquarters. The mile walk back to HQ would take me about fifteen minutes. By then, most FBI employees would have packed into their Crown Victorias and rumbled home. But plenty of personnel worked late or on the graveyard shift. One nosy person could ruin my night.

I could have asked someone from my class for a ride back to HQ or driven myself to law school and back, but I wanted to walk. Being a ghost involved plenty of walking, whether I was memorizing an area before a surveillance began or actively following a target. Successfully following someone without losing them and without being noticed requires a number of other skills too. The first is to know the target. Learning every possible detail about the target before you ever set off on their trail can transform a potentially chaotic and nerve-racking surveillance into a cakewalk. If the target embraces veganism, you know where to find them around lunchtime. If you're following a jogger or a nature enthusiast, you'd better pack comfy sneakers. If they come from a country where everyone rides bicycles, you can expect them to drive well under the speed limit.

More often than not, I'd receive only basic information about a target. Vague descriptions that might include clothing and the make and model of their car would be the only arrows in my quiver when setting off on a hunt. In those cases, my second rule, know your environment, is the key. How many streets intersect the main thoroughfare? Are there shopping malls and coffee shops that a person can quickly duck into? Do the storefronts have large glass windows that allow a target to surreptitiously watch the reflections of those behind him? How many people are on the streets, and are they walking or in cars? How are they dressed?

Every stone tells a story. Every brick in every wall and every crack in each sidewalk marks a place where a person has been. We miss all of those details when we drive through a neighborhood or race down a busy street. But when you walk the same ground, you see the graffiti sprayed across the brick. You note a child's handprint in the sidewalk. When we slow down to understand the details of the world around us we can follow my final rule: blend in.

The hallway to 9930 looked dark and haunted. The environment I knew had flipped upside down. During the day, voices carried along the narrow corridor. Good-natured shouts and muffled conversations competed with the sounds of footsteps and the click of doors opening and closing. Sometimes classic rock music from Garcia's radio would escape his office and swing down the hall toward Hanssen's SCIF. At nine thirty p.m., my footsteps echoed in the unnatural silence.

I cracked the door to my office and set my bag and coat down on my desk. If Hanssen reviewed the security log for the SCIF, I'd tell him I had forgotten my cell phone and needed to come by after school to retrieve it. Because the log showed in and out times, I'd have to be fast.

First things first. I lifted my phone handset and dialed Juliana. "Hi, honey," I said.

"Where are you?" Her voice sounded tight. "Are you at the office?"

I called her from the office instead of my cell precisely because I knew she could see the FBI number on our caller ID. "Yes," I said. "We had a server malfunction and I had to come in after law school to deal with it."

"This late at night?"

"I promised them I'd come back and handle it after law school," I lied. "I didn't want to miss class."

"Well, okay." Juliana yawned. "Try not to wake me when you come home."

I'd become very good at sneaking into my own home. "I won't."

We said our goodbyes and I set the phone down. Sometimes to catch a bad guy, you have to learn to be one. Lying to my wife was a start. Time to up the ante.

I activated the electronic lock on the SCIF door and left the mechanical ones alone. When I returned, I'd only need to wave my SACS badge and say open sesame to get back in the SCIF.

The nearby stairwell took me three floors down to the sixth floor. All along the hallway, computer boxes rested on small wheeled carts. I wondered if these were part of Assistant Director Dies's dream to put a computer on every agent's desk.

I passed a blank door that concealed key-copying equipment for if I ever found a way to relieve Hanssen of his keychain. Farther down the hall, past the servers and IT support, and administrative offices that built the foundation for the Information Resource Division, I found O'Leary's office. Not far from there, I spotted the closed door to his conference room. His unlocked conference room.

I slipped through the door and closed it behind me before flicking on the lights. The prints O'Leary had arranged on the walls came right out of the men's country-club handbook. One scene showed two men rowing a boat into choppy waters. Another displayed the idyllic expanse of a golf course. A sand trap dominated the bottom corner, danger hidden among the placid green. My favorite was a hunting scene. Two men and a woman in proper English coats chased a fox across a misty countryside, dogs baying at their heels.

The framing had likely cost more than the prints. Stained wooden frames surrounded triple matting in an array of complementary colors. The glass was pristine. I lifted one off the wall and flipped it over. On the bottom corner the artist had signed his name and added a number on the carefully stapled paper that sealed the print in the frame.

I doubted O'Leary wanted to lose these, but needs must when the devil drives. It took some time to liberate a cart. Each computer box I removed went onto a different loaded cart. I then arranged the remaining carts to fill in the space where my purloined one had rested.

The three prints fit in the cart perfectly. After a moment, I also wrested the hangers off the wall with a letter opener, and took the letter opener and a stapler while I was at it. I felt a little like the Grinch as I backed out of the room. I'd taken O'Leary's art; now all I needed to do was get back to 9930 before Cindy Lou Who came out for a cup of water. The only explanation for someone moving prints at nearly ten at night was art thievery. And I couldn't exactly show my badge and use the national-security investigation excuse inside FBI headquarters.

Voices sent me scurrying back into the dark conference room. I peered out the cracked door into the hall and considered my folly. Even if I managed to get the art back undetected, O'Leary would ask to see the surveillance tapes from the cameras that protruded like angry eyes out of every hallway corner.

A famous Soviet poster from World War II portrays a woman in a red kerchief who holds her finger to lips in the universal gesture for silence. The translated Russian verse says the following:

> *Keep your eyes open.*
> *These days*
> *Even the walls have ears.*
> *Chatter and gossip*
> *Go hand in hand with*
> *Treason.*

At FBI HQ, the walls essentially did have eyes and ears. I'd have to ask Garcia to work some magic to make this evening disappear.

When the hallway quieted, I maneuvered the cart through the conference-room doorway and locked it behind me, then dashed down the hall to the elevator. I pressed the Up button and thought of the annual Vegas trips my uncle John organized. My brother David and I would join the Italian side of my family for a weekend of drinking, cigars, great food, and plenty of gambling. I rarely gamble, but watching my uncle and his cousin Joe at the craps table was like racing down a crowded highway in a Porsche 911 with no brakes—all adrenaline with no care for consequence. You survived as long as luck held. This late at night the odds fell in my favor, but I reminded myself of Uncle John's number-one rule about gambling: Know when to walk away.

My heart relaxed as the doors opened. I dragged the cart into the empty elevator and moments later across the silent ninth-floor hallway to Room 9930. A rare sort of smile split my face. The kind that you'd never find on a Boy Scout. I used the stapler to hammer the stolen picture hangers into the walls above my desk and over the empty desk across the room. As I drove the first nail into drywall, I wondered what the monitoring team at WFO thought of my crime. By the second, I thought about Hanssen, and whether espionage delivered him the same satisfaction that stealing art had given me. I'd stolen three expensive prints from an assistant director and knew I would get away with it. I hung the boring golf picture over the empty desk and left the two men adrift at sea leaning against the wall in front of Hanssen's office.

The hunting scene went over my desk. Kate's certainty that Hanssen was Gray Suit had shaken my outlook on the case. The FBI's long hunt for Gray Suit had given the spy legendary status. Catching Hanssen was the intelligence-community equivalent of dredging Nessie from Inverness's deepest loch or trapping Bigfoot in the pine-forested mountains of Wyoming. I stared at the print I'd just stolen and made myself a promise. From that moment forward I'd no longer play the role of the fox, dodging Hanssen's questions and carrying on the chase. It was time to join the hunt.

# CHAPTER 15

# A FLAW IN THE SYSTEM

January 26, 2001—Friday

I kept my expression neutral when Hanssen walked into the office the next morning. He unbuttoned his coat with exaggerated movements, eyes shifting from one print to the other. I prepared myself for the inevitable demand that I exchange the hunting scene over my desk for the boating scene I'd left in front of his office. As usual, Hanssen caught me by surprise.

"This will do nicely." He tucked the print under one arm.

I brandished my stolen stapler. "Want me to hang it for you?"

"That won't be necessary. I'm very handy."

I flipped through my DayMinder. "We are due at the data center at ten."

A smile brushed Hanssen's face before he disappeared into his office.

I followed Hanssen through the first security door, and a guard scanned my SACS badge before admitting us through the second. We were about to get a VIP tour of FBI headquarters' data center. I scanned Hanssen's shirt, his pants, the lump in his back pocket, his shoes. Hanssen wasn't just a suspected spy, he was *the* suspected spy. Gray Suit. The game had changed, and yet it remained exactly the same.

Checking out wasn't an option. If the FBI's suspicions were true, we needed proof. I needed to find Hanssen's flaw. Either Hanssen would have to misstep, or I'd need to find hard evidence—a letter, an electronic file, or something similar linking him to Gray Suit—that a Justice Department attorney could use in order to prosecute him.

Finding flaws in a system requires the methodical collection of data over time. Successful criminals spend long hours in preparation. If you want to rob a house, you case it first. Note when the lights are on and when the family is away from home. Observe whether a dog prowls the yard, and if a cleaning service or a nanny might appear. Determine whether an alarm system protects the home. If so, does an external company monitor the windows and doors and motion sensors, or could a simple snip of an external Internet cable defeat a pricey, do-it-yourself installed wireless system?

Spy hunting presents similar challenges. My FBI Academy photography instructor always reminded us that the eye does not necessarily see what the camera does. Sometimes we miss flaws that are right in front of our face.

During one lengthy investigation of a terrorism target, I found myself standing across from a restaurant in Old Town, Virginia. The entrance was on a quiet street, with little traffic and few pedestrians. The only cover was a low stone wall. I sat on the wall, trying to look nonchalant in sunglasses and a leather jacket that belonged on the set of *Donnie Brasco*, not near-suburban Virginia.

A car stalked up the street and stopped right across from me. Another ghost, one of my colleagues, rolled down the passenger-side window and thrust a camera in my face. The SLR had a massive telephoto lens hanging off it, meant for low-light situations when using flash was out of the question.

"He's coming out with the wife," the ghost, code-named "Panther," told me. "You need to get some shots."

I grabbed the camera and stepped back as Panther sped away. Bastard. I couldn't stand there with an 80–200mm F/2.8 telephoto lens hanging off my camera. The thing looked like an assault rifle. And for a target suspected of terrorist activities, a ghost with a camera would be worse than a cop with a handgun.

A few doors down was an office building with dark tinted windows that faced the street. It made the building look as if it had put on sunglasses. And that gave me an idea. I plastered my best smile on my face and strode through the door. The guard at the internal security station looked from me to the camera hanging at my side and frowned.

"I don't want to go up," I said. "Can I hang out in the lobby for a minute?"

Skepticism curdled on his face, and he picked up his phone.

"Wait!" I raised my hand. "Did you know that Tyra Banks is in town?"

The phone stopped halfway to his face. Everyone knew the supermodel had come to town; celebrities setting foot in DC always caused a local media sensation.

"I'm paparazzi. She's right in that restaurant!" I held up the camera and turned a liability into a prop. "I just need a few shots for my editor and I'll be out of your hair."

The guard dropped the phone and came around his desk to stand next to me. Everyone loves a good story. The trick is selling the right one.

Within a few minutes the guard had called a crowd of employees down to the lobby to see the "supermodel" who would soon emerge. They pressed around me and squinted through the tinted windows toward the empty door across the way. Each jostle and shove made me smile. Some might feel crowded, but I welcomed the cover.

When the target and his wife came out, they stopped on the street in front of the restaurant and faced each other. I snapped through a roll of film and loaded another, my hands working while my eyes never left the street in front of me.

When I put my camera down, the expectant crowd murmured in confusion. Where was the supermodel?

"You have to be fast to catch those supermodels," I said over my shoulder on my way out of the building. "They know how to hide in plain sight."

So did I.

I won an FBI award for one of the photos I took that afternoon. I couldn't see the flaw with my naked eye, but the picture told a different story. The target and his wife were angry; her eyes were shot through with scorn. In one frame, the target balled a fist as though ready to hit her. The FBI exploited that flaw by turning the wife against her husband; it led to our big break in the case.

Now all I had to do was find Hanssen's flaw.

As the door slid open, cold air speckled my forearms with goose bumps. The change in temperature and the slight pressure against my inner ear as I adjusted to the controlled environment inside the data center reminded me of descending during a scuba dive. I looked around. Computer systems towered around us. IT staff hunched behind various computer screens. A few agents, distinguishable from the tech staff by the guns on their hips, wandered the corridors between the dull gray metal servers. Drop floors and ceilings gave the sterile environment a futuristic sheen. My work with Hanssen in the Information Assurance Section was theoretical; this is where the magic happened. The Automated Case System ran from here, and so did FBI NET, the FBI's internal network. I looked at Hanssen. His slumped shoulders and usual smirk couldn't hide the buzz of anticipation and hint of childish wonder that such a place sparked in every computer nerd.

We were greeted by a man with a shock of white hair and a mustache impressive enough to land him a role in a Clint

Eastwood film. He introduced himself as Joseph Kielman, the FBI's chief scientist for the Information Resources Division. Hanssen's Information Assurance Section technically fell right under the chief scientist. That *technically* made Kielman Hanssen's boss—though Hanssen's unilateral transformation of our security team into a section blurred the lines of reporting enough that the FBI probably couldn't have said who supervised whom.

Kielman had degrees in physics and biophysics and a doctorate in genetics. As chief scientist, he was responsible for the FBI's information services, laboratory, and operational technology. The affable gentleman shaking hands with my irascible boss was the closest the FBI had to Bond's "Q." I could tell that Hanssen hated him the moment they met. The contempt bubbled past his placid mask the way it had when O'Leary first walked into 9930.

Hanssen's attitude around another of his bosses revealed a minor flaw. Hanssen had little respect for those he saw above him in the chain of command. It wouldn't break the case, but it might be useful. I filed it away for later.

As Kielman showed us around, Hanssen muttered to himself or tapped on his Palm Pilot. He only perked up when Dr. Kielman mentioned ACS.

"I have grave concerns about the ACS system," Hanssen said, tapping his Palm Pilot against his leg with one hand and spinning the stylus through the fingers of the other. "The system is flawed," he continued. "All it takes is one bad bureau person to invalidate all the security."

We stopped at a computer displaying the ACS terminal, with its green monochrome screen.

Kielman placed on hand on top of the monitor. "ACS audits keystrokes, you know? We've opened a number of OPR investigations when we determine that someone is looking where they should not."

I glanced from Kielman to Hanssen. OPR meant the Office of Personnel Responsibility. You definitely didn't want to get on the bad side of the ethics investigation team. I needed to remember this conversation. In my mind, I imagined writing each sentence of the exchange in longhand. I captured the imaginary pages in my mind, college ruled and notated in thick number-two pencil.

"Is OPR any good at auditing?" Hanssen asked.

"How do you mean?"

"Can we take a document in ACS and say who accessed it?"

Kielman sighed. "It would be difficult to differentiate a pattern from the wider random access. Unless OPR was focused on a particular person, they would most likely not discover a pattern. So no, I don't think so. Not yet."

"What you are telling me," Hanssen said, "is that ACS's audit feature doesn't work unless a specific OPR investigation is opened. In other words, ACS only works as long as someone is not a spy." He turned toward the door. "I know the Russians. If there's a spy in the system, I'll find him."

"So you are saying ACS is flawed?" Kielman said.

Hanssen stretched himself to his full height. "The FBI is flawed."

He wasn't wrong. In 2003 the US Department of Justice's inspector general conducted an exhaustive review of the FBI's failures to detect Robert Hanssen. The IG's team reviewed over 368,000 pages of material from an alphabet soup of intelligence agencies. The FBI, CIA, DOJ, NSA, and State Department all fell under the task force's scrutiny. They picked apart Hanssen's personal and professional life. Family, friends, supervisors, and colleagues were interviewed for hours, their every sentence dissected for clues. No stone was left unturned.

Most of the 674-page report remains classified at the top-secret level, but a 31-page public summary uncovered major deficiencies in the FBI's approach to internal investigations.

In short, the IG concluded that the FBI's internal security was flawed, and that those flaws made it impossible to catch a trusted insider.

The IG report rattled off a laundry list of problems, some specifically related to the Hanssen case, but most endemic to the FBI. Hanssen received a background investigation when he joined the FBI, but in twenty-five years at the bureau, he never received a polygraph. He also never submitted a disclosure form detailing his finances and investments. The FBI submitted Hanssen to the only background reinvestigation of his career in 1996, twenty years after he joined, but although the background investigator raised red flags after a perfunctory review, the FBI declined to follow up. Frankly, I was shocked the investigator managed to find anything of concern in the first place. Hanssen's reinvestigation didn't involve review of his personnel file, security file, or credit reports. The investigator never even interviewed Hanssen.

Had the reinvestigation followed best practices, the FBI might have caught Hanssen early in his spying career. A review of Hanssen's personnel file and interviews with Hanssen's various supervisors would have revealed weak managerial and interpersonal skills and a narcissistic personality. Details about an early '90s Office of Personnel Management investigation might have raised an eyebrow too. Hanssen threw a female FBI employee to the ground after she confronted him over an administrative issue. Hanssen received only a letter of censure and a five-day suspension.

A deep dive into Hanssen's security file might have revealed numerous breaches. In 1992, the FBI promoted Hanssen to chief for the National Security Threat List (NSTL) Unit. The newly minted unit investigated economic espionage (the theft of secrets with the intent to provide them to a foreign agent), trade-secret theft, and nuclear proliferation. While serving as boss of the NSTL, Hanssen hacked the FBI's computer system and illegally snatched Soviet counterintelligence documents from his colleagues' hard drives. Worried that the FBI might figure out that he had knifed through their computer security, Hanssen then reported his breach to his superiors, claiming to have hacked the FBI in order to expose flaws in the system. In late 1994, the FBI moved Hanssen to the Office of Foreign Missions at the State Department, where FBI computer specialists found password-breaking software on Hanssen's computer and referred him to the FBI's security programs manager. Hanssen's excuse? He told the security chief that he had installed the forbidden software in order to connect his desktop to a color printer. The FBI didn't even bother recording the incident in Hanssen's personnel or security files.

And if he'd ever been subjected to a financial review, Hanssen's spy career would have smacked into a brick wall. His profound disregard for the FBI's ability to detect a spy in the worst possible place led him to take risks. He opened a passbook savings account in his own name at a bank a block away from FBI HQ, where he would deposit the cash left for him under park platforms by the KGB—after counting it in his FBI office.

Hanssen snuck under the FBI's radar partly because the bureau failed to properly investigate its own employees. At a minimum, Hanssen should have undergone a background re-investigation with a polygraph and interview every five years—as should all FBI employees with access to classified information. But even without the reinvestigations, he wouldn't have been able to evade capture as long as he did were it not for the FBI's lack of information security. The FBI had no systems to monitor and track access to classified national-security information, which meant Hanssen often waltzed out of FBI buildings with copies and even originals of some of the US government's most sensitive documents. He routinely accessed information in ACS that he did not have a need to know. In addition to the case information he stole and handed over to the Russians, Hanssen habitually checked his own name and address and the locations of his favorite drop and signal sites for active investigations.

Hanssen couldn't have explained away these searches the way he had brushed off installing password-cracking software and hacking his buddies. But the FBI rarely used the ACS audit function to find those sticking their noses in the wrong places.

In fact, the agency may have even helped Hanssen carry out his work on behalf of the KGB. One year before the FBI identified him as a possible mole, when the investigation was still focused on Brian Kelley, headquarters ordered the closed network WFO team to brief Hanssen on the hunt for the mole. Two agents from the Gray Suit squad shared an evening chat with Hanssen in which they sought his opinions about the identity of the mole and requested a list of Russians who might provide information on him. The FBI required everyone seeking access to the elite Gray Suit squad to submit to a special polygraph. Everyone except Hanssen. The crafty spy's list of Russian targets sent the FBI on multiple wild-goose chases, each designed to put further distance between the real Gray Suit and the FBI investigation.

Hanssen was the most damaging spy in the history of the FBI—and possibly the worst in US history. Every scrap of information Hanssen delivered to the Russians required access to highly classified documents. Good cybersecurity demands that each time someone accesses critical information, that access is noted and at some level scrutinized. From 1979 until 2001, the FBI had been ignoring one of the cardinal rules of counterintelligence: watch those with access to the keys to the kingdom. Trust, but verify.

"Let's go, Eric," Hanssen said. "We have a lot of work to do."

I hung back and stopped Dr. Kielman while Hanssen passed through security.

"Do you think I could requisition a Palm Pilot? The newest model is a Palm V." I glanced at Hanssen's back. "Actually can I have two?" Always good to ingratiate myself with the boss.

"Why do you need these?" Dr. Kielman asked.

"Every executive needs a digital assistant," I said. "If I don't get one, I'll continue to be a no-good, do-nothing, worthless clerk. Plus, one is for my boss."

A smile twitched Kielman's mustache. "That might be the best requisition request I've received. Submit the paperwork and I'll approve it."

"Thanks, Doc."

"I hope you and Bob can help improve security," Kielman replied.

My mind sped through the days ahead. If we could prove that Hanssen was Gray Suit, and catch him in the act of espionage—if I granted all of Kate's wishes—we could rebuild the counterintelligence walls that Hanssen had spent a career undermining.

Hanssen held the door open, looking back toward me when he realized I hadn't obediently heeled to his command. I masked my disgust with a cough and flashed a grin toward the doctor.

"We'll improve security, Dr. Kielman," I said. "In fact, I guarantee it."

# CHAPTER 16

# NOT A BEAR

## January 29, 2001—Monday, Early Morning

I dreamed I was on a Boy Scout camping trip. My childhood friend Christian and I shared a dilapidated army tent, which we'd set up on a collection of old pallets that someone had left in the campground ages ago. Our troop had hiked out into the deep Appalachian woods when fall edged into winter. Nightfall had dropped the temperature so drastically that all the scouts had fled to their warm sleeping bags. Sleep had nearly claimed me when a rustling broke the silence right beside my head. Christian stopped me before I could shout.

"Don't move," he said. "That's a bear."

Juliana shook me awake.

"Juliana, what . . ."

She shook her head, eyes wide, and made a harsh shushing noise. I quieted immediately and listened. Rustling right outside the window closest to my head. Not a bear. Footsteps.

The Super Bowl party had not gone as I hoped. We hadn't fought, which was a mark in the win column, but we'd gone together and spent the time apart. My buddy Mike had thrown the party in the group house he shared with a few other guys out near the University of Maryland in College Park. Viv was also there with a large number of our mutual friends.

Once we arrived at the party, Juliana paired off with Viv and the other women while I joined the guys around a newly tapped keg. Mike took one look at my face and pressed a beer in my hand.

The Baltimore Ravens annihilated the New York Giants 34 to 7. For a few hours, I let football drive my worries away. But soon enough, the game ended, the snack trays lay barren, and the keg floated in an icy bath. I found Juliana, and she drove us home.

I'm a terrible backseat driver on the best of days. After a few beers, I criticized every movement of our Jeep. Juliana had to pull over and threaten to make me walk before I would retreat into the sullen silence that got us home. That silence had continued as we readied ourselves for bed and fell asleep.

Two thoughts fought in my mind as the not-bear trudged around outside our window. Joy that my wife had decided to speak to me again. Anger that she'd done so only because a greater threat than me had shown up. The two emotions danced and caught and melted together, finally resolving into one. My anger had a target.

"Stay here," I whispered. "I'll check it out."

Juliana clutched my arm, half holding me to the bed. "What, are you crazy? Call the police."

I put my lips close to her ear. "It might be an animal."

Before she could talk me out of it, I disentangled myself from her and padded from the room. I found my shoes and threw on a heavy coat.

"This is a bad idea," Juliana hissed from the bedroom doorway.

I stuffed my FBI credentials and a heavy extendable baton from my messenger bag into my coat pockets and handed Juliana my cell phone. "If I shout, you call 911."

Before she could say another word, I was out the door.

Our apartment was tucked into the back corner of our building. Our bedroom windows looked past two feet of moss to a massive wooden wall on one side and a parking lot strewn with gravel on the other. The surrounding fences forced anyone walking to the back of the building to enter via the driveway.

I eased the front door shut and crept around the side of the building, trying not to let the gravel crunch underfoot. My ears filtered out the constant rush of street noises and car horns that are the background track to every city and focused on the noise of feet—or paws—on the dead leaves left over from the fall. The trespasser still made noises behind our apartment. Whether it was animal or burglar, I had it trapped.

"Who's there?"

Footsteps careened around the corner. A heavyset man saw me and skidded to a halt in a spray of gravel. He gripped a crowbar in one gloved hand.

"What are you . . . oh!" Juliana froze next to me.

"I told you to stay inside," I breathed.

The man took a step toward us. My heart raced, not out of fear for myself—I welcomed this fight—but for the unknown danger to Juliana. I gently nudged her behind me with my left hand and reached into my pocket with my right. For the first time, I thought about how ridiculous I must look in a winter coat over black-and-neon Grinch pajamas.

"Did you call the police?"

"No," Juliana said, her voice too fast. "I forgot the phone."

I held out my right hand and gave it a flick. The cold snick of the baton extending flooded me with courage as I faced down the shadowy form of the man standing at the end of our small driveway. We stared at each other for a long moment, each waiting for the other to move first. Then I herded Juliana back around to the front of the building, moving slowly backward to keep the burglar in sight. The moment he had enough space, the trespasser fled past us.

Back in the warmth of our apartment, Juliana called the police, and I tried not to shake through an adrenaline crash. She hung up the phone and rounded on me.

"What if he had a gun?"

"He didn't."

"But what if he did?"

"Then you should have stayed inside like I told you and called the police."

She slammed the phone into its charger. "I'm not a little girl you need to protect."

I sighed. Juliana couldn't understand the risks undercover operatives take the moment they buckle themselves into an unmarked car to chase a target through some of the more dangerous parts of Washington, DC. I couldn't tell her. The only way to operate in situations where every instinct screams for you to run is to cultivate a powerful sense of self-confidence that dips its toe into the waters of arrogance. Standing across that alley from our would-be burglar, I was certain of one thing: I was the most dangerous person standing on that loose gravel.

I guided Juliana down to the couch next to me. She pulled away, but finally relented.

"I hate this place," she said.

"Me too."

"Our nights should be like a honeymoon, not a constant fight."

I held her tight. "It will all be over soon."

"What? What will be over soon?"

I let out a deep, shaky breath. "Do you trust me?"

She barely thought before answering. "I don't know."

Her words made the room spin. I held her until the dizzying moment passed. "You can trust me. I promise."

# CHAPTER 17

# IN THE MIDDLE

January 29, 2001—Monday

Kate intercepted me in the morning as I trudged out of the Archives–Navy Memorial Metro Station, spotting me despite my heavy overcoat and the knitted cap pulled low over my ears. I felt exhausted. Juliana and I had lain next to each other in sleepless silence after we gave our report about the burglar to the police. I'd left out the part about the extendable baton and hadn't identified myself as FBI. Juliana had gallantly not filled in the blanks. But our united front for the police officer fell to tatters once the two of us crawled into bed. I'd spent the rest of the night watching shadows crawl across our ceiling.

I jumped into Kate's car. She pulled into traffic on Pennsylvania Avenue and drove past FBI HQ. Sleepless night or no, I needed my wits about me this morning. For the first time, I was going to the Washington Field Office to meet the team working on the Gray Day investigation.

Hanssen was in pocket at a doctor's appointment, but he wouldn't be gone long.

I got out of the car and followed Kate through the parking deck to an elevator. When we got out, she led me down a long hall toward a distant room at the back of the squad. I recognized several National Security Division special agents I'd worked with over the years, and as I walked by I heard a smattering of calls: "What's up, Wolf?" I shot my old colleagues a smile but couldn't stop to speak. We were heading into the nerve center.

Kate led me through the Washington Field Office. Unlike the ridiculous maze at HQ, the WFO floor plan made organizational sense. Light permeated the white stone building, contrasting with the murky gloom of the Hoover Building. Switching from Room 9930 to the clean walls and orderly desks of the WFO was like escaping a medieval dungeon and ending up on Wall Street. I stayed close on Kate's heels until she stopped before a nondescript door—the sort I recognized from my Earl Pitts days. Her badge and a key code granted us entry to a room larger than 9930 and infinitely cozier. About a dozen agents and support staff buzzed amid desks and computer monitors. Piles of paper made sometimes orderly and often haphazard islands in all the controlled chaos. In this room, Hanssen's every action became a data point in the long list of information that might lead to his arrest. I shook hands with various agents and analysts, all of them smiling, and knew that I was only one such data point. Maybe not even the most important one. Perplexed, I followed Kate to a group of analysts relaxing beside a technical station. We were at the listening post, where a team of analysts monitored all of Hanssen's darkest secrets, from phone calls to the video feed from 9930 and the GPS we'd placed on his car.

"All these people—"

"You're not alone on this case, kiddo," Kate smiled. "A lot of people have your back."

That's when I realized: I'd been compartmentalized. Not only did the FBI surround Hanssen in a fictional world designed within the FBI's most hallowed hallways, but the FBI had kept me in the dark, too, isolating me from the other players so I wouldn't know who else was part of the case. I stood on the outside looking at familiar ground. The FBI had compartmentalized the Hanssen case the way Donner's squad had sequestered itself when we went after Pitts. Both teams wanted to remove the chance that someone would carelessly divulge information about a highly sensitive investigation in passing conversation—but also to catch any other spies in case Hanssen wasn't acting alone.

Kate flicked on a bank of computer screens. The black-and-white image on the first screen was unmistakable: the edge of my desk, empty except for the picture of Juliana. The neighboring screen showed Hanssen's smaller office. The final screen showed the hallway from one of the standard FBI cameras that poke out of every corner.

"How well can you hear?" I asked.

"Barely," said one analyst. "We can make out most of what you're saying, but less than half of what GD says."

Kate dragged open a heavy drawer from a secure file safe. She sorted through the contents and selected a page of paper in a clear protective sleeve. I turned the page over in my hands. A carefully sliced-open envelope bore a one-word return address: "Chicago." The postmark was faded but still legible: "WDC 200," July 13, 1988. I flipped it over to read the letter, typed on a typewriter:

```
I found the site empty. Possibly I had the
time wrong. I work from memory. My recollection
was for you to fill before 1:00 a.m. I believe
Viktor Degtyar was in the church driveway off
Rt. 123, but I did not know how he would react
to an approach. My schedule was tight to make
this at all. Because of my work, I had to
synchronize explanations and flights while not
leaving a pattern of absence or travel that could
later be correlated with communication times.
This is difficult and expensive.

I will call the number you gave me on 2/24,
2/26 or 2/28 at 1:00 a.m., EDST. Please plan
filled signals. Empty sites bother me. I like to
know before I commit myself as I'm sure you do
```

also. Let's not use the original site so early
at least until the seasons change. Some type of
call-out signal to you when I have a package
or when I can receive one would be useful.
Also, please be specific about dates, e.g.,
2/24. Scheduling is not simple for me because
of frequent travel and wife. Any ambiguity
multiplies the problems.

My security concerns may seem excessive.
I believe experience has shown them to be
necessary. I am much safer if you know little
about me. Neither of us are children about
these things. Over time, I can cut your losses
rather than become one.

Ramon
P.S. Your "thank you" was deeply appreciated.

I handed the letter back to Kate, and she slipped the folder
into the file cabinet, then closed the drawer but didn't lock it.

"These letters are from the late '80s," Kate said. "But we
think he started his spying much earlier than that. He uses a
number of pseudonyms, and never his own name, or anything
that might refer to the FBI. He often calls himself 'B.'" She
handed me another letter. "It gets interesting."

I flipped the plastic-covered letter over and read the date:
October 24, 1985. The letter described operational procedures
for managing the complex system of signals and drops that are
the bread and butter of spy craft.

DROP LOCATION

Please leave your package for me under the corner
(nearest the street) of the wooden foot bridge

located just west of the entrance to Nottoway
Park. (ADC Northern Virginia Street Map, #14, D3)

PACKAGE PREPARATION

Use a green or brown plastic trash bag and trash
to cover a waterproofed package.

SIGNAL LOCATION

Signal site will be the pictorial "pedestrian-
crossing" signpost just west of the main Nottoway
Park entrance on Old Courthouse Road. (The sign
is the one nearest the bridge just mentioned.)

SIGNALS

My signal to you: One vertical mark of white
adhesive tape meaning I am ready to receive your
package.

Your signal to me: One horizontal mark of white
adhesive tape meaning drop filled.

My signal to you: One vertical mark of white
adhesive tape meaning I have received your
package. (Remove old tape before leaving signal.)

I scanned the mental map of Virginia the ghosts had drilled
into my head. I used to drive with stacks of ADC map books
in the back of my car. My Northern Virginia map was heavily marked up with red circles and sticky tabs for all the spies
who make Vienna and Arlington their home. "Nottoway Park.
That's right near his house."

"A five-minute walk." Kate took the letter from me. She

handled it reverently, the way a curator in a museum moves an artifact. I half expected her to snap on a pair of white cotton gloves. "He made things very convenient for himself."

"It sounds like him," I said. "The letters, I mean. The way he talks."

"There are more." Kate pointed out a whiteboard. Someone had scribbled a history of espionage from 1979 until 2001 in blue marker. Pitts and Ames had prominent spots amid a pantheon of spies and double agents. Lines spiked from each to sources they might have revealed or operations they might have compromised. Numerous question marks riddled the timeline. I noted that the name Ramon Garcia showed up in 1985. It was circled in red.

"Why Ramon Garcia?"

Kate shrugged. "Our best guess is that he chose Garcia because the letters 'CIA' are in there. He doesn't seem the sort to rely on coincidence."

"No," I agreed. "He's too much of a control freak. If this is his alter ego, he'd want it to mean something."

Kate tapped the whiteboard with a knuckle. The sound made a few analysts look up from their workstations. "Believe me, kiddo, we've agonized over it. At the end of the day we'll just have to ask him." She winked. "But first we need to catch him. We need something to tie Hanssen to Ramon."

In 1985, when the CIA and FBI lost nearly every significant human asset operating against the Soviet Union, it was a mole named Ramon Garcia who was partially to blame. It took until the fall of 2000 for the Gray Suit team to recruit a source who might shed light on those events. He had stolen the file on the Soviets' most valuable spy before leaving the KGB sometime after the collapse of the Soviet Union. After allowing it to gather dust in his attic for years, the former KGB officer turned businessman was ready to sell. The FBI expected the file to point directly to Brian Kelley, the CIA case officer they had hounded for years and code-named "Gray Deceiver."

The unnamed KGB retiree agreed to sell the file of information for millions of dollars and the promise of a better life for his family. Despite the risk of spending millions on possibly worthless information, the FBI jumped at the opportunity. The Brian Kelley case had been going nowhere. Maybe this was the spark they needed.

As the Russian defector settled into his secret new life here in the States, the agents opened the file on Gray Suit. They found letters that he'd left in clandestine drops to the Soviets over the years, and noted that each had been signed only as "B" or "Ramon Garcia"—pseudonyms meant to keep everyone guessing at his identity. Next to the letters was a cassette tape and a trash bag retrieved from one of the drop sites. Gray Suit made only two mistakes in twenty-two years of spying. The FBI had now bought both from a KGB defector.

The trash bag was the first. FBI forensics lifted two partial fingerprints off it that matched Hanssen's biometrics. While not enough to definitively prove that Hanssen was Gray Suit—he could have claimed the KGB had set him up—it pointed us in the right direction. The cassette tape held a recording of an August 1986 telephone call between a Russian intelligence officer named Aleksander Fefelov and "B" in which the two discussed a missed payment for a drop. When the FBI played the cassette tape, a senior agent who'd worked for Hanssen on a task force recognized Hanssen's whispery voice. The recording sent the Gray Suit team reeling. They'd been looking for the mole in the wrong place—and at the wrong agency—for years.

The FBI required an ironclad case against Hanssen. His combative disrespect for authority and his clever manipulation of the FBI's procedures, practices, and computer systems during his espionage career would make a successful conviction difficult. Much like in the Pitts case, a defector had traded dated information identifying Hanssen as a spy in return for money and a better life. But the source was reluctant to take the stand to testify to the accuracy and origin of the information. The former KGB lieutenant colonel Vladimir Putin had just been elected president of Russia, and he did not look kindly on his former colleagues sharing secrets with the United States. We had to bury the former Russian intelligence officer and his family deep into Witness Protection with a new name and identity.

At trial, Hanssen could have argued that the source information was circumstantial and that the defector was using an old Soviet entrapment scheme in which the KGB sought to discredit senior agents tasked with hunting Russians. Likely to succeed? Probably not. But it was risky enough that the Justice Department might be inclined to seek a lesser sentence under the more forgiving conspiracy statute. The FBI didn't want Hanssen to quietly ride out a twenty-seven-year sentence. They needed the sort of pressure that makes people reveal each and every skeleton in every closet until all the closets are cleaned out. The sort of pressure one feels when facing the death penalty.

There are two flavors of espionage in Title 18 of the Code of Laws of the United States of America. Section 794 (a) sets out the criminal violation of espionage: gathering or delivering defense information to aid a foreign government. Conspiracy to commit espionage, codified in Section 794 (c), occurs when two or more persons conspire to gather or deliver defense information to aid a foreign government. Both charges can theoretically carry the death penalty, but as the Earl Pitts case showed, a conspiracy case is not a sure bet in that regard.

In order for the FBI to deliver an airtight case of espionage to the US attorney, the FBI needed to catch Hanssen knowingly and unlawfully communicating, delivering, and transmitting documents and information relating to the national defense of the United States to representatives of a foreign government. In other words, we needed Hanssen to spy again.

We also needed to be able to tie Hanssen to Ramon and "B." Careers had slammed against brick walls looking for the mole undermining the intelligence community under these code names. If Hanssen was the spy we sought, the FBI needed every scrap of leverage available to crack his silence. It needed to connect all the dots before making the arrest. If they didn't get it right, Hanssen might walk.

The FBI's ultimate goal in seeking the death penalty wasn't to punish Hanssen—not entirely. We wanted to be able to trade the death penalty for a lifetime of debriefings. Only then could we begin to repair the damage he'd done to US counter-intelligence.

To catch Hanssen in the act, the FBI needed him to make another drop to the Russians, which is why the FBI put Hanssen in charge of the Information Assurance Section. Tasking Hanssen to a section responsible for cybersecurity gave him access to classified information. We hoped he'd try to pass it to his old friends.

But Hanssen was as smart as a fox. He anticipated that the FBI might investigate him, which is why he put his own pre-cautions in place. Over the years, Hanssen made it his job to know all the top agents—anyone who might be investigating a high-priority Russian target. Which is why he didn't know me. Though I'd investigated major cases, some of which involved Russian agents, I hadn't been on the front lines for about a year, ever since I proposed to Juliana. I also wasn't a special agent. And to Hanssen, even a ghost was little more than a *do-nothing worthless clerk*. Everything suddenly clicked into place. This was one reason I was tapped over a more seasoned agent: I was the most out-of-sight, unexpected person the FBI could find. When Gene parked in front of my apartment that frigid December morning, he'd asked me if I'd ever heard of Robert Hanssen. But that wasn't what he was really asking. His real question was *underneath* that question: *Had Hanssen ever heard of me?* If Hanssen wasn't on my radar, I likely wasn't on his—or anyone else's, for that matter. Which is why no one, not even Hanssen, would suspect me.

An analyst pulled me out of my epiphany: "He's on his way back."

Kate led me past the desks of agents that reminded me of the small team assembled to catch Earl Pitts. I glanced back before she shut the unmarked door and cut off the squad room's camaraderie. I missed those moments of gentle ribbing and jokes amid the nose-to-the-grindstone effort FBI personnel give to every investigation. I knew that all those people were working as hard as I was to catch Hanssen. But I was the only other person locked into Room 9930.

"He keeps a journal on his desk," I said to Kate. "Maybe we can find something in there."

"We copied it during the last office search. He left it out the other night, remember?"

I did. This case had taught me to mentally photograph rooms and scenes. I'd also learned to memorize everything Hanssen said, sometimes to the word, in order to log it for later.

Kate grimaced. "We're going to search his car tomorrow if you can find a chance to get him away. Also, plan for a late night tomorrow. We're going to search his office and you need to be there. In the meantime—"

"I'll keep looking."

Hanssen was Gray Suit. Gray Suit was "B" or Ramon Garcia. Ramon Garcia was the most damaging spy in American history. He was also weeks away from a drop that might end in his arrest or, if we missed it, a last payout before he took his retirement and we lost our chance. So much hinged on what I learned in 9930. But while the agents in the secret squad room had piles of evidence, I had nothing. No information, no leads, no case.

Target: Robert Hanssen

Russian mole
Gray Suit, potentially Ramon
Garcia, B
Shared nuclear secrets
Compromised overseas assets
Worst spy in American history

CHAPTER 18

# MAKING A SPY

In January 1976, Robert Hanssen joined the FBI. His credentials as a certified public accountant with a master's degree in business administration complemented four years spent on the Chicago police force to make him a good fit for the agency's Financial Crimes Division, and he was assigned to Gary, Indiana, right out of the FBI Academy. But even as Hanssen investigated white-collar criminals in the Midwest, he was dreaming of bigger things. Hanssen had grown up with a fondness for espionage. He devoured James Bond books and movies. He bought a Walther PPK pistol, a Leica spy camera, and a short-wave radio to flesh out the fantasy. He even opened a Swiss bank account. But 007 didn't belong in Lake County, Indiana.

After two years, the FBI signed off on Hanssen's transfer request to New York City, one of the great spy capitals of the world. Hanssen found his calling within the Soviet Counterintelligence Analytical Squad. His early supervisors described him as smart, technically proficient, and analytical, and they marveled at his ability with computer systems. They also considered him lacking in field operations ability and assigned him to administrative work, crushing his James Bond fantasies. Instead of working undercover against Soviet spies on the streets of Gotham, Hanssen managed the New York Field Office's counterintelligence database. He joined the FBI to hunt spies. The FBI made him a librarian.

Hanssen had married a woman whose family was wealthier than his own. He converted to Bernadette "Bonnie" Hanssen's Catholic faith and joined Opus Dei, an exclusive, doctrinally conservative order within the Church. The new couple committed to send each of their six children to private schools and to tithe a portion of their income to the charitable works of their parish. But Hanssen couldn't afford the lifestyle that he thought he deserved. His growing family would need space, and Hanssen's vision of himself required that he provide for them while Bonnie managed the home and raised their children. These financial pressures, together with the slight he perceived from the FBI and his inherent narcissism, triggered Hanssen's first decision to spy.

In November 1979, Hanssen dipped his toe into the world of espionage. While in Manhattan, he used his growing knowledge of Soviet operations to volunteer his services to Russia's foreign military intelligence agency, the Glavnoye razvedyvatel'noye upravleniye (GRU). Clever from the start, Hanssen cloaked his identity from Russia's largest intelligence service. From 1979 until 1981, he left information stolen from the Soviet Counterintelligence Unit in dead drops in exchange for around $21,000 (worth about $60,000 in today's dollars).

The GRU experiment tested Hanssen's resolve and ability. He might have continued his work for them, but in the spring of 1980, Hanssen's wife, Bonnie, found a strange letter from the GRU to Hanssen in their Scarsdale, New York, basement. Hanssen downplayed it, telling Bonnie that he had given the Soviets junk information to trick them into giving him money. The couple agreed that Hanssen would confess the crime to their priest.

The priest granted Hanssen absolution but required that Hanssen repent his sins and suggested he donate the tainted money to the needy. Hanssen ended his GRU experiment and donated nearly $20,000 to Mother Teresa's Little Sisters of the Poor in multiple $1,000 increments.

Hanssen's wife might have caught him, but the FBI still didn't have a clue. Plus, he'd handled his mistake like a true master spy. In 1981, Hanssen made his way to Washington, DC, the spy capital of the world. From 1981 until 1985, he served in the Budget and Soviet Analytical Units at FBI headquarters. He remained a librarian, but one perched in the center of the web of information flowing to and from the intelligence division. His cyber tendrils took in information from the NSA and the CIA, catching the FBI's most sensitive human assets and technical operations against the USSR. Hanssen realized that the best spies do not flash like Bond on a world stage; they manipulate information from the shadows, unnoticed and unknown.

In September 1985, Hanssen returned to the New York Field Office. This time around he supervised a foreign counterintelligence squad, which gave him access to a wealth of Soviet spy information, including the identity of the FBI's Soviet sources and informants and the locations of Komitet gosudarstvennoy bezopasnosti (KGB) defectors in the United States. Empowered by his success with the GRU, Hanssen graduated himself to the big leagues. He decided to spy for the KGB.

On October 4, 1985, the mailman delivered an odd envelope to Viktor Degtyar's home in Alexandria, Virginia. Degtyar opened the envelope and found a second envelope nestled within the first like a matryoshka doll. Stern instructions forbade Degtyar from opening the second and demanded he take it to Victor Cherkashin.

The contents of the envelope would either make or break Degtyar's career. Whoever sent the envelope knew Degtyar was a KGB Line PR officer. The KGB organized its espionage activities into distinct lines (or sections) that had different responsibilities in gathering intelligence and pursuing counterintelligence. Each line of activity came under the direction of the KGB *rezident*, a spy operating out of a KGB First Chief

Directorate *rezidentura*, typically an embassy. In Washington, DC, the *resident* was an official member of the ambassador's staff who had the covert job of spymaster. He operated out of the Soviet embassy, and all espionage lines reported to him.

Degtyar's Line PR collected information about political, economic, and military strategic intelligence and conducted active measures. Other lines pursued different tasks. Line X sought to acquire American technology and implement technical spying. Line KR gave the FBI the biggest headache. KR intelligence officers were the ones who recruited American spies.

The mere existence of the letter would inform the KGB that the FBI had uncovered Degtyar. He dismissed thoughts of opening the inner letter, or burning it in his fireplace. Either could mean prison or worse if the KGB found out.

The next day Degtyar dutifully handed the entire package to Cherkashin, the Line KR chief at the Soviet embassy in Washington, DC. Cherkashin opened the letter with calm hands. As the head of counterintelligence and security for the KGB in America's capital, he'd seen it all. He had already extracted a wealth of information out of the CIA from Aldrich Ames. What new spy had volunteered to the cagey spymaster? Once his eyes skimmed the letter, his hands began to shake.

```
Dear Mr. Cherkashin:


Soon, I will send a box of documents to
Mr. Degtyar. They are from certain of the most
sensitive and highly compartmented projects
of the U.S. Intelligence community. All are
originals to aid in Verifying their authenticity.
Please recognize for our Long-term interests that
there are a limited number of persons with this
array of clearances. As a collection they point
to me. I trust that an officer of your experience
will handle them appropriately. I believe they
```

are sufficient to justify a $100,000 payment to
me. I must warn of certain risks to my security
of which you may not be aware. Your service has
recently suffered some setbacks. I warn that
Mr. Boris Yuzhin (line PR, SF), Mr. Sergey
Motorin, (line PR, Wash.) And Mr. Valeriy
Martynov (line W, Wash.) Have been Recruited by
our special services.

To further support my bona fides Details regarding
payment and future contact will be sent to you
personally. . . . My identity and actual position
in the community must be left unstated to ensure
my security. I am open to commo suggestions but
want no specialized tradecraft. I will add 6,
(you Subtract 6) from stated months, days
and times in both directions of our future
communications.

True to his word, the mysterious spy signed the letter with the simplest of monikers: "B."

From 1985 to 1991, Hanssen handed the KGB the intelligence community's most important Soviet counterintelligence and military secrets. His first letter to Cherkashin caused enormous damage. The FBI and CIA relied on Yuzhin, Motorin, and Martynov to spy for the United States and provide critical inside information about Soviet espionage operations. After Hanssen's letter, the KGB flew each of the spies back to Moscow and tried them for espionage. After sham trials, the Soviets executed Motorin and Martynov. Yuzhin received a fifteen-year sentence. By 1991, Hanssen had also completely compromised the FBI's ACS database. The intelligence efforts of the United States against the Soviets unraveled.

Meanwhile, Hanssen counted his money at his FBI desk, laughing while the FBI looked for him in all the wrong places.

Hanssen shelved "B" in 1991 when the Soviet Union fell and Russia orchestrated a pivot from communism to quasi-democracy. The new government split the notorious KGB into the Federal Security Service (FSB) and the Foreign Intelligence Service of the Russian Federation (SVR). (The GRU continued to collect intelligence for the Russian military.) Hanssen feared that KGB spies fleeing the USSR's bloated husk would find their way into FBI nets and trade their secrets for freedom. Better to go dark until Russian intelligence sorted itself out and disappeared any defectors.

In 1990, the FBI had promoted Hanssen to the FBI headquarters inspections staff. By then, the Soviets had paid him more than half a million US dollars, and that money burned a hole in his pocket. He spent a lot of it as an inspector's aide. His assignment required travel to FBI field offices, resident agencies, and FBI legal attaché offices in US embassies across the world so that he could rate their performance. Traveling gave Hanssen an opportunity to spend some of his espionage money away from the prying eyes of the FBI and his family. He rented fast cars, holed up in lavish apartments with an exotic dancer, and acted out his James Bond fantasies.

In the summer of 1991, the FBI brought Hanssen back to headquarters and made him a program manager in the Soviet Operations Section. His unit fought to keep US technology and scientific achievements out of Russian hands. Six months later, the FBI finally promoted him to unit chief in charge of the National Security Threat List Unit. The choice position at one of the FBI's most glamorous new units should have fast-tracked Hanssen to new executive heights. Instead, Hanssen's dour personality and caustic leadership skills frustrated the team he managed. He would frequently sit in his office and listen to foreign-language tapes instead of rolling up his sleeves and pitching in with his team. In 1994 the FBI removed him from the position and assigned him to a computer squad at WFO.

While Hanssen's career fizzled and died, the FBI and CIA

hunted for the mole they'd named Gray Suit. By 1993, the FBI was pouring enormous resources into the search. The problem? The FBI focused all its investigative powers on the CIA.

The FBI's CIA tunnel vision blinded the investigation to two events that may have ended Ramon Garcia's long reign as king of spies. In the summer of 1990, while Hanssen flew around the world inspecting FBI field offices, Bonnie found $5,000 in her husband's dresser drawer. Perhaps remembering the last time she found incriminating evidence, Bonnie asked her brother for advice. Her brother happened to be Special Agent Mark Wauck, an FBI agent based in Chicago. Wauck reported the money, along with other suspicions he had about his brother-in-law, to his FBI supervisor in Chicago. The Chicago Field Office dismissed the concerns. At the time, the FBI didn't have a policy or procedure for investigating such reports. No one at the FBI questioned Hanssen about the money, and the incident never made it to his file.

In 1993, the day after his father died, Hanssen nearly self-destructed. He surprised a GRU officer in the garage of the officer's apartment building. He told the shocked Russian that he had spied for the KGB, and that he was Ramon Garcia. The GRU officer backed away from the rabid FBI agent and refused to accept a package that Hanssen insisted contained details about double-agent cases that the FBI ran against the GRU. Hanssen returned to headquarters and monitored the FBI's computer systems. The GRU officer complained about the meeting to his superiors. Russia lodged a protest against the US government, complaining that the FBI had officially sanctioned a provocation.

Hanssen sweated behind his computer monitor. The FBI opened a formal investigation that should have led directly to him. After all, the spy had broken his careful cover and even used the code name he'd given the KGB. Hanssen kept his passport and open ticket to Moscow handy in case he had to run.

But the FBI never linked the strange parking-garage

approach to Hanssen or to any other agent. Hanssen thanked God for his good fortune. His recklessness had almost cost him everything. From now on, he would be more cautious. He put Ramon Garcia back on injured reserve and silently plotted his next move. Hanssen had learned patience.

In 1995, the FBI found a quiet spot at the State Department Office of Foreign Missions to stash Hanssen until his mandatory retirement in 2001. OFM acts like a watchdog for foreign missions operating in the United States. This includes activities like registering and titling vehicles operated by the foreign diplomatic community in the United States, protecting US citizens from foreign diplomats that abuse their privileges and immunity, and ensuring that American diplomats abroad are treated well. The FBI brass figured that the OFM liaison position would be a perfect fit for a seemingly unambitious supervisory FBI agent and promptly forgot about him. During the six years he liaised with the State Department, Hanssen had no supervisor, submitted no performance reviews, and made no reports to the FBI about his work efforts. While I graduated from the FBI Academy and was thrown face-first into deep-end work, ghosting Russian targets and chasing terrorist bombers, Hanssen spent his days surfing the Internet, watching movies, and hanging around with friends and colleagues. He also spent a great deal of time searching the ACS.

For some reason, the FBI had given Hanssen unrestricted access to thousands of internal FBI classified documents for which he had no "need to know." Hanssen would routinely search his own name and address, the addresses of his drop sites and signal sites, and other identifying information to determine whether the FBI had a case open that might link Ramon or "B" to him. While in ACS he mined the FBI's database for the most sensitive espionage investigations. Ramon might have been taking a break, but Hanssen was preparing for his future.

In 1999, the exiled FBI agent contacted a known SVR Line

KR senior intelligence officer identified as "V.K." The newly formed SVR was delighted to hear that their goose would once again lay golden eggs. In October 1999, "B" received a triumphant letter from the SVR.

Dear friend: welcome!

It's good to know you are here. Acknowledging your letter to V.K. we express our sincere joy on the occasion of resumption of contact with you. We firmly guarantee you for a necessary financial help. Note, please, that since our last contact a sum set aside for you has risen and presents now about 800.000 dollars. This time you will find in a package 50.000 dollars. Now it is up to you to give a secure explanation of it.

As to communication plan, we may have need of some time to work out a secure and reliable one. This why we suggest to carry on the 13th of November at the same drop which you have proposed in your letter to V.K. We shall be ready to retrieve your package from DD [dead drop] since 20:00 to 21:00 hours on the 12th of November after we would read you signal (a vertical mark of white adhesive tape of 6-8 cm length) on the post closest to Wolftrap Creek of the "Foxstone Park" sign. We shall fill our package in and make up our signal (a horizontal mark of white adhesive tape).

After you will clear the drop don't forget to remove our tape that will mean for us—exchange is over.

The letter went on to describe a new signal site, code-named "Ellis," on a telephone pole at the southwest corner of a T-shaped intersection of Foxhall Road and Whitehaven Parkway. The pole sprouts from the sidewalk between two crosswalks near the curved brick sign for George Washington University's Mount Vernon Campus. During the morning and evening rush hour, numerous cars crawl through the intersection and give way to a single stoplight and frequent foot traffic. In the middle of the day or after the evening commute, the Ellis telephone pole stands a silent and lonely sentinel. Perfect for a spy.

Hanssen could request a dead drop by driving a tack into the pole 1.2 yards from the ground. He could do so anytime he wished, even in the middle of a crowd seeking to cross the intersection. It takes little sleight of hand to stand beside a pole and drive a tack into it.

A Russian intelligence officer would occasionally drive by Ellis looking for a spot of yellow or white. A white tack meant that Hanssen wished to request an urgent dead drop. Yellow signaled that Hanssen felt threatened and needed assistance from his Russian friends.

In addition to the bridge in Foxstone Park, the Russians offered a new drop site called "Lewis," located under a podium in the Long Branch Nature Center Amphitheater. The nature center's sprawl of paths and ponds lies along a creek of the same name, which spills from the larger Four Mile Run stream. A wilderness trail winds past the nature center's small green-sided education building to an isolated amphitheater hidden in a basin of trees. Sparse wooden benches set on rising tiers of brick and stone face a wooden stage that resembles an oversized pallet. During opening hours, a family might stumble through the quiet space, or a tour group might chatter through, seeking the meadow or Willow Pond. Occasionally the Nature Center will erect a screen between two large poles at the back of the stage and host a family movie night.

After the park closes at five p.m., the amphitheater is quiet and dark. Hanssen used a flashlight to find his way to the tens of thousands of dollars the SVR would tuck into a small depression behind the stage's back corner. They set the signal for that dead drop location on a different telephone pole.

Ramon was back in business.

# CHAPTER 19

# HAVE FAITH

January 31, 2001—Wednesday

Hanssen dashed through the main door and disappeared into his office without so much as a hello. He emerged a few minutes later with his coat still on and a scarf wrapped around his neck.

"Get your coat," he said.

"Where are we going?"

"To church."

I huddled in my coat against the chill as we left headquarters and walked about ten blocks until we reached a nondescript building on the corner of Fifteenth and I Streets. The sign above the building read CATHOLIC INFORMATION CENTER. A bookstore.

Hanssen opened the door for me, and we stepped into a cozy, well-lit interior. Pleasant staff wearing name tags pinned neatly on crisp white shirts glided through rows of bookshelves. The store was divided into three sections: Learning the Faith, Living the Faith, and Loving the Faith. Hanssen took me to the Learning section.

"The congregation here is Opus Dei." Hanssen spoke in the soft voice reserved for a library or place of prayer, which I suppose this place had covered.

At the time, all I knew about Opus Dei was that its members came from influential families, tended to hold positions of power, had to go to church every day, and dedicated their lives to the organization. Later, I learned that Opus Dei—meaning "work of God" in Latin—had been founded by Saint Josemaría Escrivá in Spain in the late 1920s. Escrivá was a Catholic priest who believed mainstream Catholics were losing sight of the true faith, becoming what we'd today consider lapsed or "grocery cart" Catholics. He sought to guide laypeople toward a special offering of their spiritual, professional, social, and family life to God.

Hanssen shared Saint Escrivá's fears about the insufficiently devout Catholics he liked to call "junior varsity practitioners." I certainly fit his description. While I tried my best to attend Mass on Sundays and, as the Jesuits at Gonzaga High School reinforced, be a "man for others," I barely scratched the surface of what Catholicism truly demanded. I lived my faith in my heart and mind, but I could have made it to church on a few more holy days of obligation.

Still, I've always felt more comfortable in the Catholicism in which I was raised, "junior varsity" though it may be, than in an organization like Opus Dei. The organization is an orthodox personal prelature of the Catholic Church—meaning it lies outside the normal Church hierarchy and reports directly to the Vatican—and has been criticized as elitist for the way it separates itself from the broader Catholic Church, as well as for its secret practices, aggressive recruiting, and tight control over its members. As a robust individualist, I knew the rigid requirements of Opus Dei would fit me like a hair shirt two sizes too small. But I also knew it could be the key to understanding Hanssen's personality.

"Bonnie sponsored me into Opus Dei," Hanssen continued. "I was a lapsed Lutheran before I met her, and not a good one at that. She saved me." He gave me a look. "If you like I can sponsor you."

I nodded, feeling a jolt of adrenaline. Juliana grew up Lutheran in an East Germany that discouraged religion. She limited her church appearances to Easter and Christmas Masses with me at St. Matthew's Cathedral. Ever musical, Juliana loved St. Matthew's exceptional choir. Hanssen's relationship with his wife flipped the script Juliana and I followed, but the similarities between us were jarring. I had sniffed out another connection between us that might help break the case, but I stood perilously close to a line I'd vowed not to cross. The investigation had taken over every other part of my life. I wanted to hold my faith in reserve.

Behind the rows of neat books and Information Center staff, large double doors led into a beautiful chapel with polished wooden pews and an ornate golden altar at the front. The rows of pews might have held a few dozen people, but only ten or so sat in silent reflection. The hushed atmosphere reminded me of drafty morning Masses at Saint Jane de Chantal, where the only noise might be a slight creak of wood or a muted cough.

"The chapel fills up every day," Hanssen said. "Masses begin at 12:05 p.m. daily after an intention service to let us pray the rosary or offer our intentions to God."

I looked at my watch. We had arrived fifteen minutes early for the Mass. I was observant to the point of paranoia as I followed Hanssen to a seat three rows back from the altar against the left-hand wall. Now that I'd been fully read into the case, I was suspicious of everyone. Most people in the chapel wore the sort of professional clothing that suggested they had stopped in from high-end K Street offices on their lunch break. More men than women sat in the pews, and most had reached middle age. The only person who stood out piqued my interest solely because he wore a leather jacket instead of an overcoat.

Hanssen knelt and crossed himself before sliding into the pew. I followed suit. After a few minutes I missed the soft padded kneelers at St. Matthew's Cathedral.

"For whom are you praying?" Hanssen asked.

"My mom," I said.

"Is she ill?"

"She has Parkinson's." I hadn't told even my best friends about my mother's illness. And my family rarely acknowledged its existence. My brothers and I would ignore our mother's slow decline, secretly pray for a miracle cure for an incurable disease, and practice willful blindness until finally, on a quiet evening, the disease would win. Why the hell did I tell Hanssen?

"I'm sorry to hear that," he said. "I'll pray for her."

Hanssen's devotion surprised me. He bowed his head and prayed silently for the majority of the Mass, hands folded around a rosary in front of him. He watched me recite Christianity's oldest prayer. His scrutiny felt like a pincer on my larynx as I spoke the familiar words, "*Our Father who art in heaven, hallowed be Thy name.*" I'd told many lies to Hanssen, each one added to a snowball of deception growing so large I could barely lift it. For once I did not have to lie. I passed his test of my Catholicism, and felt dirtier for it. Using that sanctuary to help me win a case for the FBI robbed a small part of God's light.

The second time Hanssen looked up, he glanced at the guy in the leather jacket. The two waved to each other. A second later, the man bowed his head and hurried from the chapel.

When a primary target contacts someone we don't recognize or know, we call that person an UNSUB—an unknown subject. UNSUBs are of particular interest to investigators because identifying them can sometimes break a case. I knew a team of ghosts haunted the Information Center, waiting for Hanssen to depart. I had no way of warning the team that someone they'd want to check out had just left. Of course, the UNSUB could have been anyone—a neighbor, a passing acquaintance. But without investigating, it was impossible to know.

When the Mass concluded, Hanssen brought me back to the Living the Faith section of the bookstore. He selected a palm-sized book and handed it to me. *The Way*, by Josemaría Escrivá. The tiny book outlines 999 points for meditation and prayer, each as practical as they are instructive. Hanssen insisted on buying it for me, which struck me as oddly sentimental. How could I make sense of a man who presented himself in a devout and spiritual manner, said all the right things about his faith, and prayed the rosary every day, but who simultaneously betrayed everything he claimed to stand for?

"My brother-in-law, Bonnie's brother, is a priest in Rome," Hanssen said as we headed back into the frostbitten day. "Bonnie and I attended John's initiation into the priesthood. The event was glorious." We paused at an intersection to let cars go by. "Rome is a majestic and beautiful place. Bonnie and I loved our time there."

Hanssen rarely spoke in such an effusive manner and scarcely mentioned his wife. He would drone on for hours about spies and computers, but those discussions were professorial and clinical. Standing within his lunchtime church had triggered a change in his demeanor that both concerned and excited me. I couldn't decide whether our shared faith had sparked Hanssen's sudden collegiality, or if he had finally come to trust me. Or maybe, just maybe, a drop might happen soon. Was this a sign?

I needed to encourage his sudden vulnerability. I swallowed my prior vow to separate my personal life from the case and took a leap—I spoke about Juliana.

I told Hanssen that she was studying international business at American University, and she hoped to eventually work with American companies that wanted to do business with Russia.

"Maybe we should be worried about you, Eric," Hanssen said. We cut through a short alley, brick walls all around us. "Your wife is from Communist Germany. Maybe she was sent here to recruit you. You've heard of a honey trap?"

An old joke calls espionage the second oldest profession. You can guess the first. A honey trap combines the two. Spies have used women to seduce secrets out of men since civilization began. The Red Sparrows were some of the most famous honey traps. Beautiful women, each trained in sexual exploitation and entrapment at their school in Kazan, Russia. A Sparrow would seduce a man with access to information into providing a small government secret. After the first breach hooked the target, a Russian intelligence officer—call him Boris—would use the indiscretion to blackmail more secrets from the newly entrapped spy.

Modern honey traps can use both women and men, but they're always attractive and seductive and prey on the most basic of human needs. Just like the Sparrows of old, once a honey trap hooks the target over a one-night stand or sometimes a lengthy relationship, Boris shows up to blackmail additional secrets.

I grabbed Hanssen by the shoulder before he could step off the curb and into the path of a bike messenger. The grungy bicyclist hollered and shot us the finger before speeding away.

"I'm teasing about the honey trap, Eric." Hanssen waited for the white Walk sign to flash before venturing out into the street again. "Thank you for rescuing me."

"Death by bike messenger would be a terrible way to go," I said.

He smiled. "That it would."

The Gray Suit team needed Hanssen hale and hearty. If a tangle of bicycle, messenger, and the hard, cold street sent him to the hospital, he couldn't make a drop for the Russians. And if he didn't steal secrets and attempt to hand them over to a foreign intelligence service, we'd never be able to definitively link Hanssen to his alter egos.

I'd like to think that these clinical thoughts ran through my head before my hand shot out and pulled Hanssen back onto the curb. But consideration for the case came after. I'd joined the FBI to protect people. Even master spies.

We walked another few blocks in silence. Occasionally Hanssen's crooked gait would send his shoulder into mine. I would curse under my breath and push back. I found it hard to think about anything other than whether he bumped me on purpose or because of the way he limped when he walked.

"Do you and Juliana plan to have children?" Hanssen asked.

With the smallest insinuation, he knew how to get under my skin. Juliana and I did plan to have children, but not until I graduated from law school and she had her business degree. Eventually, I would lobby Juliana to have children earlier than we had planned so that we could fulfill my mother's wish to hold a grandchild. But now, newly married and full of my youth, I couldn't imagine adding another person, even a tiny one, into the cramped space of our lives.

For the first time, Hanssen didn't let the silence hold. He told me it was God's plan for all of us to have children—that it was my duty as a Catholic to bring children into the world. I tried to demur, to blame the delay on Juliana's schoolwork, but Hanssen dug in like a dog playing tug-of-war with its favorite slipper.

"Juliana should stay home and raise the children," Hanssen said.

I laughed, not without malice. "I'm an FBI analyst in a new section that still hasn't defined itself," I said. "Juliana is an international business student. She'll probably make more money than I will." I reined myself in. We only had one more block until we'd arrive at headquarters.

Hanssen grabbed my arm. Danger skidded across his face. "You'll ruin your marriage," he said. "Men are not meant to be supported by women. Your genetic code demands that you make money and provide for the family. Juliana's demands she stay home and nurture the children. Anything different goes against biology."

He didn't seem to care that my genetic code had just saved him from a gruesome bike-messenger-related death. "Sometimes we have to do what we need to make ends meet," I said. "Biology has nothing to do with it."

"You can't argue against biology," Hanssen said. "Besides, there are ways to make ends meet."

"Like what?" I asked.

Traditionally, spies have used one of three motivating factors to convince a person to betray their country: greed, blackmail, and ideology. We all understand greed. You have two mortgages on your house and are struggling to pay the tuition for your children's expensive private school. I offer you $50,000 to plug a thumb drive into a computer and execute the program I've placed on it. A simple double-click of your mouse, and your financial problems evaporate. Your company will be fine; they have plenty of money to spare.

We also understand blackmail. Now that you have committed a crime, I own you. Your supposed one-time breach of trust just became a long-term recruitment. I haven't told you who I am, but a whisper in the wrong ear and you lose your job. At worst, your children grow up while you serve a lengthy prison term. To sweeten the deal, here is another $25,000. Once you're hooked, you are worth less.

Though repugnant, greed and blackmail work. But ideology—belief in a system of common ideas and ideals—is the most complicated and powerful tool of espionage. If I can convince you to betray your duty or allegiance to your country because you think more like me, or look more like me, or we have the same religion and politics, blackmail becomes irrelevant and greed the cherry on top. The heroes and villains of espionage depend on what color flag you salute.

Hanssen put a solemn hand on my shoulder. "God will help you find a way."

"Then God better come up with an extra thousand dollars a month so Juliana and I can afford a bigger place with a spare room for a nursery." The spite in my voice surprised me. For once I didn't have to invent my feelings. "I mean, they give us access to all of these secrets, ask us to protect the nation, but pay us less than an administrative assistant at a law firm. Then they wonder why people become spies."

Hanssen's somber voice agreed with me. "That's why you always find the spy—"

"In the worst possible place."

Hanssen smiled. "Now you're getting it."


Hanssen had made Room 9930 a place of somber reflection. The few pieces of art I'd stolen at his behest scarcely broke the monotony of the stark white walls and industrial furniture. When Hanssen wasn't lecturing me, it was silent except for the coughing and wheezing of the computer workstations and the occasional belching of the HVAC unit. The austere environment fit Robert Hanssen's personality like the black suit he wore each and every day. I recognized Hanssen's good qualities. He cared for his family and preached the importance of marriage. He had a sharp mind and an almost preternatural understanding of the flaws in the FBI's information-security protocols. But he was also Dr. Death, who had led some of our most important intelligence assets to sham trials and cold graves.

I sat behind my desk at ten p.m. and watched agents turn Hanssen's quiet kingdom into a festival of camera flashes, white gloves, and hushed conversations. Kate had picked me up from law school and brought me back to headquarters for a thorough search of the office. The specialized forensic team needed me present to officially let them into the SCIF and to testify to any evidence we found. I knew they would leave no stone unturned, from pulling up carpet to hunting in the ceiling with flashlights; Earl Pitts used to hide his money in the drop ceiling of his office. Hanssen would scoff at such carelessness.

"Are you gonna call her?" Kate sat in one of the chairs in front of my desk. Where Hanssen might have slumped, Kate sat forward, elbows rested on her knees, ready to spring forward into action.

My hand brushed the white handset next to me. "How about you call her."

Kate scoffed. "Trouble in paradise?"

I watched agents arrange pictures of Hanssen's office on our whiteboard. A large instant camera flashed and whined and belched large puzzle squares that together formed a whole picture. I had warned them that Hanssen was meticulous to the point of obsession. Thank God they listened. I'd have to clean up any mistake made by the forensic team with my temperamental boss.

"Call Juliana," Kate said. She picked up the copy of *The Way* Hanssen had bought me. "He really bought you this?"

I had read through the small book and found myself agreeing with many of Escrivá's thoughts. The inspirational devotions are a mixture of simple lessons, like Number 14, "Don't put off your work until tomorrow," and more dogmatic ones, like Number 286, "There is nothing better in the world than to be in the grace of God." After skimming through all 999, I kept coming back to Escrivá's first:

> *Don't let your life be barren. Be useful. Make yourself felt.*
> *Shine forth with the torch of your faith and your love.*

Hanssen had placed his mark on the world. In indelible ink. I wanted to do the same—but for the right reasons.

I dialed my home number reluctantly and answered Kate's question while the line rang. "Yes. It was like a different person gave it to me."

"How do you mean?"

"More . . . vulnerable," I said.

Juliana picked up the phone. I spent the next few minutes lying to her about yet another manufactured server crash. I kept my voice calm and my words short, very aware that Kate was listening even as she politely looked away from my train wreck of a personal life.

"Wait," Juliana said. "Are there people there with you?"

"Of course. This is an all-hands-on-deck moment. My whole team is here."

"Okay," she relented. The tension drained out of me. "I'll be asleep when you come home."

"I'll be quiet."

I hung up and hid behind my closed eyes for a few heartbeats. When I opened them, Kate's sympathetic expression didn't help.

"She probably thinks I'm cheating on her," I said. "Server crash. Lame. I wouldn't even know what to do if a server crashed."

"Relax," Kate said. Ever the optimist. "You're doing fine."

"Make me a promise," I said. "When this is over, assuming Hanssen doesn't shoot me and hide my body in a dumpster . . ."

She grinned. "Assuming."

"Assuming that I live, and we win, you're coming to dinner with me and Juliana so you can explain all of this to her."

"*When* we win," Kate said. "You're on." She sighed. "As for tomorrow, you're supposed to drive Hanssen to the CIA."

"Bingo," I said. "He's been looking forward to it."

"Like a kid the night before Christmas?"

"I couldn't have put it better."

"Expect a no go."

My shoulders slumped. "What?"

"The director is having second thoughts about sending public enemy number one over to the CIA. Freeh's calling Tenet first thing tomorrow a.m."

"Why would he do that?"

Kate flashed her trademark grin. "It's complicated."

"Understatement of the decade." I stopped myself from putting my face in my hands. Hanssen would go ballistic when he heard the CIA had canceled his trip. "Let me guess, the FBI spends years tailing the CIA when everyone knew that Kelley wasn't the guy, and now the CIA gets to say 'I told you so.' "

"No comment."

"We're nearly wrapped here." An agent I didn't know strode out of Hanssen's office and took a seat on the empty desk beside mine. He was an older man, and he wore his blue sport coat over a work shirt. His gun and badge rode a thick leather belt and pointy-toed cowboy boots peeked out from his worn jeans. He looked like a middle-aged Chuck Norris.

Kate suddenly became very interested in *The Way*. She kept her face neutral and stared at the book.

The agent we'll call Chuck took in the chairs guarding the entrance to my workstation sanctuary and laughed. "I hear we might need to change your code name, Werewolf."

"Why's that, sir?"

"GD seems to have taken a liking to you." He chuckled. "Maybe we should call you Boy Toy."

Kate stayed mum.

"I'll stick with Werewolf." I tried not to growl.

Chuck laughed and slapped his knee. "Just joshing you, Wolfie." His face got serious all of a sudden the way a sunny day will yield to a gathering storm. "Not everyone wanted you for this."

I stayed silent.

"Oh, there were arguments both for and against." He ticked them off on one hand. "Not an agent. Not trained. Not a veteran going up against a veteran. Too much of a maverick. That one from one of your supervisors." He held up the other hand. "Then the good stuff. Knows computers. Understands espionage. Not afraid to break a rule or two to win a case. That was from Gene McClelland." He shrugged and let his hands fall. "At the end of the day, the pros beat the cons."

Still nothing from Kate.

"Why are you telling me this?"

"A lot is riding on this case, Wolf. You don't want to be the guy that makes all the naysayers right about you."

*Great pep talk, Chuck.*

"He's got this," Kate said.

*A touch little and a lot late, but thanks, Kate.*

Chuck nodded. "I hope so." He stood to follow the rest of the search team out and turned to Kate. "I'll let you know what we found tomorrow. Doesn't look like much." Then he focused on me again. "We think GD might be recruiting you. Let him."

With that bombshell dropped, Chuck left the building.

Kate set the book on my desk and patted my shoulder. "You should read this, Eric."

"Why?"

"Looks like you're joining Opus Dei."

## CHAPTER 20

# BREAK THE ROUTINE

February 1, 2001—Thursday

The digital clock on my desk flashed 12:00 in angry red characters. This was odd because I couldn't remember putting it there. Words on my computer screen melted and ran before my eyes, elusive little bastards that required supreme concentration to wrangle back into place. Someone had forgotten to turn the air on in 9930. My shirt stuck to my back and when I wiped my hand across my forehead, it came away wet.

"I told you not to screw this up, kiddo." Kate sat across the office near the Internet computer, her face buried in my copy of *The Way*. "Now you're in for it."

Hanssen's office door slammed open. The boss stormed through, his face twisted into the snarl he'd worn in the parking garage when I challenged him. "Were you in my office?"

My phone rang. Juliana on the caller ID.

"I have to get this," I said. "It's important."

Hanssen drew a handgun from the holster on his hip. I recognized the Smith & Wesson Model 60 snub-nosed revolver that he sometimes wore at his ankle. The .357 Magnum rounds could punch through a car door and keep traveling.

"It's too late for that," Hanssen said.

The gunshot crashed through the small room.

I sat up in bed, sheets tangled around my legs. A frantic scan showed that I was in my bedroom, and I was the only one there. The morning chill struck my sweat-soaked nightshirt like a whip. I ignored the cold and hunted for my ringing phone.

"Hello?"

Juliana's voice answered. "It's me. I left early."

"Okay." My mind wouldn't turn on. The violent dream still demanded my attention. My psychology degree reminded me that dreams simulate threats in order to enhance the cognitive mechanisms we need to avoid threats in reality. If so, my reality needed an exorcism.

"I'm on my way to class. I'm mad at you, but I didn't want you to be late for work. You always forget to set an alarm."

I turned the rusty crank that started my brain and decrypted her words. Mad. Late. Alarm. "Oh, crap!"

"Seriously, Eric!" Juliana said in the sort of tone reserved for uncooperative children. "Are you just waking up?"

The meticulous office search had dragged on. By the time I got home, the witching hour had come and gone. I drafted a novella to Kate about Hanssen's field trip to church and then agonized my way through the elements of *mens rea* and *actus reus* in criminal law. By the time I had joined Juliana in our bed, the winter sky had lightened.

"I have to go," I said.

"You'd better run," she replied.


The dream lingered like the smell of old moth balls on a winter coat pulled from storage. It hounded me on my frantic Metro ride and raised concerned glances from security when I burst through the turnstyle at headquarters. Hanssen had a lot of rules. First among them was punctuality.

I paused at the door to the SCIF, one hand on the latch, my forehead pressed against the cool metal. I gathered the tattered remains of my strength into a tight ball of resolve and dragged the mask back onto my face.

"So sorry, boss!" I injected cheer into my voice and stepped across the threshold into 9930. I dropped my coat and bag, woke up my computer, and scanned my FBI NET messages. One look at the memo waiting for me crushed any thought I had of surviving the day. I wanted to curse out loud. Instead, my leaden fingers hit Print.

"Our car wouldn't start." I glanced up from my desktop. "I had to help Juliana jump the . . ."

Hanssen's face stole away my false cheer. I knew without a doubt that my dream portended more than just my fear of failure. Any moment now the gun would appear.

His voice cracked the silence between us. "Follow me."

I paused to retrieve the single sheet of paper from the printer beside my desk and followed Hanssen into his office. The memo was still warm. It hung from my fingers like a living thing.

Hanssen stopped me and pointed to the TV stand next to the door. I looked from the television, still displaying a CCTV view of Pennsylvania Avenue, to the wooden stand, to Hanssen, perplexed.

"See anything?"

"No, boss."

He dragged me down to the floor until I was kneeling beside him. A hand that could have palmed a basketball pressed the back of my head until our faces met across from one leg of the stand. "See anything now?"

"I see your blue carpet," I said.

"Moron," Hanssen spat. "Idiot."

We throw those words around, but "moron," "imbecile," and "idiot" used to have clinical meanings within psychology. A moron is a person with an IQ between 51 and 70—at least 30 points below average. An imbecile scores between 26 and 50, and an idiot lower than that. Hanssen always started with "moron" and bottomed out by calling me an idiot. He knew his taxonomy of insults.

I summoned the remaining scraps of my youthful bravado,

shrugged off Hanssen's hand, and scowled. He traced a minuscule impression in the carpet next to the leg, maybe a few centimeters square. "This leg has been moved."

We clambered to our feet, livid and eyeing each other like two boxers entering the ring.

"So?"

"Were you in here?"

"I might have bumped it," I said.

It gave me small comfort to know that, for once, I hadn't made the mistake that boiled Hanssen's blood. But I'd have to take the fall for the search team. I found myself missing my SSG days, when I knew I could always disappear. There was no disappearing in 9930.

"I'll be more careful," I said, eyes downcast, penitent.

"I see everything," Hanssen said, his breath hot on the top of my head. "Do you understand?"

I looked at the sheet of paper in my hands and knew the office climate would shortly progress from miserable to thermonuclear. Less than a month in, and Hanssen was already following me into my dreams. The investigation was all I thought about; Juliana had become the ghost. The lies weighed down my body and my mind, exhausting both. At home, that emotional baggage found its release—which is why undercover work has some of the highest divorce rates in the FBI, and in law enforcement as a whole. It locks you away from your loved ones. It turns your whole world gray.

Hanssen grabbed the paper out of my hands, crumpled it into a ball, and tossed it toward his wastebasket. It bounced off the metal rim and landed on the floor. The Information Assurance director had canceled Hanssen's meeting with the CIA due to a scheduling conflict—or at least that's what I'd told Hanssen.

The truth is, I'd lied. There was no scheduling conflict. The FBI director had had a come-to-Jesus moment about sending the most damaging spy in US history over to the CIA to discuss cybersecurity. Our sister agency would hardly take kindly to our allowing the newest target of the investigation into its nerve center. And, of course, the FBI and the CIA already weren't on the best terms regarding the pursuit of Gray Suit, given how many years our agents had spent tracking the wrong man in the wrong agency.

Much of the reason Hanssen's spy career lasted as long as it did is that, with the occasional exception, he was meticulous and cautious. Hanssen had access to an abundance of information about the Russians, but he also understood that sharing too much of that information could at some point implicate him. He realized that once the leaks clearly pointed back to the FBI, the FBI's hunters would begin to look inward. And every FBI employee, from the greenest academy graduate to the savviest veteran, knows that once the FBI starts looking in earnest, the arrest is only a matter of time.

To keep himself out of the FBI's crosshairs, Hanssen often shared intelligence about operations that were controlled by the CIA, so that the leaks would point to a mole within that agency. In other words, Hanssen orchestrated a cover story within a spy story. He fed his KGB handlers information about CIA technical penetrations of Soviet and Russian operations, the identities of KGB spies who were secretly working for the CIA, and, most important, specific details about the FBI's investigation of State Department official Felix Bloch. So when the leaks came to light, the FBI turned its attention to the agency known to harbor rotten apples—most recently Aldrich Ames and James Nicholson—and settled on a new target: the man who had led the CIA's investigation of Felix Bloch, CIA officer Brian Kelley.

In the spring of 1999, Hanssen learned that an FBI/CIA joint task force pursued a target code-named "Gray Deceiver." Within a day of discovering the case, Hanssen peeled away the FBI's security and discovered the target's true name. Hanssen had never heard of Kelley, but the situation suited him. We say that there are no coincidences in espionage; everything is suspect. Well, Brian Kelley lived right around the corner from Hanssen. When the FBI began investigating Kelley, they zeroed in on his jogging route, which wound through nearby streets and parks, including a small park where Hanssen would leave secrets for Russian intelligence officers under a wooden bridge.

Kelley's bad luck provided cover for Hanssen and destroyed Kelley's life. Kelley passed a polygraph test, turned his back on an FBI false-flag operation—an FBI agent posing as a Russian intelligence officer—and denied every accusation that he was a Russian spy. But the CIA still suspended him for over a year while he fought to clear his name. Meanwhile, Hanssen laughed from his house around the corner.

The FBI's focus on Kelley resurrected Ramon Garcia. Hanssen missed the excitement and satisfaction that only espionage could inject into his otherwise placid family life. Ramon hadn't loaded a moonlit drop or pressed a thumbtack signal in a telephone pole for six years, but he hadn't let his spy skills wither, and he'd been collecting and storing critical investigation documents mined from ACS since he went dormant in 1991.

Hanssen set a goal to collect $100,000 from the SVR, enough to stay under the radar and stabilize his flagging finances until he could retire in April 2001 with a full pension. Hanssen could then mothball Ramon after a final, legendary exchange of secrets. A swanky consulting job or maybe even an executive position at an information security company awaited him. And Brian Kelley would take the blame.

Hanssen stood up from his desk. Without glancing down, he slipped a hand into his blue shoulder bag and slipped out his Palm IIIx. He jabbed a finger toward me with one hand and jammed the Palm into his back pocket with the other.

"Our whole afternoon is wasted." Hanssen threw up his hands.

Shit happens. Best to sit quietly and wait out the storm.

Hanssen paused his tirade and glanced around the office, hands on hips. "I'm leaving for the day."

This raised my eyebrows. "Really? Where are you going?"

"Last I checked, you report to me." Hanssen grabbed his coat. "Out of my office."

The SCIF door closed behind Hanssen. I listened for the beep that meant it had locked and slumped down into my chair. Half a memo on procedures to enhance the ACS's interface lay forgotten on my screen. I was more interested in how Hanssen had acted when I'd just pulled a very plush rug out from under him. Last-minute changes in schedule set my boss into the same rage as a challenge to his authority. He didn't appreciate being disappointed or caught off guard.

My pager chirped. Kate. I glanced around the empty office; the memo could wait.

I met her in her car, parked a few blocks away from headquarters. "We need something," Kate said as she scanned my observation notes from the day before. The analysts believed that Hanssen's next drop was imminent. We couldn't risk pushing him over the line from suspicion to paranoia, but we needed the evidence that would connect him to Ramon and "B."

"Palm Pilot," I said. "He keeps it in his left back pocket. Always that pocket. When he sits down he puts it in his briefcase beside his desk. When he stands back up, the first thing he does is reach for it. It's a reflex . . . a—"

"Routine," Kate said.

We all have routines. Some of us hang our car keys on a hook when we come inside—always the same hook, so the keys are always available when you need to leave. Wallets go on the same counter or dresser. Routines like these protect us from embarrassment, even danger. Criminals have routines too. Ghosts are trained to watch for them, especially when tracking

Russian targets. Does he slow down at that telephone pole each time he drives past? Does she use the same mailbox every third Thursday of the month? If so, maybe that's a clue.

Hanssen had a subtle routine to protect his Palm IIIx personal digital assistant. He kept it in his left back pocket. Always. When he sat down, he reached back and drew the Palm out of his pocket and slid it into his blue briefcase. The same practiced motion happened in reverse when he stood. I knew the PDA was encrypted. I wanted to know the secrets locked within.

I explained to Kate that Hanssen took it everywhere he went—even to the bathroom. It never left his side. Kate folded my notes and put them away.

"We need to get him away from it," she said. "We need to break the routine."

# CHAPTER 21

# OUT ON A LIMB

February 5, 2001—Monday

Sometimes shadows are braver than people. Mine stretched across the rectangle of light that carved a block across the floor into Hanssen's empty office. The running joke I kept with myself likened the boss to a vampire. His tall and lanky frame, shrewd eyes, long fingers that might have coaxed music from a piano if he hadn't turned to a computer keyboard instead, the dim, single-bulb lamp that barely illuminated his office—all gave credence to the nickname Dr. Death. But maybe he had other reasons for the way he acted.

The FBI had ostracized and ignored Hanssen. Fellow agents described him somewhere between genius and creep, and few sought his company for lunch or hallway chatter. Hanssen had wanted to chase spies through dark city streets and make contacts under the bright lights of casino gambling tables. The FBI had dashed his James Bond dreams by closeting him with analysts and techies. The irony is, his skill with computer systems and information security was exactly what the bureau needed to stop the tsunami of cyberattacks on the horizon.

Today, the best cyber companies and major corporations have hired all the hackers of yore. These men and women, in jeans and hoodies, with beards and with hair dyed pink, sit at executive tables beside company officers in bespoke suits. Their voices are heard and celebrated, where stodgy executives once scoffed before dismissing them. The FBI's inflexible culture and infamous resistance to change missed the bandwagon. FBI agents who couldn't lead or manage fell to the ranks of the forgotten, no matter what other skills they possessed. Those who could climb the thorny agency ladder stepped on Hanssen's face on the way up.

None of this excuses Hanssen's espionage. He was still a green agent the time he first sold out to the GRU; he had barely scratched the surface of FBI's hierarchy. The bureau may have played a part in driving Hanssen toward espionage, but Hanssen's decision to betray his country rests squarely on his shoulders. Hanssen could have helped save the intelligence community. Instead, he helped destroy it.

Now I had to destroy him.

Juliana and I had negotiated a truce that I knew wouldn't last. We'd joined my parents for dinner the night before. The ritual had become a biweekly event. My parents would order from our favorite local restaurant, Hong Kong, and open a bottle of wine. If all the wine disappeared over the course of the evening, Juliana and I would spend the night and drive back into the city in the morning.

We usually looked forward to our visits to suburbia. My youngest brother, Danny, still in high school, occupied my old room. During weekend breaks, my brother Sean might sneak home from the Naval Academy for a home-cooked meal. On the rarest of occasions, David, the oldest of my three younger brothers, would cross the country from Hollywood. A hallmark of the O'Neill clan is our fondness to come together. Juliana fit right in. Usually.

Earlier that evening we'd almost had to turn the car around just a few blocks from my parents' house. I had just slapped on my blinker and merged onto the off ramp toward Connecticut Avenue. The white spires of the Mormon Temple thrust above the dark tree line like spears of light reaching toward the stars.

On every other drive Juliana oohed and aahed at the building Washingtonians fondly called the Castle. Not this time. Our heated argument collapsed the world to our Jeep's front seat.

"Why do you have to study Russian anyway?" I asked. The Capital Beltway disappeared behind us. "Russia is our enemy. We should let the language rot."

Juliana's sigh sounded more like a growl. "I like the language." She slammed her shoulders back into her seat and crossed her arms. "I grew up speaking Russian, for God's sake."

"You grew up under Russia's thumb, more like." I jerked the car into the number-one lane and ignored an angry car horn. "You're brainwashed."

"The only one who is brainwashed is you." Juliana's voice plunged to a calm that should have rung warning bells throughout my head. "You've changed since I came here to live. Since you transferred, or *TDY'd* or whatever it's called in FBI-speak." She jammed a thumb at her chest. "*I'm* the same person."

Anger distorts the right and the true. Juliana is a gifted musician and student, with an incredible ear for languages. I'd stolen her away from her quiet little village and dumped her in an Eastern Market dungeon. Now I was attacking her for one of the traits I admired most.

Juliana warmed at dinner. She played the role of the dutiful daughter-in-law and spent most of her time with my mother. Watching them together made me fall in love with Juliana all over again.

The skill I had just chastised Juliana for made her one of my mother's closest confidantes. Parkinson's had stolen my mother's true voice. What remained defeated my ear and frustrated my thin patience. My dad often joked that "Juliana speaks Vivian." My mother's forced words and thin, robbed-of-breath voice were just another language for Juliana to master.

That evening, in the attic, we lay a handbreadth apart in a little iron-framed bed. I glanced at her and watched shadows cross her face. I could always look at my Juliana and see that laughing girl in Capitol City Blues Café. One person can promise an entire future. If you let them.

The old Victorian house whispered to us in creaks and pops as it settled for the night. We exchanged amorphous apologies that solved nothing but chipped the walls enough for an embrace. We made a date for Valentine's Day, and I promised to open up about everything.

I wanted out of this case. The FBI wanted Hanssen wrapped up in paper and a bow for the Justice Department prosecutor. I'd have to take some risks if I wanted to align both goals.

Hanssen himself put the idea into my head. He'd told me that Boy Scouts finish last, and challenged me to steal the art from an assistant director. What he meant was that winners take risks. It took a spy to help me remember the lesson behind all of my best successes as a ghost.

I'd forgotten the crazy places I'd climb for the perfect camera angle, or the way I'd talk my way into buildings or through security. I took risks to ghost my targets. Hanssen was the biggest target of all.

I followed my shadow across the threshold into Hanssen's office.

The smaller room raised goose bumps on my arms even though one thermostat regulated all of 9930. It wasn't because I feared that Hanssen would jump out from behind his desk. The last I'd heard from Kate, a team had him headed west on Massachusetts Avenue past Dupont Circle.

I moved slowly with patient purpose past the spot where the search team had shifted Hanssen's TV stand and bought me a face pressed into the thin carpet. My hands found each other behind my back in quiet agreement not to touch anything.

Then I saw Hanssen's messenger bag. Five minutes later I called Kate.

"Remember when you told me never to search GD's office?"

Kate sounded harried. They had followed Hanssen to his old haunt at the Office of Foreign Missions and had no clue why he'd returned. "Yeah. Don't tell me you—"

"Guilty," I said. "But before you get mad, hear me out." Kate held her tongue. I took that as an okay to continue. "I went in his office. I didn't touch anything. But then I saw it."

"Saw what?"

"His bag. He never leaves it." I shifted the phone to the other ear. "I mean never. I couldn't pass it up."

"Okay . . . so you called me right away, right?"

"Wrong." I unclenched my jaw. "I searched it."

"Oh. My. God. Eric." Kate's voice dropped to a hushed whisper. I could hear her moving. "You took a colossal risk. What were you thinking?"

This time I stayed silent. Waiting.

"What did you find?"

Probably best that Kate couldn't see my grin. "Bad news is that he took his Palm Pilot." I didn't bother stating the obvious. Hanssen had taken his car, so he had his keys. "But there is a data disk. And a current passport, financial statements, a computer disk, and a cell phone I've never seen before."

Kate's footsteps echoed. "I'm coming there now. Don't touch anything else."

"I wouldn't dream of it," I said. "Did I mention that he never leaves his bag behind?"

Her car roared to life. "I get it." She paused. "Aw crap, Eric. I don't know whether to scream at you or hug you."

"The Versa data card is eight megabytes," I said. "I looked it up. Five hundred pages per megabyte. That's potentially four thousand pages of information."

"You did your homework."

"I prefer the hug over the shouting."

---

Hanssen spent most of his day bumping into former State Department colleagues at the Office of Foreign Missions. I spent several slow, agonizing hours nervously anticipating Kate's report on what the team found after they copied the devices and I put them carefully back where they'd come from. At around three p.m., Hanssen returned to grab his bag and left just as abruptly. I logged the time and let Kate know he'd rushed right back out of the office. The SSG team wouldn't have any downtime.

I also told her I planned to leave early myself, hoping she'd clue me in on whether they'd found something. The edge to her voice worried me. She told me to meet her on our usual corner. She'd drive me to school, and we'd find some coffee on the way.

"I told the team that I authorized the search," Kate said. We'd found a quiet table in the back of a deserted Così coffeehouse around the corner from GW Law. Two large coffees steamed on the table between us.

"You covered for me?"

"That's part of my job. Your job is to make sure I don't have to."

I was all out of apologies. "I'm tired of being a Boy Scout."

Kate rolled her eyes. "What does that even mean?"

"Something Hanssen told me."

She tapped the table with a finger. The sound echoed like a fist punched through a snare drum. "Try not to take advice from spies."

I sipped my coffee, then cut to the chase. "What did you find? Tell me you found something."

Kate couldn't hide her grin. "Oh, we found something, all right." She handed me a sheet of paper. "This letter was drafted around March 14 of last year. We got it off the Versa card you found in his briefcase."

My eyes scanned the page and then widened. I said a silent prayer of thanks for my seat. I doubt my legs would have held me.

I have come about as close as I ever want to
come to sacrificing myself to help you, and I get
silence. I hate silence. . . .

Conclusion: One might propose that I am either
insanely brave or quite insane. I'd answer
neither. I'd say, insanely loyal. Take your pick.
There is insanity in all the answers.

I have, however, come as close to the edge as
I can without being truly insane. My security
concerns have proven reality-based. I'd say, pin
your hopes on "insanely loyal" and go for it.
Only I can lose.

I decided on this course when I was 14 years old.
I'd read Philby's book. Now that is insane, eh!
My only hesitations were my security concerns
under uncertainty. I hate uncertainty. So far I
have judged the edge correctly. Give me credit
for that.

Set the signal at my site any Tuesday evening.
I will read your answer. Please, at least say
goodbye. It's been a long time my dear friends,
a long and lonely time.

The letter was signed "Ramon Garcia."

Kate bubbled with excitement. I looked up and she nodded.
"I know, right? It gets better." She handed me a second sheet of
paper. "This one is from a month later. We think June 8, 2000."

I read the letter addressed to Hanssen's *Dear Friends* twice.
The words gave me more satisfaction than every Director's
Award I'd ever won as a ghost. In it he enclosed a rudimen-
tary cipher algorithm that would protect the dates and times

of their meets in subsequent drops. He cautioned the Russians to rein in the GRU and mentioned a Russian diplomat named Gusev that I remembered from my SSG days.

Two paragraphs raised my eyebrows. The first referred to his favorite piece of technology:

```
One of the commercial products currently
available is the Palm VII organizer. I have a
Palm III, which is actually a fairly capable
computer. The VII version comes with wireless
internet capability built in. It can allow
the rapid transmission of encrypted messages,
which if used on an infrequent basis, could be
quite effective in preventing confusions if the
existance of the accounts could be appropriately
hidden as well as the existance of the devices
themselves. Such a device might even serve for
rapid transmittal of substantial material in
digital form.
```

The second blasted the United States in a way that sounded all too much like Hanssen:

```
The U.S. can be errantly likened to a powerfully
built but retarded child, potentially dangerous,
but young, immature and easily manipulated.
But don't be fooled by that appearance. It is
also one which can turn ingenius quickly, like
an idiot savant, once convinced of a goal. The
purple pissing Japanese (to quote General Patten
once again) learned this to their dismay.
```

"Holy shit," I said.

"You betcha." Kate left the letter on the table between us. "What do you see?"

I slurped my coffee and tried to keep my voice from cracking. "First off," I said, skimming the rest of the letter, "he misspells all sorts of words. 'Algorythm' should be 'algorithm.' 'Existance' instead of 'existence.' He even misspells 'ingenious' and 'laundering.' " I shook my head. "I misspelled a word once on a memo to GD. He circled it five times in red."

"We think it's a cover. Ramon makes spelling mistakes. Hanssen doesn't."

I tapped the name Gusev, remembering the case. The FBI had arrested Russian diplomat Stanislav Borisovich Gusev in December 1999 for espionage. The Russians had somehow gotten a bug into a seventh-floor secure meeting room right outside Secretary of State Madeleine Albright's offices. They'd listened into dozens of high-level conferences before we captured Gusev and disabled the bug.

"My ghost team caught this guy," I said. "We followed him to the State Department and caught him acting weird. When he wasn't walking around the street, he was trying to park his car just right." I picked up my messenger bag and put it on an empty chair next to me. "Gusev would make weekly visits to the park outside and would put his bag on the bench beside him while he ate his lunch." I took the bag off the chair and put it back on the floor beside me. "When he left, he'd pick up the bag."

Kate smiled over her coffee cup. "You kept your eye on the bag."

"Bingo," I said. "We saw that when he put his bag down, the wooden bench flexed." I joined my fingers together in front of me and then bent them downward. "When he picked up the bag, the bench sprang back." I leveled my hands.

"That bag was heavy."

"You'd have made a great ghost, Kate." I dropped my hands. "Way too heavy for that little bag. He had a recording device in it. Every week he'd sit and eat his lunch and capture the feed from the bug in the conference room."

"How did they get the bug in the conference room?"

I grinned. "That's classified."

Kate scoffed. "Anything else tickle you about the letter, Sherlock?"

I squirmed in my chair. "He signs it Ramon. . . ."

"Obvious."

"I told you the Palm Pilot was important."

"You also just broke the case."

Now was not the time for a smug grin. Instead I let the gravity of these letters sober my enthusiasm. "It's really him, isn't it?"

"It's him. Hanssen is Ramon. We could arrest him today."

"So let's go get him."

Kate shook her head. "Arrest him now and we have a clear case for conspiracy. Arrest him after he makes a drop at a known drop site to the Russians and the best lawyer in the world can't save him."

Kate's phone rang. She held up a finger for silence, and her smile evaporated. After a few moments of tense silence, she hung up and looked at her watch.

"It's 5:37 p.m. Hanssen just drove past the Foxstone Park sign real slow."

My skin pebbled. The Foxstone Park sign was the signal spot for drop site Ellis. Hanssen would check for a signal from his Russian paymasters to let him know they were ready to receive a drop. I'd later learn that he checked the same sign three times that night. "I think someone just walked across my grave."

"You and me both," Kate said. She looked at me. "It's happening soon."

I pointed out the third paragraph of the letter that definitively tied Hanssen to Ramon. "We need to get that Palm Pilot away from him. If he's using it to exchange information . . ."

Kate picked up her coffee cup and finished my thought. "That's where we'll find the jackpot."

We knocked cups in a silent toast. I took a sip and set mine back on the table. My coffee had gone cold.

# CHAPTER 22

# THE WORST OFFENSE IS DEFENSE

## February 9, 2001—Friday

The information I'd found on the memory card had offered solid evidence of the connection between Hanssen and Ramon in a case that so often seemed to be all questions and no answers. The Gray Day task force didn't start popping the Champagne, but confident smiles replaced perplexed frowns, and a full day's work on Hanssen suddenly meant more than it ever had before.

I wasn't ready to join the revelry. Spies are slippery. The world of espionage thrives on excuses, alibis, cover stories, and manipulation of the truth. Hanssen had made spying an art form by actively leapfrogging his pursuers. We had plenty of evidence, but we needed more.

The spy who named himself "B" and Ramon had blown wide holes in the US counterintelligence infrastructure. Hanssen handed over nearly two decades' worth of critical information that undermined our spies and shattered top-secret operations to collect intelligence from our Russian adversaries. He damaged the FBI and CIA so deeply that neither agency understood how far the cracks ran. Catching him wasn't enough. We needed to *enlist* him to tell us where he'd hidden all the bodies.

I played my role. Equally Watson to his Sherlock and Robin to his Batman. I listened and took notes as Hanssen covered the dry-erase board in marker while describing his thoughts on security theory. I nodded at his soul-searching soliloquies about his place in the world and what we leave behind when we go. The upcoming drop—that secret that we both knew but would never share—had turned him excitable. When he stepped out of his office, I never knew whether he would lecture me about the death of religion in the United States or the new technology that might solve one of the FBI's many security problems.

We continued to dance, or play chess, or whatever relationship best suits two men who are never certain which is the spy and which is the hunter. But one thing had given me the slightest upper hand. Hanssen didn't know that I knew that he would soon make a drop to the Russians. I had the winning cards in my hand. But I'd still have to call his bluff.

The morning after Hanssen shined a flashlight at the Foxstone Park sign, he appeared at my desk. For a tall guy who walked with a slight limp, he could move with preternatural quiet when he wanted to. Hanssen would have made a good ghost.

"Get your coat," he said. "We have a meeting this afternoon."

I floundered and pulled a shiny new Palm Pilot from the breast pocket of my suit jacket. My hands fumbled with the stylus as I opened the calendar. "What meeting? I didn't know we had a—"

"I am capable of setting up my own meetings." Hanssen nodded toward the Palm. "When did you get that?"

"They came in today." I opened my desk drawer and presented a neatly boxed Palm V to the boss.

He looked at the device with disdain and fished out his beefier model. "I've written the encryption on this myself," Hanssen said. "Those idiots in FBI IT couldn't crack it if their lives depended on it." He brushed the Palm V away—"You can take that one back"—and handed me a business card.

The name on the front read Victor Sheymov, Invicta Networks. Sheymov was the founder of Invicta, which provided encryption services to the government and private companies. I'd later learn that Sheymov was a former Russian spy.

The KGB recruited Sheymov in 1971 at age twenty-five to serve in its communications division. His knowledge of systems soon saw him promoted to senior manager and troubleshooter, an important role that provided him a breadth of knowledge about the KGB's structure and operations. One of his job duties included ensuring the security of encrypted KGB communications throughout the world. His role was so critical that the KGB assigned a minder to watch Sheymov, protect him if necessary, and, most important, eliminate him if he sought to defect.

As Sheymov rose in power and gained access to the Kremlin's secrets, he grew disillusioned with communism and the corruption of the Russian elite. Many KGB activities hastened the unease Sheymov felt, including a plot to assassinate Pope John Paul II and an intelligence penetration of the Russian Orthodox Church. While on assignment in Warsaw, Sheymov hatched a plan to evade his KGB minder and make contact with the CIA. According to Sheymov's memoir, *Tower of Secrets*, in 1980 he combined his knowledge of the inner workings of the KGB with a heroic effort by the CIA to help him escape with his wife and daughter across two closely guarded borders into Austria. Hanssen would later tell me that the CIA faked Sheymov's death and ultimately extracted his family through Finland, and that Hanssen personally conducted Sheymov's debrief when he arrived in the United States.

Sheymov was one of those rare, somehow untouchable defectors, most likely because the KGB bought the story that he and his family had perished. They wouldn't learn the truth until ten years later, likely when he wrote a memoir that exposed the KGB's structure and espionage practices. By then, Sheymov had already spent his secrets in debriefs to the US intelligence services, and any further action against him by the FSB would risk sparking an international incident in exchange for petty revenge.

Hanssen checked his watch. "We leave in fifteen minutes."

"I'll reserve a car."

I took five minutes to find Garcia and reserve the black Tahoe. Five more minutes to make him swear that it would be waiting when we reached the parking sublevel. I spent the final moments in a stairwell filling Kate in on our unannounced departure. She planned a search of Hanssen's car while we met with Sheymov in Reston.

Garcia kept his promise. Hanssen and I climbed into the black Tahoe and sped onto Route 66 toward Virginia. It would take us over thirty minutes to drive there and as many to return. Kate's team would have plenty of time to accomplish their search. I'd have plenty of time to shoot the shit with Gray Day.

As soon as we got in the car, Hanssen returned to our conversation about marriage and children. He still had a stick in his craw about my boast that Juliana would out-earn me. I had to promise to win the bread for my hypothetical future family to shut him up.

The meeting with Sheymov and his team fascinated me. Invicta had developed a hardware device that Hanssen thought could protect the FBI's systems while, at the same time, making them run more efficiently. Invicta's device, if it worked as promised, would mask the location of FBI computer systems, making it hard for an external attacker to identify a particular computer by continually changing the IP address of that computer. This would solve the conundrum of how to allow an FBI employee to access classified information and the Internet on the same machine. Sheymov's product was an early hardware solution for creating what we now know as virtual private networks. Today most VPNs rely on software to mask a user's computer from Internet eavesdroppers. Millions of people around the world use software VPNs. Citizens under the thumb of authoritarian regimes like China and North Korea quietly use them to access websites and bypass restrictions on content. Savvy computer users across the world use them to explore the Internet anonymously, to hide their identities from government surveillance and marketing agencies, or to secure their transactions from cyber thieves. Sheymov's solution was to protect computer systems by using hardware to establish a point of defense—like a gateway—before information ever arrived on the user's computer.

During the Hanssen investigation, most agents hadn't yet been issued official FBI email addresses. We used external email addresses from providers like AOL, Yahoo!, and Hotmail to send and receive personal email. In retrospect, this wasn't the best idea, considering that in 2013, cyberattackers (believed by the intelligence community to be Russian and working on behalf of the Russian government) breached Yahoo! and stole all of the company's 3 billion user accounts. Yahoo! took three years to discover and disclose the breach and spent another four investigating it.

In 2016, Yahoo! disclosed that a second attack in late 2014 had stolen an additional 500 million user accounts. This time the FBI uncovered evidence that pinned the breach on the Russians. In March 2017, the Department of Justice indicted four Russian agents for the 2014 breach of Yahoo! and theft of accounts that included names, email addresses, telephone numbers, dates of birth, passwords, and some encrypted and unencrypted security questions and answers. The defendants included two officers of the FSB and two criminal hackers with whom they conspired to bust into Yahoo! But because the United States and Russia do not have an extradition treaty, the Russian government cyber spies remained outside the DOJ's reach. That same year a cyber attacker who went by SunTzu583 offered over 1 million decrypted Yahoo! and Google accounts for sale on the dark web, the Internet's black-market underbelly.

But financial and political motives for hacking often go hand in hand. In early September 2017, the credit-reporting agency Equifax disclosed that unknown hackers had obtained sensitive personal and financial information for millions of consumers. The attack began in May 2017 through a known exploit in back-end software for web applications called Apache Struts. A security researcher had told Apache about the flaw, and Apache had published a patch that would fix it. Unfortunately for Equifax and many American households, attackers learned about the vulnerability before Equifax managed to install the patch. The attack continued until July 2017 and siphoned consumer data from 148 million American households, including Social Security numbers, birthdates, addresses, 200,000 credit card numbers, and dispute information for 180,000 Americans. The dispute information is most concerning because it included personal identifiable information that sophisticated attackers could use to gain entry into medical records, bank accounts, employer email accounts, and internal networks—virtually anywhere that a person may have an online presence. State-sponsored attackers are universally blamed for the Equifax attack. Many are pointing the finger at China. I'm still betting the Russians are behind the breach.

Why would Russian intelligence want to steal Yahoo! accounts and possibly steal consumer information from Equifax? Simple. Infiltrating email accounts allows spies to collect credentials that provide access to particular networks they're targeting and create virtual trusted insiders within those networks. Because most people use the same username and password over multiple accounts, and rarely activate two-factor authentication, stealing information about one account can open the doors to many others—from online bank accounts and corporate email accounts filled with valuable intellectual property to sensitive government databases. Armed with an insider account, a Russian spy could monitor government-agency systems to inform policy decisions and collect information on US defense and attack capability. Russia can also use email espionage to boost their flagging economy by gaming our stock market with insider information and stealing cutting-edge technology before we build or develop it fully and send it to the market. The breach of Yahoo!, which the company's board blamed on "failures in communication, management, inquiry and internal reporting," also allowed FSB spies to wade through the accounts of diplomats, journalists, Russian officials, and politicians critical of the Kremlin. Considering how the Kremlin treats dissidents, the Yahoo! breach may still have deadly implications.

For all his talk about counterintelligence, Hanssen spent most of our time at the Information Assurance Section focusing on prevention. He sought a way to stop external attackers from accessing internal FBI computer systems that could access both FBI NET and the Internet on the same machine. Searching for hardware and software solutions at Invicta was Hanssen's response to the first requirement of effective cybersecurity: technology.

People and process are the other two requirements, and the ones many companies trip over. Even the best security technology is just window dressing if employees aren't trained to use it effectively. With the right combination of technology and training, companies can gain visibility into attacks as they occur in real time. They can watch the attack land, figure out where it originated, and track how it moves within a system once the breach occurs—called the "attack killchain" in cyber lingo. Actively hunting for threats is the key to discovering attacks before they can do irreparable harm. But in order for threat-hunting to work, cybersecurity and counterintelligence have to play nicely with each other.

Equifax had invested in sophisticated security and had hired one of the top security threat research teams to protect its data, but an alleged dispute between the company and its security consultants just before the breach may have slowed the company's threat hunting. And when people aren't actively using technology to hunt spies, bad guys slip through the cracks. In other words, in a world where spies have become hackers, cybersecurity professionals must become spy hunters. They can never relax their guard.

But spies don't use a single playbook; they write the next attack as they go along. Hanssen attacked the FBI's most vulnerable point, internal computer systems, during a time when institutional bias had the FBI searching outward for a mole instead of inward. While the FBI sought to defend the United States from Russian spies, Hanssen attacked from within, using misdirection and detailed knowledge of security systems and procedures to protect himself. Through the years, he'd been able to siphon off information not because Russia had managed to hack FBI NET, but because with Hanssen on their side, they didn't need to. The FBI wasn't securing themselves from their own people. As long as Hanssen pointed the FBI in the wrong direction, Russia was guaranteed to win the cybersecurity game.

Hanssen smiled a lot at Invicta. My dour and withdrawn boss was flaunting an amicable, friendly, and likable side. I understood what was going on: Hanssen had taken me on his job interview. The FBI faced time pressure to catch him not only because he was about to make a drop but also because he might get a better offer in corporate security. Spying may have fed Hanssen's ego, but so would a cushy corporate job with stock options.

Meanwhile, I had another, more pressing, problem: Hanssen cut the meeting short without warning or explanation. We bid Sheymov's team a cheerful goodbye and hurried down to the car. I didn't have time to call Kate or to send a page from the two-way pager on my hip. I tried to slow-step our way through the parking lot, but Hanssen would have none of it.

"I have other appointments," he said. One hand jiggled the keys in his pocket and the other made a winding motion in the air. "Get in the car."

———

I started the car and pulled out of the Reston parking lot in full grandpa style: extended stops at intersections, exaggerated care when changing lanes, driving five miles under the speed limit.

Hanssen's patience vanished. "If you don't drive like you have somewhere to go, you can walk and I'll take the wheel," he ordered.

My mind raced. I fought to keep my eyes off the clock, a certain sign to Hanssen that I was worried about the time. If Hanssen walked straight to his car as soon as we arrived at HQ, he'd find the silver Taurus missing. Judging by his anxiousness to get back, this was a real possibility. It's impossible for someone to boost a car from the garage of one of the most secure buildings on earth; Hanssen would know the FBI had moved it. This would kick him in the pants hard enough to somersault him way over the suspicion line and into Paranoiaville.

I had to stall without rousing his suspicions. I made a turn off Route 66 onto the streets that would take me across the Key Bridge and into Georgetown.

"Where are you going?" Hanssen asked. He had this habit of tapping the dashboard with his index finger when I drove. It reminded me of my father teaching me to drive when I was fifteen and on a learner's permit. Dad would put his finger on the dashboard and tap faster when I accelerated too aggressively. I hated it then, and I hated it more now.

"I'm taking us back to headquarters," I said.

"Why didn't you take the parkway?"

I glanced over at him and raised an eyebrow. "Boss, I'm SSG, remember? This is what we do for a living. M Street is a short-cut."

He crossed his arms and slumped back in his seat. Having divorced his finger from the dashboard, he tapped his foot.

Anyone who has lived in the DC area for two weeks, or gone shopping in Georgetown once, could call my bullshit. The M Street traffic nightmare never ends, and for once Murphy helped me out. A truck had broken down in the middle of the two-lane road, and streams of cars had to squeeze by on the right. I drove us into the queue and choked back a smile.

"Moron," Hanssen said. "Imbecile!" He balled one hand into a fist. "Idiot."

The words barely penetrated anymore. The traffic would give the search team plenty of time to sew up the car and get it back to Hanssen's parking spot before I drove into the garage.

Before I could congratulate myself, Hanssen's seat belt spun away from his chest and clinked off the glass window before slamming home. He grabbed his bag from between his feet and shot me a dismissive glare. "I'll walk the rest of the way."

"Boss, wait, I—"

My phone shocked us both. I held up one hand and fumbled for my phone with the other. Hanssen tracked the black Nokia on its way to my ear.

Kate's voice. "Where are you?"

"I'm sorry, Juliana," I repurposed my panic into anger and pushed it into my voice. "I'll remember to pick up dinner." I paused. Kate remained silent. "No law school tonight, remember?"

I glanced at Hanssen. He sat, stone faced, one hand on the door handle.

"I'll try to be home on time," I said. "I'm stuck in traffic right now on M Street. I might be a little late."

Hanssen's sigh belonged in junior high school drama class. He scowled and opened his door.

"Juliana, I have to go . . ."

Hanssen got out of the car and walked up M Street, blue bag swinging off his shoulder. Sitting in the car, alone, I understood Hanssen's game. His odd mannerisms, the way he pushed his shoulder into me, his clicking pen and jingling keys, the way he insulted with one breath and complimented with the next. Hanssen was playing a game of balance.

As long as Hanssen was forcing me to react to him, my investigation was bound to fail. I spent so much time trying not to screw up the case I had tried to win it only once, when I'd dared search Hanssen's office. Boyd would have told me that each time I reacted to Hanssen, the spy changed the circumstances of our battle and forced me back into a never-ending OODA loop. I had to break the loop and make Hanssen react to me.

I ended the call and slammed the car into park. Angry Washingtonians screamed at me with their car horns as I slid across the front seat and chased after Hanssen.

"Boss, boss, wait!"

He turned and looked from me to the flashing hazard lights of Garcia's Tahoe. "What the hell are you doing?"

"I need you to get back in the car."

He stopped. Hanssen didn't just stop moving or talking, he went cold. No jingling keys or clicking pens. No foot tapping or finger pointing. His stillness was menacing.

"Why?"

An undercover case comes before everything else in an operative's life, especially when that case puts billions of dollars, numerous careers, and the security of the United States on the line. Relationships suffer. Birthdays are forgotten. Friendships fizzle. Dates sit alone in cafés waiting for you to appear. You flush away those things that matter to you, all in the pursuit of winning.

And sometimes, during that pursuit, you reach deep inside yourself for inspiration. These are the moments that make undercover work the dirtiest business in counterespionage investigations. I'd already sacrificed my faith. I had one quiet part of myself left to give.

"It's Juliana, boss," I said. "I need your advice."

He waited.

"We had a big fight last night." Totally true. "It was because of you." Also true.

Hanssen's head shifted to the side. It was subtle, but his nonverbal cues let me know he was listening.

"Juliana told me she doesn't want to have kids for a while," I said. "I brought up what you told me yesterday, about kids being the purpose of marriage. She didn't take it well." I glanced back at the shouting drivers and honking horns. "I thought we could have some time to discuss it in the car, but I didn't know how to bring it up."

"Do you swear?" His eyes bored into mine, equal to any lie detector.

"No," I said. "I'm not going to take the Lord's name in vain just to make you feel better." I turned to walk away. Then stopped. "I need your help!"

I didn't need to act or lie to project my indignation. How dare Hanssen test me when I had just poured my heart out to him? I spun and walked back to the car, feeling Hanssen's eyes on my back, willing with all my might for him to follow. With wooden motions, I returned to the driver's seat of the Tahoe and fastened my seat belt.

Hanssen spent the slow drive back to the office lecturing me on the purpose of marriage and the role of the man and the woman in the marriage. I smiled and nodded at the right points, and knew that nothing he told me would ever fly with my very independent wife.

I stopped the Tahoe beside Hanssen's silver Taurus and hoped that this time the search team had lined the tires up precisely in the parking space. But Hanssen focused on me with a face that slowly softened. He told me that marriage presents challenges and that my first responsibility as a Christian was to my home. I recalled a passage from *The Way*. "By good example good seed is sown; and charity compels us all to sow." I'd let Hanssen in to a personal struggle with Juliana. Hopefully he'd jump at the opportunity to lead by example.

"There are ways, Eric." Hanssen paused with one foot outside the door. "You just have to have faith."

"I have faith."

"Then everything will work out fine."

He wished me a good night and turned toward his car. I watched him back out and turn toward the ramp out of the garage, then shifted the Tahoe into drive. Before I could pull forward, Kate leapt into the passenger seat.

"Cutting it a little close," I said.

She eased the sidearm she concealed under a short sport coat and leaned back. "What do you think he meant?" She fell silent as I parked the Tahoe back under Garcia's Reserved sign.

"Have I told you, you'd make a good ghost?"

"A few times." She grinned.

"I think he's one of those people that thinks money solves all our problems." I slapped the car in park. "I don't think money has solved his."

"Good answer." She vibrated with excitement. "Jackpot."

"Jackpot?"

"We searched the car. Smooth move turning on M Street, by the way."

I wasn't in the mood for jokes or congratulations. I'd done my job, but I felt dirtier for it.

"Okay, then." Kate's excitement sobered. "Here's what we found while you kept him away. He stashed a roll of white medical tape and a box of Crayola colored chalk in the glove compartment."

"Useful to set a signal."

"You betcha." She flipped open a small memo pad. "We found a cardboard box in the trunk. Inside were seven classified documents that he printed from ACS. Some of them are classified secret and have to do with counterintel investigations."

"Which ones?"

She chuckled. "That's classified."

"Har-har."

"No, really. Need-to-know." Her eyes hardened. "Bad stuff for the Russians to get ahold of."

"What else?"

"We probably should have paid better attention to those

green ledger books on his desk. He has six of them full of classified information." She consulted her memo pad. "Here's the kicker."

"You mean there's something better than a bunch of secret docs in his trunk?"

"In a way. He has clear packing tape and dark Hefty garbage bags back there too."

"Exactly what Ramon used in his drops."

"Bingo."

"So we know he's a spy. And we know he's probably Ramon. What's next?"

She opened her door. "We want to prove it without a doubt. We put everything back exactly the way we found it. He's going to make a drop, Eric. It's right around the corner." Her voice deepened into a growl. "We're going to watch him do it."

Kate walked away. I parked the Tahoe, pulled the keys from the ignition, and sat for a long time in the FBI garage considering the narrow space between saving the day and blowing the case. On the chess table of my investigation, Hanssen and I had only a few more moves. This was the endgame.

# CHAPTER 23

# SHENANIGANS

February 14, 2001—Wednesday

Kate and I spent Valentine's Day huddled over plans to catch a spy. Hanssen had kept me late, and then I had to suffer through two glacially slow law school lectures. A clock had started ticking in my head, a staccato accompaniment to my life. I couldn't sleep, couldn't concentrate, and couldn't make my wife happy. Only winning the case mattered.

"You're distracted," Kate said. We sat in a little-used hallway on the sixth floor of headquarters. A few chairs that looked to have migrated from an office in the 1970s gave us a quiet place to plot the next day's operation. Kate's smile had fled. The intensity of the moment had sucked up all the humor in the room.

"I'm focused."

"You better be." Kate steepled her fingers in front of her lips. "Go through it again?"

I shook my head. "We've been through it enough times. I've got this."

"Then what's really bothering you?"

"In a nutshell? Juliana." I thought about the evening before. I had skipped class last night so Juliana and I could spend some time together. We'd gone to the Three Amigos restaurant in Eastern Market, a family-run, low-cost Tex-Mex joint that we both loved. The chicken/steak/shrimp choices all tasted the same under thick salsa. And they probably warmed the tortillas from a bag. But we didn't go there for the food. We went for tall pitchers and salted glasses.

"We went out last night for margaritas," I said.

Kate laughed. "Now we are getting somewhere."

I wished I could say the same about my relationship with Juliana. Her life behind the wall separating East and West Germany cheated her childhood of many of the things we take for granted. The intense colors and wild variety of choices in supermarkets overwhelmed and fascinated her. In those early years, trips to the local Safeway for a loaf of bread and bananas might cost us hours. She'd never seen a mango or avocado before coming to Washington, DC. I took her to Perry's in Adams Morgan for our first official date and she fell in love with sushi by candlelight. But it was her first margarita that had sealed the deal.

"We joked and had a great night." I slumped back into my chair.

"Until?"

"Until I told her that I'd miss Valentine's Day."

Kate raised an eyebrow. "Eric, Germans don't celebrate Valentine's Day. They do something much cooler in July. The *Loveparade*. Everyone dresses up and goes a little crazy."

"It's not about Valentine's Day for her." I quoted Juliana's words. "It's about making plans and sticking to them. I let her down."

"The job can be like that," Kate said.

"I also told her about going to dinner together on Tuesday next week at the Hanssens'."

Kate sighed. "We still aren't sure how to handle that."

"We may not have to," I said. "Her exact words were: *You're trading our night together for a night with a boss you don't even like?* Then she laughed out loud. But not in a happy way."

I didn't tell Kate about the chilly walk home that had nothing to do with the winter air or about the night I'd spent on our lumpy couch. I didn't mention the red brochure left artfully on the coffee table. The one titled "American University Abroad—Russian Studies in Saint Petersburg." Some things were better left unsaid.

"Ouch!" Kate patted my shoulder. "But there's good news!"

I stopped inspecting my shoelaces and lifted my head.

"This will all be over soon." She snapped her fingers. "That is, as long as you don't screw up tomorrow."

## February 15, 2001–Thursday

Hanssen's best friend, Jack Hoschner, was visiting from Germany and the boss couldn't stop talking about it. As I listened to him boast, I fought to quiet the ticking clock that now thundered in the back of my head.

When Kate had finally released me from our Valentine's Day planning session, I hurried home. At the base of the Metro steps, a vendor sold me roses out of an ancient umbrella stand filled with water. I exchanged a battered ten-dollar bill for six wilted roses wrapped in a sheet of bright-red paper. Six roses for six months of marriage.

You cannot buy a woman's affection with flowers. Juliana had dropped the roses on the kitchen counter before retreating to the bedroom. I arranged them in a vase and left them on our coffee table before following her to bed. When I woke the next morning, I found the apartment empty and the roses shoved in our kitchen trash.

Now I listened with half an ear to Hanssen spin stories about Jack, the military attaché stationed in Bonn, Germany. Today was the true pivot point of the Gray Day case. Kate and I had bet the house on stealing Hanssen's Palm Pilot. I needed my mind honed to a razor focus. Instead it drifted back to our apartment and six flowers poking over the lip of our trash can.

"Jack would make a great spy," Hanssen said. "He does munitions work for the army. Has great access."

"Good thing he's not a spy, then." I didn't have to engage

Hanssen in conversation today, only keep him sitting behind his desk. Thankfully, something had ignited the boss's chatty streak. I just had to give him a few nudges.

"Oh, you never know, Eric." Hanssen spun his pen over the back of his hand like a stage-show magician. "You find spies in the strangest places." He gave it a few clicks and I checked the urge to snatch it from him. Only a pretense of friendship with Hanssen remained. If the FBI had decided someone needed to choke him out, I'd have been first in line.

"Are you and Juliana still coming over to dinner on Tuesday?"

My smile hurt my face. "We wouldn't miss it."

Hanssen's invitation had given the FBI conniptions. I had used Juliana as a pretext to speak with Kate on numerous occasions. If Hanssen asked Juliana about even one of those fake phone calls, the investigation might unravel. I had also used my wife to excuse everything from arriving late for work to talking Hanssen back into the car on M Street. The FBI couldn't allow Hanssen to interrogate her over a dinner table.

On the other hand, Hanssen's house was a black hole that the FBI couldn't penetrate. Hanssen's wife or one of his many children was always home. We couldn't get a technical team inside. The best we could manage—a feat in itself—was to purchase a home down the street. Undercover FBI agents played house there, pretending to be a married suburban couple while spying on the Hanssen household from upstairs windows. It was good enough to call the family in and out of the Hanssen residence, but no substitute for embedding technology in the walls.

If I could strut into the Hanssen home on Talisman Drive with an invitation, the FBI would at a minimum have a memorized layout of the home's common areas. I could also spot any potential items of interest. A gun safe would have to be factored into any arrest plan. The search teams would want to know about any locked file cabinets. The tech crew might even hand me bugs to place if an opportunity presented itself.

Of course, to accomplish any of this, the FBI needed Juliana onboard. Kate would have to read Juliana, a German national, into the biggest case the FBI had ever run. The idea gave the FBI brass heartburn and paralyzed them in endless debate. They didn't know that I had yet to talk my recalcitrant wife into showing up on my arm.

"I'd still like to see that Walther PPK you keep talking about," I said. "Now, that's a real spy gun."

Hanssen stretched. Panic that he might stand up woke me to the situation and forced a surreptitious glance at my watch. Not yet! I needed him to sit a little longer.

"The same model Bond used in *Dr. No.*" Hanssen slouched back into his chair and I relaxed back into mine. "German engineering at its best. Did you know that a firearms expert wrote to Ian Fleming and convinced him that Bond should fire a PPK?"

"I had no idea."

"You're married to a German. Translate *Polizeipistole Kriminal.*"

I let him see my discomfort. "I don't actually speak German."

"How can you be married to a German and not speak her language?" Hanssen waved a finger at me. He might as well have also jammed a dunce cap on my head. "It means 'criminal police pistol.' The Walther was developed for undercover German police."

I briefly wondered whether they let you watch Bond films in prison. "Makes sense."

"Especially since the Walther PPK uses a 7.65mm round, common all over the world. Very accommodating to Bond's jet-setting lifestyle." Hanssen looked like he'd just sucked a lemon. "Now Bond uses a P99. The more modern version of the—" He looked up as the door beeped. "Who could that be?"

"Don't get up." Garcia strode into Hanssen's office with O'Leary in tow. "Do you have lunch plans?"

Hanssen waged a war against his scowl and lost. "I have important things to—"

"Nonsense." O'Leary looked pointedly at the painting hanging over Hanssen's head. "Nice print, by the way. I have one just like it."

"Yes, well . . ."

O'Leary slammed a twenty-dollar bill on Hanssen's desk like an actor sweating for an Oscar. Hanssen's prize pen rolled onto the floor, and murder raged in his eyes.

"I heard you think you can shoot," O'Leary said. "Should we put it to the test?"

Hanssen choked back the apoplectic response I'm sure he wanted to throw at the ADIC and fought to be deferential. "This isn't a good time—"

"Bullshit," the ADIC said. "It's always a good time to shoot." He pointed at Garcia. "Rich is in."

Hanssen looked from one superior to the other. I knew well the fake smile he wore on his face. It mirrored the mask I'd carried around for months.

"Fine," he said.

Hanssen retrieved his gun, his ear protection, and a pair of yellow-tinted shooting glasses from his desk drawer. Distracted by the superior agent standing over him, pissed at the unexpected interruption to his monologue, and angry at what he saw as a challenge to his authority, Hanssen, for the first time, did not reach down and scoop his Palm IIIx out of his bag.

I froze. Only my eyes moved to watch them leave through the main office area and out the big SCIF door. I watched them on the monitor in Hanssen's office, tuned to the security camera that looked down the hallway toward the elevator. I willed them to get on it.

Only when the doors closed did I take a breath. Patience. I waited, counting Mississippi until my pager buzzed at my hip. I brought the dull screen to my eyes and read the magic words. "In pocket. Shooting."

Then I moved.

There's a term of art for tricking a target into doing something you need them to do: shenanigans. A more technically inclined person might call the art of manipulating someone social engineering, but I'm half Irish. In Hollywood, the hero might casually pass Hanssen and distract him with a bump while slipping a deft hand into his back pocket to steal the Palm Pilot. Three problems with this scenario. First, we needed to remove the Palm IIIx from his possession long enough for a team to copy it before he realized he'd misplaced it. Second, I'm neither an illusionist nor a carnival thief. Third, would you want to put your hand that close to Hanssen's backside? Since pickpocketing wasn't an option, we needed a plan that would distract Hanssen and force him to break his routine. The shenanigan Kate and I scripted relied on everything we'd been able to learn about the spy so far.

When the agents running the case asked me to do things that seemed crazy—like making Hanssen angry—they did so in order to develop a detailed psychological profile of the spy. Each of Hanssen's reactions became a data point. Over the many hours of conversation between Hanssen and me, we'd discovered that he had contempt for authority, an overwhelming hubris that would have made Oedipus weep, and a passion for firearms. I'd also just learned that he didn't take well to changes in plans.

Kate and I combined these four data points, and the result was a wonderful shenanigan. We would surprise Hanssen with the sudden appearance of an assistant director—someone with more authority than Hanssen—who would demand that Hanssen change his schedule. I suggested that they go shooting. Hanssen talked about guns all the time and routinely promised to take me down to the firing range. The other day he'd told me that the best way to solve crime in Washington, DC, would be to make firearms legal and put one in every house.

Kate gave the operation a green light, and then we planned it from every angle. We weren't going to deal with a case of the missing Tahoe again. I had to make sure that Hanssen was sitting down when the director barged in, because if he was standing, the Palm would be in his back pocket. The timing had to be perfect.

So when Hanssen seated me across his desk to talk about his best friend and *Dr. No*, I sent a secret page to Kate. Then, after Hanssen trailed his superior out of the office, another agent kept Hanssen in pocket down in the shooting range. I'd also timed, at a sprint, the distance from the range to Room 9930. It took nine minutes at the most aggressive pace. Hanssen was an old guy with a limp. I didn't see him moving faster than a walk. His pride demanded a sense of decorum.

When I finished counting to 100, I knelt before Hanssen's bag. The briefcase sat at an angle against the side of his desk, dark blue canvas with brown accents. Four zippered pockets surrounded the central organizer for papers. With exaggerated caution, I opened all the pockets and sorted through the contents, searching for what I hoped and prayed would be the key to bringing Hanssen down.

A smile spread across my face. It felt almost strange—I hadn't smiled a real smile since the first time I'd entered Room 9930. In one of the pockets, the Palm IIIx rested next to a plain gray floppy disk. Hanssen's sanctum sanctorum. I drew them both from the bag like Arthur rescuing Excalibur from the stone. A quick search of the other pockets revealed the same 8MB Versa Flash Memory card I'd found during my previous search. I took that too. Then I ran.

A tech team waited three flights down on the sixth floor. For weeks, they'd sweated in a small, unmarked room, surrounded by various computer systems and machines. I never did manage to steal Hanssen's keys, but I woke them up with something better.

Kate met me at the door. "Do you have it?"

I showed her and nodded. I didn't trust my voice.

"Follow me."

She knocked a few times, and the door cracked open. I

handed over the Palm, floppy disk, and memory card. The tech team got to work.

Ghosts harbor a supreme amount of patience. We sometimes sit for hours staring at a front door or taillight, hoping that the target will move. You can listen to a lot of talk radio and NPR in the surveillance business. Now I found stillness impossible. I bounced on my toes, straining to look over the tech's shoulders, sweating each tick of the progress screen as the devices copied.

"It's encrypted," said a tech. "We'll have to clone it and break the encryption later."

"Do what you have to do," Kate said. She turned. "You wait outside."

"What, like guard the door?" I said.

"No, genius. You're making everyone nervous."

If nothing else, the Hanssen case had taught me humility. I slinked out the door and stood under the fluorescent lights of a cold, white hallway. I put my hands in my pockets and continued to bounce away the energy that sparked like static off a wooly coat.

My pager buzzed.

I brought it to my face and read the words: "Out of pocket. Coming to you."

Kate pressed the Palm, memory card, and floppy disk into my hand the way an Olympic runner passes a baton. I scooped the devices into my arms and sprinted for the stairway. Nine minutes. I had at least nine minutes before Hanssen stormed into 9930 looking for his digital assistant.

The secret about counterespionage is that, even at the highest levels, it can be pretty boring. James Bond never spent lonely hours watching someone innocently stroll through a park, or poring through documents and records looking for the financial irregularity that might break open a case. But sometimes, when your adrenaline is pumping and you're racing against the clock, you can't help but feel like the kind of spy you read about when you were a kid. This was my Bond moment.

I dashed into the SCIF, slammed the door behind me, and slid to a halt in Hanssen's office with three minutes to spare. Piece of cake.

One look at Hanssen's bag and my cocky grin fell away. Sweat beaded between my shoulder blades and traced a slow path down my back. My stomach recalled the moment before every test I'd forgotten about, every teenage traffic ticket I'd have to explain to my parents, each time a girl had laughed and turned away. . . . My vision sank and spun, growing dark at the periphery. I grabbed the edge of Hanssen's desk and wrested control of my breath.

I had opened all four of the bag's pockets and held three devices. My empty, traitorous mind only recalled that the floppy disk went with the Palm Pilot. I couldn't even remember pulling the memory card out of the briefcase.

My wrist was shaking, which made telling time difficult. Two minutes? Three minutes? How much did I have left? I glanced at Hanssen's TV, with its surveillance feed of the hallway. Still empty.

Brains can do weird things under stress. Instead of focusing on the bag, I recalled an Auburn University lecture on hypnosis. A guest lecturer had visited our psychology class in the basement of Haley Center and had hypnotized a student into recalling a license plate from his childhood. Panic made me think I could close my eyes and visualize the Eric from minutes ago taking the devices out of the bag. I stilled my breathing and sought an impossible Zen state.

The door to the SCIF beeped. My eyes snapped open and sought out the monitor. Hanssen was at the door to 9930. I made a sign of the cross, dropped the devices in the bag, zipped up all four pockets, hurtled out of Hanssen's office, and dove into my chair. My breath calmed and my hands stilled. If I'd gotten the pockets wrong, there was nothing to be done about it now.

Hanssen shoved the door open and glared at me. I frowned and looked up from the keyboard I pretended to type on. A beat of sweat tickled my hairline and I pasted a bored poker face across my writhing anxiety. *Please, please, please stay there*, I thought.

"Did you win?" I controlled my voice and rode into the eye of the storm.

Not a word in answer. Hanssen searched my face and then abruptly turned toward his office. The door slammed behind him.

I let my head slump toward my chest. The energy that'd had me so on edge in the tech room had fled. I was tired of playing four-dimensional chess with Hanssen. Tired of second-guessing myself. Tired of fighting with Juliana. Tired of long nights in front of a laptop in a dark room typing observation notes after two hours of law school lectures. Tired.

I heard Hanssen unzip his bag.

I thought of all the time and extraordinary effort that the FBI had poured into this case. Kate told me that this was the biggest investigation the FBI had ever run. They'd trusted me in the center of it. I couldn't let them down.

By this point, Hanssen had shoved his Palm back into the seat of his pants. Either I'd gotten the pocket right or I hadn't. Either I put the memory card in the right place or I didn't. Either the floppy disk was sitting at just the right angle against the Palm or it wasn't. You don't go to Vegas with those odds. A smart person would have left 9930 and started running. Of course, a smart person would have memorized which pocket he'd pulled the Palm Pilot from. I'd made a mistake, which made it my duty to correct course.

A simple calculus determined how the Gray Day case would end. If Hanssen emerged from his office with his usual level of dissatisfaction, I'd gotten the pockets right and just had to downplay his suspicion. If he stormed out of his office, I'd gotten the pockets wrong. And if I ran away, Hanssen would know he'd been caught. The spy would cut and run, hole up in Russia somewhere, and the FBI would get nothing. If I stayed at my desk, maybe, just maybe I could talk my way out of this. "Hey, boss," I'd say. "I tripped over your bag. Stupid me. Everything fell out and I put it back for you. Those zippers just spontaneously popped open. . . ." Who was I kidding? He would shoot me and use his open plane ticket to board a flight to Moscow.

I couldn't run. I wouldn't run. Instead, I leapt.

"Were you in my office?" Hanssen leaned over my desk, his face inches from mine. I imagined I could smell gunpowder on his breath.

"We were both in your office, boss." I controlled my face with an effortlessness that surprised me. "I left that memo in your inbox. Did you see it?"

He held my gaze. I knew the trick of his silence and refused to let the awkwardness loosen my tongue.

"I never want you in my office again."

"Sure thing, boss," I said. "Anything else?"

Apparently not. Hanssen shouldered his bag and left.

I waited until the door closed behind him. Counted the moments until he reached the elevator at the end of the hall. Imagined the doors closing before he dropped toward the parking garage and his silver Ford Taurus.

Then I let myself fall apart.

# CHAPTER 24

# SMOKING GUN

February 16, 2001—Friday

Hanssen sat across from me with his hands pressed between his knees the way one might sit to pray. His eyes traced the faux wood laminate along my desk until they rested on Juliana's portrait. He spun the small frame until Juliana was smiling back at him.

"You are a lucky man, Eric," he said.

I couldn't help my smile. "She took that picture the day before she came to America. It's my favorite."

"You two should have children." He forestalled my objections with a raised hand and then turned the picture back around. His long, methodical fingers placed the frame in precisely the spot where it had previously been. "Bonnie and I are looking forward to seeing you both on Tuesday night."

I weighed my answer. Hanssen's moods over the past two days had swung wildly from melancholy to elation, and everything in between. I hid my feelings better, but I was just as unsettled. The curtain was about to fall on our relationship. And while the costume I wore still fit, the role had long begun to chafe.

The day was Friday, February 16, 2001, three days before Presidents' Day. Juliana and I had plans to spend the long weekend with friends in Delaware. Hanssen would be with his oldest friend, Jack, visiting from Germany. We might never see each other again.

"Juliana's excited. We both are." I squared my eyes to his as

I told the lie. A skill Hanssen had taught me. Juliana still had no intention of making the drive out to my boss's house on Talisman Lane, and the FBI still hadn't committed to letting her. The entire investigative machine of the bureau waited on Sunday night. I had played all my cards. Hanssen had one left to toss on the table.

I glanced at the clock. The day had faded behind us, not that you would know in the cave the FBI had locked us in.

My boss flashed a rare smile and stretched himself out of the small desk chair. "You have law school, and I need to pick up Jack."

I nodded to hide my frown. Hanssen had not fully committed to recruiting me. I had hoped to hand Kate a cherry to put on top of the investigation I'd bundled up for her. After Sunday, the chance would likely pass me by.

Kate had met with me a few days after Operation Palm Pilot with a beaming smile that had her walking on tiptoes. She caught me outside the cafeteria during my lunch break and took me to a small out-of-the-way hallway where the 1960s had abandoned two bright orange couches.

"We've got him." Kate slammed her balled fist into her palm.

"I thought we already had him," I said.

"Yeah, kiddo, but now we *really* have him. You got us our smoking gun."

I held my breath.

"The data card had a new letter. The last one he'll ever drop." Kate's smile might have frightened small children. "We decrypted and decoded the Palm. He's going to make the drop on Sunday at eight at night. We even know where."

"Seriously?"

She sat back crookedly to avoid a stain on the upholstery. "How do you think we should arrest him?"

My eyebrows climbed my face. "You're asking me?"

"You know him better than anyone."

"Okay." I collected my thoughts. "He despises authority. He once told me that he should be director. He also doesn't like to be surprised or challenged."

"What would you do," Kate asked, "if you were calling the shots?"

It took me seconds to answer. I'd thought long and hard about this already. "Have an older agent that he trusts, maybe a friend, meet him somewhere isolated. You want to be away from his family or people that know him. Definitely nowhere near his house."

Kate smiled. "Go on."

I told her my plan. On some pretext, I'd drive him to an empty parking lot, maybe the one outside the Tech Division at Quantico. We had planned to drive out there next week anyway. I'd park the car and then get out without a word. As I walked away, a senior agent would walk over and get in. He'd smile, shake Hanssen's hand, and say: "We know everything, Bob. Tell us how you did it."

"He's desperate to talk," I said. "He's the guy that got away with the perfect crime and can't tell anyone. But he wants to. That's why he writes all those buddy-buddy letters to the Russians."

"You'll make a great agent," Kate said. "You just outlined our plan B."

"What is plan A?"

The way Kate had paused before answering lent a crushing gravity to her next words. "We bring him down on Sunday."


Hanssen pulled his office door shut. I blinked my eyes and returned to the present.

"Good night, Eric," he said on his way out. As the door closed behind him, he stopped it with a shoulder and pushed it all the way open.

"I forgot my coat," he said.

I logged out from FBI NET and started to shut down. "Want me to get it for you?"

He grinned. "Bet I can get to my office, grab the coat, and get back before this door shuts?"

"You're on."

Ten seconds later, he caught the door with one hand, nearly crushing his fingers. His jacket and briefcase hung from the other arm.

"Told you," Hanssen said. He turned to leave. "Have a nice holiday weekend, Eric."

"Boss?" I blurted out, feeling at once that the end had come. He stopped and looked at me. "I'll catch you later."


Each year I threw a winter party with my closest friends at my parents' beach house. The year before I left for college, my parents began construction on a gray sandpiper home in Delaware, blocks from the beach. My father named it Villa Viviana, after my mother. Mom so loved the home away from home that when she could no longer use the stairs, Dad had an elevator installed.

My mother guarded use of the beach house the way a chatelaine kept the keys in a medieval castle. Friends and family each begged a week or weekend at the home over the summer. Equipped with a spreadsheet and calendar, Mom used complex mathematical equations to distribute the few open times fairly.

Since returning from college, I had taken the path of least resistance and begged weekends at the house in the autumn or winter, when only wind haunted the small beach town. I've always preferred a cabin, good friends, endless wine, and a fired-up grill over late nights at loud clubs or packed house parties. One weekend at the beach house, my buddy Christian looked over the railing of a high deck down to where Juliana and another friend rollerbladed on the empty street. "Are you going to marry her?" he'd asked around the edge of a cigar.

"I'm not sure," I replied, without taking my eyes off the way she spun in quick circles, laughing behind golden hair that whipped across her face.

"You should."

Months later, I proposed.

The day after I said goodbye to my boss for what would be the last time, I caravanned with a group of friends to Villa Viviana. We arrived in the early afternoon and, after unloading bags and bickering over rooms, rushed to the shore. It was a beautiful day. The bright sun in an azure sky made the beach sparkle golden. During the high season, soft waves reach toward vacationers sitting under umbrellas or sunbathing on towels. In winter, the deserted beach is stark and beautiful, quiet but for the roar of the ocean pounding the sand.

A seagull spun in a lazy circle overhead, hopeful that one of us would drop a kernel of popcorn or a Goldfish cracker. A few of my friends pointed out the bird with delight. I scarcely noticed it. My thoughts were two hundred miles inland.

The Hanssen investigation had consumed nearly three months of my life. In that time, my law school grades had suffered, my marriage had stumbled out of the starting gate, and my mother's worsening condition had been an iron weight inside my chest. I was out in the middle of the ocean treading water, and I was desperate to come to shore. Still, I found myself fervently repeating a prayer that blocked out my friends' banter and Juliana's concern in equal measure.

*Please don't let him be arrested on Sunday. Let it be Tuesday.*

Part of me needed to hand Hanssen over to the arresting agents myself in order to close this tense chapter of my life. Like a hunter on a quest for the mythical white stag, I wanted the satisfaction of the kill. Without it, I worried I'd never be able to dispel the case from my mind.

Now I stood leaning against that same deck where Christian and I had once shared cigars and looked at the empty street below. Laughter and the occasional gleeful shriek escaped the twin sliding doors behind me, revelry from a party I had planned but never truly joined. Juliana escaped the merriment to ask that sensible question that rarely gets a straight answer in any relationship. "What's wrong?"

I looked at my still-new wife and thought of the first time I had taken Juliana to Villa Viviana. My father and I had shared a glass of Glenfiddich beside a nautical bar that he'd rescued from an old ship. We'd leaned our elbows on the heavily polished wood and toasted my impending marriage and future.

I've always turned to my parents for advice. In matters of the heart, my mother held court. For advice about how to overcome life's various beatings, I turned to my father the way the ancient Greeks sought out an oracle. We'd clinked glasses and said "Cheers"—our ritual performed—and then I sought my father's counsel.

"Dad," I had asked, words slow and careful, "law school, marriage, work—how did you balance it all?"

"We took turns caring for you," Dad had said. "I'd come back from law class in the afternoon in time for your nap. Your mom and I would spend a few hours together over a late lunch and then she'd leave for her night shift at the hospital. We spent all our weekends together."

My parents didn't suffer through law school. They thrived. My father didn't trudge to school at night after a full day of work. He was a day student who spent quiet evenings reading me bedtime stories while my mom worked as a maternity nurse. They could turn off the part of their brains that worried about work in order to be fully with each other, and with me. I didn't have that luxury.

"You look tired, Eric." Dad had offered the only advice he could. "You should get more sleep. Sleep is a weapon."

Now I looked at Juliana and wished that I had taken my father's advice about sleep. I had neither the mental elasticity to spin a placating lie nor the patience to answer politely. Instead I gave the answer responsible for the majority of marital battles. "Nothing."

Maybe Juliana sensed the way my thoughts spun with anticipation. Or perhaps she was tired of chasing an argument that the last two months hadn't resolved. She shook her head in that knowing way that always makes me wonder if she can read my mind and folded me into a hug.

I kept my FBI cell phone close and my pager on my nightstand. The phone felt hot in my hand, a viper waiting to strike. An early ring meant that Hanssen had gotten cold feet and escaped to Moscow. The case would implode, and fingers would point in every direction. I knew plenty of those fingers would be pointed at me. I'd made enough mistakes to warrant the blame.

I made Juliana trade me her introvert stripes so that she could play the role of host for the weekend. I spent the weekend in a bubble of misery racing down a river of stress. My FBI-issued Nokia never left my side. It came with me on beach walks and rode in my pocket to dinners and during drinks. I grimaced where I should have laughed and watched the distant waves while friends bonded behind me. By the time the weekend limped along to Sunday, I'd made myself an outcast.

## February 18, 2001—Sunday

Hanssen had the best Sunday of his life. His children returned to the Hanssen homestead with grandchildren in tow to enjoy a late brunch, church services, and plenty of laughter. Hanssen and his best friend, Jack, spent some time throwing a Frisbee out back with the family Labrador. The perfect day stretched onward toward evening. Jack loaded his bags in the back of Hanssen's Taurus, and they drove to Dulles Airport with plenty of time for Jack to board his return flight to Germany.

On his way home, Hanssen parked his car up the block from Foxstone Park. He hugged his brown tweed sport coat close and stepped out into the chill. After a short visit to his trunk, he strode along the deserted sidewalk toward the bright red park sign. He scanned through the surrounding trees, an easy task given the bare branches of winter. At this late hour, just after seven p.m., no dog walkers braved the cold, and joggers had long since retired for an hour of TV before bed. The pawns lived their mundane lives in their quiet homes, paying bills and muddling through meaningless office jobs. Hanssen's life had a purpose bigger than that of all the bureaucrats with their fancy suits and manufactured promotions. He was water seeping up through a crack in the concrete, quietly undermining the foundation.

In the center of the park, Hanssen stopped on a small wooden-and-steel bridge. He leaned on one railing, looking down toward Wolf Creek's thin trickle of water past icy banks. The gray sky hung heavy with the promise of snow. All the better to cover his tracks.

Hanssen looked and listened. A dog barked, momentarily startling him, but the echo came from far away. Distant traffic from Route 123 droned like waves on a beach. He was alone.

Minding the mud along the creek bed, Hanssen stepped off the bridge and clambered under it. He fished a package out of his sport coat and slid it into the superstructure. He'd wrapped the package in dark trash bags and packing tape, following a routine that had carried him through decades.

Once satisfied that no one could spot the dead drop, he climbed back onto the bridge and smiled. He had just loaded his final drop to the Russians after twenty-two years of spying. He knew that no other spy could match his body of work. None of them had lasted long enough to try. Now Hanssen would go dark. This was his farewell.

He retraced his steps toward his car and placed a piece of white tape on the Foxstone Park sign to signal his Russian friends that his secrets waited under the bridge. At Hanssen's next stop, he would collect his payment: $50,000 that would help secure the many things his growing family needed. He'd included a warning of sorts in his last letter. Something had aroused the FBI "sleeping tiger."

After Hanssen made the drop, he retraced his steps back to the car. He fished his keys from a pocket, then dropped them. Two vans screeched to a halt on either side of his Taurus. Camouflaged agents rose like apparitions from the gloom of the park around him. SWAT team members swarmed out of vans, their rifles at the ready.

Hanssen began to raise his arms but was grabbed by FBI agents before they cleared his waist. "The guns are not necessary," he said quietly.

Rough hands pulled Hanssen's arms behind his back and handcuffed him. His former colleagues told him to stand with his legs apart as they patted him down for weapons. Hanssen suffered the indignity in silence. He'd lost his final gamble.

"What took you so long?" he said.

# CHAPTER 25

# UNDERSTANDING

February 18, 2001—8:15 p.m.

**W**hat is with you?" Juliana asked.

Rain drizzled from the evening sky, blotting out the tail-lights of the traffic ahead. I clicked on the windshield wipers.

"What do you mean?"

"You were distracted all weekend," she said, glancing at the phone on my lap. "You carried that thing around the entire time."

"I'm sorry," I said, and meant it. "Stuff is going on at work."

She turned away, watching Route 295 as it curved along the banks of the Anacostia River toward the brightly lit monuments of downtown DC. Juliana and I had spent the majority of our drive from the Delaware coast in silence. To say I had a lot on my mind was an understatement.

My cell rang, and we both jumped. Emotion fell away and I raised the phone to my ear. Either way, at least I'd have my answer.

"It's Kate. It's done."

The words sent my stomach into free fall. I put on my blinker and eased right through traffic toward the shoulder. My hands shook on the wheel. "Do you need me to come in?"

"No. Nothing for you to do now." She paused. I could hear voices in the background. "You were right, Eric."

"The Palm?"

She shouted at someone, her voice muffled, then turned

back to me. "The Palm gave us where and when he'd make the drop to the Russians, right down to the hour. He showed up and we got him."

My world narrowed to Kate's voice in my ear. The Palm Pilot also sealed an airtight connection between Ramon Garcia, "B," and Hanssen. It was our smoking gun—a unicorn in intelligence investigations. Ever since Gene had smiled out his car window at me on that Sunday morning back in December, the FBI had piled lies upon lies like weights on my back. They all fell away to be replaced by the hand-shaking realization that I'd shot the moon and won. I'd helped catch the biggest spy in FBI history. What came next?

"Look," Kate said, "I need to run. We can talk on Tuesday. We're searching Hanssen's house right now."

"Wait!" I stopped her before she hung up. "Can I tell Juliana?"

Quiet on the other end of the phone. Then, finally: "Just immediate family. We're trying to catch the IO when he comes to service the drop. We don't want the story out."

Catching the Russian intelligence officer tasked with picking up Hanssen's drop wasn't necessary to fully prosecute Hanssen, but it would give the State Department explosive ammunition against Russia. Right now, none of that mattered to me.

"Just Juliana," I said.

I finished easing the car over to the shoulder, one set of tires into the grass. Trucks screamed by with such force that the wind of their passing rocked our Jeep Cherokee. It all felt like a dull blur.

"Tell me what?" Juliana said softly.

"I need to tell you about Hanssen."

She folded her hands in her lap and waited. Half in a dream, I told Juliana the entire story, from Gene showing up at our apartment, to the truth behind all the lies I'd told her throughout. I told her about going to church with Hanssen and the FBI searching his car. I told her about replacing the Palm Pilot and the way we'd said goodbye. I told her about Kate, and how she'd shepherded me through an ordeal that forever molded my life. I told her I loved her, and always would.

When I finished, she looked at me for a long time. Her eyes found mine and held them. I feared that she would condemn my dishonesty or kick me out of the car, vow to return to Germany, or tell me to move back in with my parents.

When she finally spoke, she said a few perfect words.

"Now I understand."

I leaned over and kissed her. My final leap in the Hanssen investigation would guide the rest of my life. Hanssen had never found real happiness. I'd found the path to mine.

On Tuesday morning, Kate met me in Hanssen's office. She waited quietly while I turned a slow circle. Most of Hanssen's possessions waited in banker's boxes along one wall. Different FBI agents working the case from behind the scenes had taken the rest; trophies from the biggest espionage case in FBI history. An agent I had never met carefully inventoried the contents of my desk. Everything was evidence, including a floppy disk containing my criminal law exam outline. I hoped they'd give that back to me.

Kate puffed out her cheeks and exhaled. "We still have to finish the search of his house and inventory this office. We'll talk to his wife and kids. We hope he'll plead guilty."

I thrust my hands into my pockets. "I never got his keys."

Kate laughed. "I never told you this, but there were two squads working this case at the end, and we had a bet as to who could collect the best evidence." She leaned a hip against Hanssen's desk and glanced around the office before continuing. I wondered what would become of this dreary place that had forever changed my life.

"I received a telephone call on Saturday telling me I had

won that bet." Kate's eyes met mine. "It was because of your ability to pick up Hanssen's Palm Pilot."

She asked me what I planned to do next. I didn't know. Maybe I'd apply to work in the real Information Assurance Section; maybe I'd go back into the field.

"You know, Eric," Kate said. "Most FBI agents spend a career chasing a case like this and never find one." Her eyes softened. "You did a great thing here."

"Can you think of a better time to leave?"

She laughed. "Nope. You can only go down from here."

I leafed through the green ledger books I'd never been authorized to touch and righted a picture of Hanssen's family that the search team had knocked over. I picked up Hanssen's pen. Clicked it a few times for good measure.

"Can I?"

"I think you've earned it," Kate said.

I pocketed the pen and walked away.

## CHAPTER 26

# THE FUTURE IS
# YESTERDAY

The FBI lauded the Gray Day squad and handed out awards and commendations to numerous agents. In late February 2001, Louis Freeh and newly appointed Attorney General John Ashcroft met in an HQ auditorium with every individual who worked the Hanssen case, from agents and ghosts to support staff and analysts. As Director Freeh gave one of his final addresses to the FBI before his resignation and Ashcroft told us that Hanssen would remain one of the most damaging spies in US history, a number of hardnosed agents blinked away tears.

I sat apart from my former colleagues in the SSG and on the Gray Day team. I was the first investigative specialist in FBI history to work undercover directly against a spy, and I might be the last. Now I didn't know on which side of the investigation I belonged.

I returned to ghosting the streets and watched from the sidelines as information about Hanssen's long list of crimes became public. His espionage included material on our nuclear program and an assessment of the KGB's efforts to compromise it. He compromised our methods to retaliate against a large-scale nuclear attack and elements of our defensive strategy if the bombs fell. He provided the Soviets with a tactical edge by passing along our continuity-of-government plan—where we send our president and vice president, the cabinet and Congress, and everyone else who matters most during a catastrophic attack.

Hanssen gave up detailed "ways and means" for how we protect ourselves and how we hunt spies. He burned covers and put at risk countless operatives working on foreign soil and quite possibly fellow field operatives in Washington, DC. He gave the Soviets our protocols for conducting counterintelligence. The Soviets were able to plan a counterattack to defeat every move we made; it was like the United States was coaching a Super Bowl team against a rival who knew each play before the offense set up at the line.

Kate must have known some of this, maybe all of it, but she hadn't told me. I understood. Had I known, my anger might have compromised my ability to calmly collect the facts against Hanssen. I would not have seen the man through the spy and would have never found a way to relate to him. I had to act like a young man finding my way, not a spy hunter seeking to take down Russia's top mole.

I realized that Hanssen had placed the FBI through a constantly resetting OODA loop. For two decades, neither his KGB handlers nor the teams of FBI investigators discovered his identity. They couldn't even nail down in which agency he was hiding. Each time investigators closed in on Hanssen, he'd change his actions, forcing the FBI to observe new information, reorient, decide, and act. Hanssen used pseudonyms and dropped information stolen from other agencies to mask his location. When our highest sources in the Soviet Union reported that a mole hid within our intelligence community, Hanssen gave up Martynov and Motorin to his KGB handlers. Soviet intelligence flew them back to Moscow and put a bullet in the back of each of their heads. No lengthy trial. No celebrity defense attorney or media firestorm. No appeals process or pleas for clemency. Picture a dark hallway, a shadowy figure, and a loud gun. Russia doesn't waste time with traitors.

One afternoon, after watching a Soledad O'Brien report on CNN, I scooped up my phone and speed-dialed Kate to confirm a story. The network was reporting that the FBI and the NSA had bored a tunnel under the Russian embassy on Tunlaw Road in Washington, DC. At the end of the tunnel, sophisticated listening devices captured conversations in the embassy above and fed us a constant stream of raw intelligence. Golden information. One of the most expensive and complex tricks of espionage in history. Also a total waste of time. Even before US engineers completed the tunnel, Hanssen had keyed Russia into its existence.

During all the years I spent chasing Russians out of the embassy, I'd never realized an FBI tunnel was right under my feet. I'd never had a need to know. I traded a few curses with Kate about how Hanssen's betrayal had likely led investigators down hundreds of useless rabbit holes. If the Russians know that there's a super-secret tunnel under their embassy and we have round-the-clock analysts drinking pots of coffee and listening to every conversation, and the Russians know that we don't know that they know, what can they do? They can laugh behind their hands while feeding us false information, years of false information, every word manufactured to make us chase our own tail.

An FBI friend of mine once told me that it wasn't what Hanssen did that made him want five minutes alone in a room with the spy, it was what Hanssen *undid*. Every step we took toward securing our nation—to defeat spies and recruit assets, to follow those who wanted to do us harm, to bring out of the shadows those working against us—the Russians skipped a step ahead of us. And when the United States can't conduct counterintelligence—when the information brought back by our CIA and NSA is defective, or when we can't investigate the spies swarming around cities like Washington, DC, and New York—buildings fall and people die.

In March 2002, Robert Hanssen pled guilty to thirteen counts of espionage, one count of conspiracy to commit espionage, and a final count of attempted espionage. The maximum penalty for each count is the death sentence. Hanssen had a good lawyer. The government agreed to take the death penalty off the table and offered Hanssen life in prison with no chance of parole or reductions in his sentence for good behavior. In return, Hanssen agreed to cooperate fully and truthfully during intelligence community debriefs and to provide the FBI with all information regarding his criminal activity and espionage. Hanssen agreed that his debrief would be a "lifetime commitment" that would include answering questions; turning over all writings, documents, and materials relating to his espionage; and submitting to polygraph examinations. Hanssen ended up getting his first FBI polygraph shortly after his arrest.

The government agreed not to collect on a $1,437,000 forfeiture judgment against Hanssen that represented the proceeds of his espionage, including the $50,000 the FBI found under the Long Branch Nature Center pavilion at the Lewis drop site. Bonnie would keep a survivor's annuity portion of Hanssen's retirement pay (about $40,000 per year), the house she and Hanssen shared, and the three cars they owned. She would also learn that her husband had dishonored every aspect of their marriage. Hanssen had posted strange and vivid sexual stories about Bonnie on public message boards, installed a camera in their bedroom so that his friend Jack could watch the couple in their most private moments, and gave money and a car to an exotic dancer he met during frequent trips to a popular downtown DC strip club. On the balance sheet of their lives, Hanssen did their marriage far more harm than good.

When the magnitude of Hanssen's betrayal became public, the FBI faced a hailstorm of questions, recriminations, and finger-pointing. As Ashcroft and Freeh prepared to explain to the inspector general how the FBI had failed to identify Hanssen as the mole for so long, I was coming to understand the beauty of Hanssen's law. The FBI couldn't catch Hanssen because they were looking in all the wrong places. It wasn't until the FBI thrust me into Room 9930 with Hanssen that they introduced an unknown variable that broke Hanssen's OODA loop and beat him at his own game. Meanwhile, Hanssen taught me to be a better spy.

In May 2001, I took a deep breath and walked away from the FBI. I considered completing my law degree and returning as a special agent or Justice Department attorney, but I knew that if I were to remain in that world, only undercover operations would fulfill me. I chose Juliana, our marriage, and a career that would keep us together, not tear us apart. I improved my grades, polished my résumé, and applied to law firms.

I never forgot Hanssen's law.

In the aftermath of the investigation, the Senate Select Committee on Intelligence and the attorney general asked the Department of Justice Office of the Inspector General (OIG) to review the FBI's performance in the Hanssen case and make recommendations for reforms that would, hopefully, prevent another breach. The OIG made twenty-one recommendations. By September 2007, the FBI had implemented the majority of them, and it went on to make sweeping changes to internal security. Today, the FBI's internal counterintelligence and computer security programs hunt spies from within as voraciously as the men and women of the bureau investigate external threats. The counterintelligence walls that Hanssen dismantled over twenty-two years of espionage are now bulwarks of defense that leave few places for future moles to hide.

Most important, the FBI leapt into the computer age. Programs to detect improper computer usage and to enforce "need to know" when accessing information prevent the abuse of databases that thrilled Hanssen. The FBI's systems now audit access to critical cases in real time and sound an alarm when someone dips fingers where they don't belong. The security exploits and self-name searching in the ACS that Hanssen routinely abused are things of the past. Finally, the FBI remembered that in every organization, employees are the best security surveillance system. All FBI personnel must now graduate from security-education-and-awareness training to help them spot violations.

These changes would ensure that no spy from within the FBI ever surpassed Hanssen as the worst spy in the FBI's history. But what about the spies from without?

In December 2015, I opened a letter from the Office of Personnel Management. The OPM oversees all policy created to support federal human resources departments, with all that entails: overseeing health-care and insurance programs, administering retirement and benefit services, assisting federal agencies in hiring new employees, providing federal investigative services for background checks, and creating leadership training programs. If you've ever been a federal employee or applied for a federal job, the OPM probably has a file on you. Mine included my Social Security number; address; date and place of birth; residency, educational, and employment history; foreign travel history; and information about immediate family and personal acquaintances. The letter informed me that all of this personal information could have been stolen in a security breach that was later traced to hackers affiliated with the Chinese government. Following the letter's instructions, I signed up for the free credit-monitoring service OPM had offered as an olive branch. Numb fingers typed my information into yet another database that the US government could allow to be compromised.

I thought I knew what Hanssen had meant when he spoke of the spy in the worst possible place. But as I reread my OPM letter, the same one received by millions of current and former government employees, I realized I hadn't fully grasped his insights. That half sheet of paper changed everything.

In March 2014, the US Computer Emergency Readiness Team (US-CERT) notified OPM that data was bleeding from its network. US-CERT is the organization in the Department of Homeland Security responsible for analyzing and reducing cyber threats, providing threat warnings, and coordinating incident response to attacks. When US-CERT calls, you listen.

Over the next few weeks, OPM and US-CERT worked together to monitor an attacker in OPM's systems and gather counterintelligence. Unfortunately, while our cyber pros thought they had the breach contained, they missed an accomplice. On May 7, 2014, a second attacker posed as an employee of an OPM background investigations contractor and used the contractor's credentials to slip into the OPM system. The virtual trusted insider installed malware and created a network backdoor, all unnoticed by OPM. By the end of May, OPM pulled the plug on monitoring the first attacker, kicked them out of the system, and patted itself on the back for a job well done, not knowing they'd only taken out a sacrificial lamb. Meanwhile, the virtual trusted insider had free rein.

Cyberattackers aren't all cold, calculating criminals. Most have a sense of humor. The virtual trusted insider registered a domain named opmsecurity.org that they used as a command-and-control center to manage malware operations against OPM. The domain was registered to Steve Rogers, aka comic book superhero Captain America.

With a little help from Captain America, the virtual trusted insider stole detailed files and personal background reports on more than 22 million current and former federal employees, plus 5.6 million fingerprint records. These records included SF86 forms, used for background investigations into those seeking a security clearance. Imagine writing down your entire life story, including everything that you might say about yourself but that you'd rather no one ever find out. You've just completed a 127-page SF86 employment application. The form reviews thirteen adjudicative criteria that the government uses to decide whether to trust an employee with classified information, including supporting documentation and the notes a background investigator takes during an interview. These criteria include not only information about the applicant's allegiance to the United States and any friends or business contacts in foreign countries but also information about criminal history, sexual behavior—especially criminal or extramarital—how lousy your finances are, how much booze you drink and whether you've experimented with drugs, and even if you've ever downloaded music illegally. In any case, not the sorts of things you'd like in the hands of a foreign intelligence service.

It took OPM until April 2015 to spot the virtual trusted insider, and only after an OPM contractor notified US-CERT about suspicious network traffic related to opmsecurity.org. By then, Chinese intelligence service attackers had used OPM's servers like a public library for nearly three years. The earliest malware detected on OPM's network dated back to 2012. They'd been hiding in the worst possible place.

Hollywood would have us believe that hackers work alone, striking from dark basements and cold warehouses in places like Belarus, penetrating servers with magic codes that knife through defenses like little silver cyber ninjas. Others in our government paint a similar picture, conjuring an overweight man in his twenties sitting in a basement (probably his mother's), hammering away at a computer while pounding energy drinks and munching on bags of Fritos.

These representations are dangerously misleading. The hackers of yore are gone. Most of them have joined tech companies to help find and fix vulnerabilities in networks and systems—what's known as "white hat" hacking. Those who remain aren't lone-wolf anarchists. They're spies: intelligence service experts trained to use traditional spy craft to recruit individuals at targeted organizations and steal their access to information. These spies are sophisticated, devious, and well funded—and they're behind all of the major security breaches we've experienced this century.

We once filed documents in towering cabinets, coded and

organized by secretaries who held the keys to the kingdom. Spies would loiter in bars outside government buildings, waiting with a friendly ear for evening alcoholics looking to complain about the boss or bureaucracy. They would search out highly placed individuals who had a secret they wanted buried, those who had lost faith in America or those in financial distress who needed fast cash to make ends meet. After long recruitment periods that involved sham friendships, bribes, and often threats, these marks became the perfect inside men to extract the paper that held the secrets. But, as businesses and government agencies began to trade the file cabinets for computer systems and servers, cell phones and laptops, thumb drives and cloud-based computing, spies had to evolve.

Which is exactly what the Russians did. While the United States, stunned by the 9/11 attacks, focused on counterterrorism, Russian military and intelligence services invested in cyberwarfare. As early as 1999, Russia's state security services used cyberattacks to spread propaganda and disinformation. In 2013, Russia's Ministry of Defense established a cyber unit responsible for offensive and defensive cyber operations such as using malware to compromise critical infrastructure command and control systems. Today Russian intelligence often contracts out these attacks to nongovernmental freelance proxies, including criminal groups, mercenaries, and unemployed students. When the attacks are inevitably traced to Russian soil, the government enjoys deniability. In the last few years, computer-security experts have caught attackers with ties to the Kremlin sneaking around in systems that manage US electric power grids, air-traffic control, mass-transit systems, and oil and gas networks, to rattle off a few.

According to the US intelligence community's 2015 Worldwide Threat Assessment Report, Russia is one of the "most sophisticated nation-state actors" in cyberwarfare, and Russian hackers are renowned for their inventiveness and sheer programming power. The report goes on to warn that "Russia is taking information warfare to a new level, working to fan anti-US and anti-Western sentiment both within Russia and globally." By using Russian state-controlled media to publish false and misleading stories that discredit the United States and build sympathy for Russian positions, Putin gets to control the narrative—to devastating effect.

There are no hackers; there are only spies. Hacking is the necessary evolution of espionage. Just as the FBI had looked in all the wrong places for Hanssen, the United States and our allies had missed the mark in preventing cyberattacks. The Russians still have spies in the worst possible place. But today, many of those spies don't even know that they're compromised.

# CHAPTER 27

# THERE ARE NO HACKERS, ONLY SPIES

On Friday, May 12, 2017, North Korea started a pandemic that made the world look up and listen. Bright-red screens popped up on more than 200,000 infected computers worldwide, with a mocking message demanding that users pay $300 in Bitcoin to the attackers before a countdown timer expired and all their data disappeared forever. Those who did pay quickly learned that the ransom demand was a hoax: all the data was already gone. More than 150 countries desperately fought the attack, but resistance was futile. The malware leapt across borders at the speed of thought, worming its way through businesses and government agencies, wreaking havoc in banks and universities, shutting down airports and bringing hospitals to a standstill.

After infecting a Windows computer, the WannaCry ransomware worm encrypted files on the hard drive, making them impossible to access, then demanded a ransom payment in order to decrypt them. WannaCry was so deadly in part because it relied on some of the best hacking tools that exist—tools that were created by the US government. As espionage has evolved, American spy agencies have evolved with it. The FBI has focused on defending against the new threats. But the NSA and the CIA are on the offensive, developing secret attack tools that exploit vulnerabilities and flaws in computer operating systems to quietly infiltrate, disrupt, and collect information. Together, they create a virtual arsenal that complements the United States' kinetic military might.

Unfortunately, it's much easier to steal a few thousand lines of code than a nuclear warhead. In 2016, a group called the Shadow Brokers raided the NSA's Tailored Access Operations (TAO) program, which attacks foreign computers to gather intelligence. On April 8, 2017, they published the password to access some of TAO's secret hoard of attack tools within a ranting political post. Less than a year later, the CIA lost the keys to what WikiLeaks named Vault 7—the CIA's cyberoffensive stockpile. In one of the largest document leaks in the CIA's history, WikiLeaks released thousands of pages outlining sophisticated tools and techniques the agency allegedly used to break into mobile phones, Internet of Things (IoT) devices, and computers. The leaks are a catalog of offensive hacking tools that include instructions for compromising a wide range of common devices and computer programs, including Skype, Wi-Fi networks, PDFs, and even virus scanners. If you believe WikiLeaks, the entire archive of stolen CIA material consists of several hundred million lines of computer code. It was like putting a virtual gun in the hand of every angry hacker on the planet.

One software vulnerability lost in the NSA hack was named EternalBlue. EternalBlue works by exploiting the Microsoft Windows operating system Server Message Block, a network file-sharing protocol that allows applications on a computer to read and write to files and to request services that are on the same network. In other words, attackers could use the vulnerability not only to install malicious software on vulnerable computers but also to use that malware to "talk" to other computers on the same network and spread itself like the viruses our children routinely bring home from school. It was EternalBlue that had made WannaCry spread so quickly and effectively.

The NSA knew that EternalBlue would likely come back to haunt it. As soon as it discovered the attack, it informed

Microsoft, which immediately solved the problem by releasing an inoculation, what's typically called a "patch," which fixes the vulnerability that the virus was designed to exploit. But even though the patch was released well before the WannaCry attack took place, at least 200,000 computers hadn't installed it.

In fact, the vast majority of data breaches result from out-of-date software. In June 2017, havoc struck Ukraine. On Ukraine's Constitution Day, the country's government, banks, and largest power companies scrambled to work around computer systems locked by black screens with red letters stating "Oops, your important files are encrypted." The Ukrainian Interior Ministry called the attack, dubbed NotPetya, the biggest cyberattack in Ukraine's history. Cyber spies had launched the attack by compromising a software update mechanism built into M.E.Doc, an accounting program used by firms working with the Ukrainian government, and spread it by using the same EternalBlue exploit that WannaCry deployed. Ukraine's security service immediately accused Russia, which had begun making military incursions into Ukraine in 2014, of starting the second pandemic. The CIA later agreed with "high confidence" that the Russian GRU had launched the attack, one of many to occur after the Russian annexation of Crimea. But the damage wasn't limited to Ukraine. Nearly 100,000 computer systems fell prey to NotPetya, including systems in both Ukraine and Russia, throughout Europe and North America, and as far away as Australia.

WannaCry and NotPetya—indeed, most of the most damaging cyberattacks we've seen in the past few years—are both examples of what's called ransomware, a cunning malware that encrypts digital files and demands a ransom to unlock them. Often the attacker tricks human targets into infecting their own computer systems by enticing them to open an infected attachment or click on a malicious link. Ransomware attacks are so successful that they have grown faster than any other cybercrime in the last five years, rising from an estimated $350 million in damage costs in 2015 to $1 billion in 2016 and

$5 billion in 2017. We are not stopping the problem. Cybersecurity Ventures, a global cybersecurity researcher, predicts that global ransomware damage costs will exceed $11.5 billion annually by 2019.

Successful ransomware attackers target soft targets, those with inferior security and the most to lose if their computer systems are locked away. Small and medium-sized businesses in the health-care, technology, energy, and banking sectors are often primary targets. These attacks can break a company. According to a 2017 IBM and Ponemon Institute study, the average cost of a data breach is $3.62 million. Cybersecurity Ventures estimates cybercrime will be responsible for $6 trillion in damage annually by 2021. If data is the primary currency of our lives, cyberattackers have their eyes on the vault.

In the last two years, the most critical and devastating cyberattacks have targeted individuals via email. These "spearphishing" attacks are often highly personal, requiring dedicated analysis and research of the target, which they then leverage in order to socially engineer a person into providing account access without their knowledge. Infiltration, subterfuge, disruption, and recruitment: the tools of a spy.


On a Saturday morning in March 2016, John Podesta, chairman of the Hillary Clinton for President Campaign, received an email from the Gmail Team telling him to change his password immediately. Podesta used his john.podesta@gmail account to run the business of the campaign, weigh in on critical decisions, influence and set strategy, and occasionally call out people for foolishness or join in on attacks against Republican rivals and stubborn constituents. Like many people with an email account, Podesta used his Gmail as a kind of second brain. If someone were to read through the 50,000 or so emails of his within Google's hidden vaults, they would find a rapidly searchable catalog of his thoughts as he wrote them.

The email from the Google Team would cause even the most dispassionate person to feel a sinking sense of dread.

```
From: Google <no-reply@accounts.googlemail.com>
Date: March 19, 2016 at 4:34:30 AM EDT
To: john.podesta@gmail.com
Subject: Someone has your password

Hi John
Someone just used your password to try to sign in
to your Google Account john.podesta@gmail.com.

Details:
Saturday, 19 March, 8:34:30 UTC
IP Address: 134.249.139.239
Location: Ukraine
Google stopped this sign-in attempt. You should
change your password immediately.
CHANGE PASSWORD https://bit.ly/1PibSU0

Best,
The Gmail Team

You received this mandatory email service
announcement to update you about important
changes to your Google product or account.
```

The thought that someone might have tried to hack into his account probably didn't surprise him. The FBI had briefed the campaign about the possibility that the Chinese or Russians might try to steal their information. None of this was news to Podesta, who had written a 2014 report on cyber privacy for President Barack Obama. He knew his way around a cyber-attack or two.

Anyone with a little cybersecurity training would think the

email looked fishy. The account came from no-reply@accounts
.googlemail.com, which looked a lot like a legitimate address,
but the location was off. Ukraine. Russia had it in for those
guys, and the political fallout from Ukraine's decision to turn
its back on Mother Russia had turned Ukraine into a hot zone
for hackers and cyberwarfare. It was possible that this warning email was a Ukrainian attempt to compromise the email of
the most *I'm with Her* of Clinton's cadre. The email looked legitimate, but appearances were deceptive. Podesta ignored the
email's instructions.

Then Podesta did what all executives with far too many responsibilities have done since the beginning of time: he handed
the problem off to someone else. Podesta forwarded the email
to Sara Latham, his chief of staff, and before ten a.m., his efficient staff had forwarded the email twice and received the counsel of Charles Delavan, the IT helpdesk manager for the Hillary
campaign. Latham and Podesta received Delavan's reply:

```
This is a legitimate email. John needs to
change his password immediately, and ensure
that two-factor authentication is turned on
[for] his account.

He can go to this link: https://myaccount.
google.com/security to do both. It is absolutely
imperative that this is done ASAP.
```

Delavan meant to say "this is **not** a legitimate email," but
damn you, autocorrect. Had he picked up the phone and had
a conversation with Sara Latham or, better yet, gotten in his
car and driven over to Podesta's house, no one would have
clicked on the link. In Delavan's defense, had Podesta's team
followed Delavan's instructions to the letter, Clinton's chief of
staff would have changed his password from within Google's
secure website. Had the Clinton campaign pursued sufficient

cybersecurity, Podesta would have used an internal and monitored hillaryclinton.com address that leveraged two-factor authentication and robust encryption rather than a personal
Gmail account. Instead, one click changed everything. Latham
included Milia Fisher, Podesta's special assistant, on the chain,
and although it is unclear whether Podesta, Fisher, or another
staffer clicked on the link in the original email, the act trans-
formed Podesta from a kingmaker to a virtual trusted insider—a
compromised mole who had no knowledge of his treachery.

The link transported Podesta to a fake website mocked up
to look like the Google Gmail password-security page. He entered his current username and password and then the new
password he crafted to keep the Ukrainians out of his business,
thank you very much. He then closed the site and went back to
his day. Mission accomplished.

Within moments, Russian cyber spies compromised Podesta's account. The email was sent by Aleksey Viktorovich
Lukashev, a senior lieutenant in Russian military Unit 26165 located in Moscow. He was using a Russian-based email account,
hi.mymail@yandex.com, which he spoofed to make it look like
it came from Google. The use of Ukraine as the "location" on
the email address and a corresponding IP address that led to
a Ukrainian city was gallows humor. Russia had test-fired the
same attack against Ukraine to disrupt the most pivotal election campaign in the nation's history—one that grew out of a
February overthrow of the prior pro-Russian government. On
May 21, 2014, four days before the election, a hacktivist group
called CyberBerkut triggered an attack on Ukraine's Central
Election Commission computers. The attack destroyed hardware, corrupted software, and disrupted the internal network.
Twelve minutes before polls closed on Election Day, CyberBerkut posted false election results to the election commission's
website. Russia's TV Channel One aired the fake information.

The Russians, of course, did not stop with Podesta either. In
March 2016 Lukashev and his comrades compromised at least

ten computers and numerous individuals at the Democratic Congressional Campaign Committee (DCCC) through email attacks. The Russian spies used a control server they leased in Arizona to monitor individual employees' computer activity or steal passwords. They then used this compromised network access to spread the attack. In April 2016, the Democratic National Committee discovered a breach that the FBI had been warning them about for months. The FBI had informed the DNC in September 2015 that Russian hackers had compromised at least one DNC computer. The DNC IT department found no malware after scanning the system and apparently chose not to share the FBI's concerns with the DNC's senior leadership. In November 2015, the FBI called again. Now the DNC computer was transmitting information back to Russia. A few months later, Podesta clicked his devastating email link.

A month after that, the DNC finally installed cybersecurity tools that spotted the breach. Too little, too late. The Russians had already stolen what they needed. When you don't hunt the threat, the threat hunts you.

Democrats wrung their hands as private emails and confidential memoranda appeared online like revenants, resurrected to destroy the party. In July, WikiLeaks published nearly 20,000 emails from the DCCC and DNC's servers. As an encore, WikiLeaks distributed nearly 60,000 pages of emails from Podesta's account in October and November 2016. The fallout included the resignation of the DNC chairwoman and most of her top party aides, a scandal that sidelined a number of leading Democrats, weeks of negative press that called into question the honesty and integrity of the Hillary campaign, and unlimited fodder for Trump's Twitter account.

A July 13, 2018, indictment from the Robert Mueller investigation accused Lukashev and eleven other Russian GRU officers of hacking into the computers of US persons involved in the 2016 presidential election, stealing documents from those persons, and staging the release of that information in order to interfere with the election. To mask their connection to Russia, the twelve cyber spies used false identities and exploited a network of computers located across the world funded by cryptocurrency such as Bitcoin. These "middle server" computers acted as proxies to obscure the connection between the Russian attackers and their victims at the DCCC, DNC, and Hillary Clinton campaign. Essentially, the Russians created a modern Moonlight Maze.

Russia has long sought to influence and undermine elections and the political process of rival nations. In attacking the DNC, Russia played the role of the provocateur, testing the United States' response at the same time it sought to destabilize us. If recruiting sources to steal information is Espionage 101, then Russia's attack on the DNC, its propaganda meddling in the Syrian conflict, its infrastructure attacks on Ukraine, and the electoral interference with then-candidate, now French president Emmanuel Macron's campaign all constitute spying on the master's level. The Russians acted in order to see how we'd react, and in the process we showed them the cracks in our systems.

The influence campaign against the US election did not stop with the release of damaging information stolen from the Clinton campaign. Russia also blended covert intelligence operations with outreach through state and private media, using paid social-media trolls and official news stories to establish a narrative that the US election system was compromised at best and corrupt at worst.

In September 2016, the cybersecurity company Carbon Black, Inc., conducted a study of voters in the United States to determine whether Russia's meddling in our election had American citizens concerned. As Carbon Black's national security strategist, I was keen to learn how Russia's espionage could affect the hearts and minds of American citizens. The sobering results showed that more than half of US voters thought that the upcoming election would be affected by cyberattacks.

Despite constant media appearances by cyber experts, including me, assuring Americans that our voting system—which, unlike Ukraine's, is decentralized and remains primarily unconnected to the Internet—could not be compromised, half of those surveyed thought our electronic voting machines could be hacked during the election sufficiently to change its outcome. One in five voters was so concerned about this possibility that they considered sitting the election out—which would mean more than 15 million voters potentially staying away from the polls over cybersecurity concerns.

In July 2017, we decided to check back in. Carbon Black polled 5,000 eligible voters to determine how all the talk about election cybersecurity that dominated the media might affect upcoming elections. This time one in *four* voters said they would consider not voting in upcoming elections over cybersecurity fears. More than 200 million voters are registered in the United States—that's more than 50 million people potentially sitting out the 2018 midterms or the 2020 presidential election. Russia doesn't have to change a single vote to influence our elections. It only has to make Americans think it can.

A January 2017 Intelligence Community Assessment called the Russian efforts to influence the 2016 US presidential election "the most recent expression of Moscow's longstanding desire to undermine the US-led liberal democratic order, but these activities demonstrated a significant escalation in directness, level of activity, and scope of effort compared to previous operations." In other words, Russia is only getting started. And other countries, like Iran, China, and North Korea, have invested wholesale in Russia's playbook.

Influencing the hearts and minds of American voters is only the tip of the Russian cyberattack spear. Russia has long sought a tactical military advantage against the United States to complement its aggressive cyber espionage and disinformation efforts. In our connected world, any future military engagement will be fought on a new battleground—rather than missiles, it will be cyberattacks that seek to disrupt, deny, and destroy.

On March 15, 2018, the Department of Homeland Security and the FBI issued a Joint Technical Alert that highlights Russia's attempts to compromise our critical infrastructure. The DHS and FBI released the alert to coordinate with new US sanctions against Russian agencies, individuals, and intelligence services charged with meddling in the 2016 US presidential election, including the Russian "Troll Farm" that used Facebook ads to exploit divisions in American politics. The alert highlights a multistage intrusion campaign by Russian cyber spies to target and compromise US government agencies and the US energy, nuclear, commercial, water, aviation, and critical manufacturing sectors dating back as early as 2016. Although this is the first time the US government has publicly confirmed that foreign attacks are targeting our infrastructure, cybersecurity professionals have long known that numerous countries have probed for ways to shut down our nation's essential functions.

Russia has long succeeded in stealing our data. More recently it has exploited the political fractures and divisions that make us shout inward instead of scrutinizing outward threats. The next phase of Russian active measures is to directly disrupt—and perhaps threaten—our lives. To beat Russia and other foreign countries, terrorist groups, and fringe organization cyberattackers, the United States needs a different playbook. We'll need a new way of thinking to beat Hanssen's law.

# CHAPTER 28

# UP ALL NIGHT

Protecting my PC, locking down servers, backing up data, securing the cloud—all of these issues keep me up at night. Ever wondered if someone is watching you through your laptop camera or the new home-security system you just bought off eBay, or maybe through your new smart-home device? Did you open an email attachment or click on a link that made you think twice when your screen flickered? Do you have concerns about the future of autonomous cars and networked robotics and whether these innovations will open us up to future tragedy?

I do. After leaving the FBI, I realized that it wasn't enough to ride through towns shouting that the cyber spies were coming. My success in Room 9930 had come when I'd broken Hanssen's OODA loop of his action and my reaction. Once I made the spy react to me, I'd discovered where he kept the information that would undo him.

On the streets as a ghost, we don't blindly follow targets from point A to B. Surveillance is an art form that predicts targets' behavior and makes judgment calls on where they will be before they make a turn or take a step. Ghosts don't follow people. We hunt them.

Understanding where a spy will attack is the first step in neutralizing espionage. Actively monitoring all activity in that worst possible place is the next goal. Organizations that combine cybersecurity defense with active threat hunting thwart spies, both from without and within. Even wannabe spies.

Gregory Allen Justice worked the graveyard shift as a mechanical engineer for a US defense contractor in California. His job focused on operational security testing for commercial and military satellites deployed by the Air Force, the Navy, and NASA. While he did not have access to information classified by the US government, Justice did work on defense-group systems that help the US military communicate. Not the sort of information you'd like the Russians to get their hands on.

In early 2016, Justice was brooding over his financial woes. His wife had a medical condition that confined her to their bedroom. In three years, Justice had paid nearly $6,000 in medical expenses to doctors, hospitals, and clinics. In March, he had told his wife to cancel all of her medical appointments for the foreseeable future. Not only were they broke, but there was no way to get her to the appointments: his car wouldn't start, and he didn't have the money to fix it. Justice's situation looked grim, but he had a plan. Gregory Justice would become a spy. The name he chose for himself: Brian.

The world of espionage fascinated Justice. He loved James Bond and Jason Bourne and was fully caught up on the first season of *The Americans*. In the past two years he'd prepared himself for his clandestine career by purchasing $4,344 in online courses. He mastered "Spy Escape and Evasion," explored "Delta Defense LLC," and learned from "Legally Concealed" and "Fight Fast." He located addresses and phone numbers for the Russian embassy in Washington, DC, and the Russian consulate general in San Francisco. All he needed was something of value to trade.

In November 2015, Justice plugged a USB thumb drive into his defense contractor workstation and accessed folders of files that contained satellite-design information. He had swiped his security badge at the entrance to the defense group building where he worked on his employer's campus. He'd swiped his badge again at the door to his work area, then inserted the badge into his computer to log in with a unique PIN. He'd typed the PIN again to access a collaboration and storage workgroup database controlled by an access list. Much like Hanjuan Jin a decade before him, Justice took the secrets he could use to buy himself out of debt. He also had to keep his superspy lifestyle going.

While his wife lay in her bed, Justice kept a supermodel on the side. It didn't matter that Justice hadn't ever made the trip to her Long Beach apartment. The woman Justice knew only as Chay looked great in the pictures she had emailed to him. In return he sent her cash. Loads of it. From December 2015 until May 2016, Justice sent Chay a total of $21,420 and gifts through Amazon.com totaling $5,916.09, which included a grill, furniture, a Dyson fan, two televisions, and an iPhone 6s.

Successfully infiltrate his employer. *Check*. Keep his Bond Girl happy. *Check*. Now Justice needed to get paid.

He mailed a printout of a satellite schematic to a captain at the Russian embassy in Washington, DC, but then couldn't get the guy on the phone when he called. Justice called again and left a message for the captain and waited to hear back. A few days later, in February 2016, his phone rang.

The man on the other end identified himself as a representative of Russian intelligence and set up a meet. Over the next four months, Justice met with his new SVR handler five times and shared a number of phone conversations. During their first meeting, Justice offered him the moon: "So what I'm offering is basically everything on our servers, on our computers. The plans, the test procedures, that's what I have access to." He asked his contact to call him "Brian" and said, "I know it's not like real life, but I like spy movies."

Each time they met, Justice handed over secrets on a thumb drive in return for an envelope of cash. He'd count the hundred-dollar bills and sign a receipt. He would return to his overnight shift at the office and load another thumb drive with satellite information to trade. As soon as he had a free moment, he'd send his Russian money directly to Chay.

Justice never made it to his sixth meeting. In July 2016, the FBI arrested him and ended "Brian's" short espionage career. The first time Justice had stuck an unauthorized USB drive into his workstation, his employer alerted the DOJ. The FBI sent a team to ghost Justice and intercepted his call to the Russian embassy. Much as they had built a case against Earl Pitts, FBI agents began a false-flag operation and used an undercover FBI employee to dupe Justice.

In total, the FBI paid Justice $3,500 for restricted satellite technology that thankfully never made it to Russian intelligence. Caught red-handed, Justice pled guilty to one count of attempted espionage and one count of attempted violation of the Arms Export Control Act, which prohibits sending certain technology to a foreign power. On September 18, 2017, a federal judge sentenced Justice to five years in prison. Justice made a pathetic spy, but had a good lawyer. He had faced a maximum of thirty-five years.

Justice's employer had no idea that one of its employees was playing spy. But it didn't need to, because it was monitoring the worst possible place: the database that contained the company's most sensitive information. The best security technology focuses on the place closest to the human that will either make a mistake, as Podesta did, or turn traitor, as Justice tried to do. We call these points of access to information "endpoints." The moment Justice stuck a thumb drive into his workstation—an endpoint—his employer's security tools logged the potential breach. Security professionals examined the threat and called in reinforcements.

Endpoints are the new doorways into the worst possible place, and hunting threats requires that we secure all of them.

Without security that actively hunts threats, a rogue employee like Hanjuan Jin or Justice can steal information directly from an employer or a government agency. But it is not enough to focus security inward. Even the most security-conscious employee can be tricked into opening an attachment or clicking a link. Humans will always make mistakes. By turning each endpoint into the most secure room in cyberspace, we can prevent most breaches and limit the damage done by the ones that sneak through. By collaborating across a vast network of endpoints that leverage big data and analytics, instantly updated from the cloud to allow us to orient to the best decision, we may be able to prevent all of them.

Imagine a collaboration of consumers, organizations, agencies, and businesses aligned in a common network of shared information. Any attempt to breach a single laptop or execute malware through an unfortunate mouse click by one member will instantly inoculate every other device on the network. Deep-learning analysis of all these devices in the cloud will allow a cybersecurity AI to identify and even predict attacks. An entire community of cybersecurity operations will simplify down to a single recurring OODA loop, one that continually resets and defeats attackers.

Nobody wants to go back to file cabinets and typewriters. But new tools require new forms of security. Hanssen was just the beginning, and wannabes like Justice serve as a stark warning of what the future may hold. It's not enough to stop the spies who are already within. We must hunt the threat before it hunts us. Otherwise, one email or one misplaced thumb drive may be all it takes to undermine the foundations of American society.

Hanssen and I never defined "information assurance" during the two months we spent together at the FBI's newest section, but we achieved the objective of the Information Assurance/Technology Team. We taught the FBI a new law for espionage's cyber revolution. In the years since, I've updated Hanssen's law to fit our modern espionage problems. In a nod to my old boss, I call it O'Neill's law:

*Hacking is the necessary evolution of espionage.*
*There are no hackers; there are only spies.*
*We must hunt the threat before the threat hunts us.*
*Because the spy is always in the worst possible place.*

If cybersecurity is the future of counterintelligence, the future is yesterday. In order to prevent breaches, cybersecurity must leverage real-time analytics and mountains of data instantly to identify vulnerabilities before the attack occurs, spot attacks as they happen, and future-proof the attacks of tomorrow. Only then can cyber defenses orient to decisions fast enough to outpace increasingly aggressive and clever attacks. We focus security on the endpoint to move that security as close to the human operator who will make a mistake that lets the spies in or, like Robert Hanssen, turn traitor. But the solution isn't as simple as securing our devices. Amateurs may hack machines, but professionals hack people.

The Hanssen investigation teaches us that the best spies and attackers embrace advances in technology to carry out traditional espionage goals. Cybercrime has followed the spy playbook. All attacks are now espionage, and to defeat the wave of continually evolving attacks, cyber professionals must become spy hunters. Understand the attackers, discover their flaws and vulnerabilities, actively seek them out, and neutralize them when they attack. Security is an exhausting journey that defies even a momentary lapse of guard. Only by hunting the cyber spies will we be able to create a world safe from cyberattacks. Only then can we beat O'Neill's law.

# EPILOGUE

July 2001

Dim light stretched through the low windows into my living room. The afternoon had crashed into evening without warning. I thought about turning on a lamp, but left the moment to shadows. Some conversations sounded best in the dark.

My brother snatched a Jack Daniel's bottle from the coffee table. He poured two glasses with the cultivated flourish of a bartender. David had spent long evenings slinging spirits across stained oak bars in London, saloon counters in Austin, wild clubs in New York City, and finally at a quiet little beach bar near Hollywood. He'd long since traded his bartender license for a Screen Actors Guild card, but he could still make a perfect pour.

We clinked glasses. Most people forget that Washington, DC, was built on top of a swamp. After nearly a year, Juliana and I still hadn't convinced our landlord to repair our struggling air conditioner. The thin trickle that struggled out of the vent barely flapped a purple ribbon Juliana had tied there when we moved in. My glass sweated condensation against the sticky humidity that slowed the nation's capital to a crawl. The lone ice cube floating in the brown liquid wouldn't last long.

"So you're telling me," David said, "that this guy all over the news. The master spy. You caught him?"

"I *helped* catch him."

The last time I'd seen Hanssen, I'd told him, *I'll catch you later.* I doubt he appreciated the joke. Days before my conversation with David, Hanssen had made a deal to plead guilty to fifteen counts of espionage and conspiracy to commit espionage. I had since left the FBI, but still jumped each time the phone rang. If the judge rejected Hanssen's plea and sent the case to trial, Kate would call me in to testify, a possibility I was dreading.

Despite my knowing better, I'd asked Kate whether I could visit Hanssen in the Pennsylvania federal penitentiary where he awaited the judge's decision on his guilty plea. I'd wanted closure on a case that had dominated and defined my young life.

The FBI debated and then denied my request. Kate put it best: "If he knows it was you that betrayed him, he'll rattle the bars of his cage."

"Okay." David rolled his eyes. "You helped catch him. But that was your *boss*?"

"You wouldn't want this guy to be your boss," I said. "Did I tell you about the time he practically massaged my back?"

I told David about Hanssen's favorite nickname for me. And how he would call out his "idiot" for every imagined mistake. I described the way I had surrounded my desk with chairs to enforce my personal space. My eyes fell as I recalled near misses and desperate gambles. The case had taken everything from me and had left me wrung out and empty.

"Why did he do it?"

I shrugged and hid my smile. "No one knows."

David's sigh called to mind years spent in a small room fighting over which of us got the top bunk. My grin broke through. "But I have a pretty good idea."

Most of us rinse and repeat our lives. We are content to wake and sleep, work and play. To carve out happiness in family and friends, children, and achievement. But some want more. Robert Philip Hanssen was the greatest spy in US history. His reign lasted over two decades in a time when espionage required immense skill and patience. Breaking his record will be next to impossible in a world of WikiLeaks and ransomware.

Hanssen's dreams demanded greatness. Heroes work and toil to scrape out their place in history. Villains take shortcuts. But both heroes and villains stretch to touch the infinite. Spying made Hanssen feel that he belonged to something far greater than himself. To the Russians he was an unknown national hero. To his family, he was a provider and a role model with uncompromising morals. I've always viewed Hanssen as a tortured man who balanced his love of family and religious faith against the pulse-pounding euphoria that rushed through him every time he dropped secrets under a bridge or saw a line of tape on a telephone pole.

During a quiet moment near the end of our time together, Hanssen sat across my desk from me and said, "Children are amazing. The best of what we are. You leave something of yourself behind in your children, Eric. They make you immortal." I didn't understand my old boss then, but I do now. The birth of my own children years later completed this last of Hanssen's lessons. Our children reflect the best of what we are and what we have to give. Hanssen had played the villain for most of his adult life, but he had also brought good into the world in the children he left behind. I'd like to think that he chose to plead guilty and abandon a lengthy court battle to keep his family out of the spotlight, and to ensure that they kept their home and part of his pension.

In the sentencing memorandum, the US attorney wrote: "For all the words that have been written about him, for all the psychological analyses, the speculations about his motivation, and the assessments of his character, this is, at the end of the day, all that really warrants being said about Hanssen. He is a traitor and that singular truth is his legacy."

"Hanssen's attorney argued that Hanssen was insane," I told my brother. I flicked on the desk lamp that Juliana had bought me when I left the FBI and joined DLA Piper as a new associate. Light pooled across my computer workbench and tinted everything the green of the glass shade. "Hanssen must have hated that."

"I read that his psychologist said he had demons." David shivered. "Maybe he was the demon."

Hanssen's insults and quips, morals and lessons rattled around in my head. Good and bad. "He wasn't a demon," I said. "He was cold and calculating. He planned every act with the precision of a master machinist. He knew every act of spying was wrong, but did it anyway. But he wasn't completely evil. He was . . . gray."

Hanssen had refused to answer a single question throughout almost ten months of sweat-soaked, stale-coffee interrogations: *Why did you do it?* His words—*The "why" doesn't matter*—fit his personality. He pled guilty to his crime in return for his life and to ensure that his family kept their home, cars, and his twenty-five-year FBI veteran pension. The plea agreement required Hanssen to submit to a lifetime of questions from four commissions. Many of his interrogators repeated the same questions until Hanssen could memorize each word. The several hundred hours of debriefings included polygraph examinations, psychological evaluations and testing, and a requirement that Hanssen waive both attorney-client privilege and a priest-penitent privilege.

Our investigation had brought him low, but the master spy clutched at one last fragment of power. The interrogators emptied Hanssen's mind, but could not breach the tiny lockbox where Hanssen hid his "why." He'll likely take that answer to his grave.

The FBI had the first crack at Hanssen's debrief. After all, the spy had gutted the bureau in a way that would take decades to repair. The CIA director formed a Hanssen Damage Assessment Team (HDAT) to assess the interagency repercussions of Hanssen's breach. Judge William Webster, the only person to have served as both FBI director and director of the CIA, led the Commission for the Review of FBI Security Programs. Finally, the inspector general of the Department of Justice got a crack at the captured spy. Each of the four commissions wrote a letter to the US attorney to evaluate nearly a year of wringing secrets out of Hanssen. If they found his answers honest, Hanssen's plea deal would stand. If the balance of commissions called Hanssen a liar, the spy would face the death penalty.

The US attorney received four letters and probably wished he could go back in time and insist on three commissions, or five. The FBI and Webster Commission judged Hanssen's responses predominantly truthful. HDAT and the CIA gave Hanssen a resounding thumbs-down. No man wishes to hold the fate of another in his hands. Fortunately for Hanssen, the US attorney split the difference in Hanssen's favor. On May 10, 2002, a US district judge sentenced Hanssen to fifteen consecutive sentences of life in prison without the possibility of parole.

"The FBI ostracized Hanssen," I said. "He wanted to be James Bond, but they made him a librarian." I thought about the piano that Juliana and I still couldn't afford. "The boss . . . Hanssen . . . needed money to support his growing family and couldn't make ends meet."

David frowned. "He did it for money? That's lame, man."

"In the beginning, yes." I started to pace. Four steps from the desk to the window and then back again. "But after enough promotions he made enough to survive." I looked at David. "Imagine the thing that you are the best at—or that you want to be the best at."

"Like acting."

"Sure. Imagine you're Leonardo DiCaprio after *Titanic*. Literally on top of the world. Do you give it up because you've just made enough money to keep you comfortable?"

David smirked. "I wouldn't give it up."

"Neither could Hanssen. Spying made him more than himself. He was a cookie-cutter FBI agent, but he was a master spy."

"But you said he was gray?" David shrugged. "Was there anything good about him?"

We are all chasing shadows, good and bad. Hanssen exploited the FBI's flaws and did incalculable damage to this country. But his interrogation and the countless pages of analysis that followed dragged the FBI into the modern world. The bureau instituted mandatory polygraph examinations before upgrading clearances. Task forces began to look inward before a disgruntled employee could turn traitor. Dinosaur systems like the ACS were scrapped for modern databases with strict audit trails. The FBI's Laboratory Division, Operational Technology Division, Criminal Justice Information Services (CJIS) Division, and the Information Technology Branch pushed to hire STEM professionals to carry the FBI into the information age. A Cyber Division was formed to catch cyber terrorists, cyber spies, and computer criminals. Agents learned to turn on computers. Everybody got a mouse.

"Want to hear something weird?" I asked.

"Anything!"

"I heard a rumor about Hanssen's last drop. More like a whisper of a rumor."

David leaned forward. Our conversation had haunted the room and I wished I had turned on more lights.

"In his final drop to the Russians, Hanssen left a final present for those he called his friends." I jabbed my chest with a thumb. "My name and information, with a note to recruit me. Hanssen told them I'd make a very good spy."

He was right.

# AUTHOR'S NOTE

February 18, 2018

I began writing this book in May 2001 after I walked out the front doors of the FBI's Washington Field Office for the last time. The investigation had isolated me not just from my friends and family but also from my colleagues and team members in the FBI. With the exception of Kate, I could discuss the case with no one. A great deal of emotional baggage builds up when an investigation closes you into a dark box. I put it all in writing. I recorded the facts of the case in classified surveillance logs that I turned over to the FBI. I dumped the rest into private journals and notes, often rambling, that memorialized the oddest conversations with Hanssen and reminded me which days locked in Room 9930 made the biggest impact on my life.

I had left the FBI to resurrect my marriage and to practice law. In the cracks between reading legal briefs and arguing cases, reconnecting with family and friends, and all the overdue quiet moments with my wife, I wrote the first draft of this book. But I couldn't share it with anyone until I received permission from the FBI to tell my story. The FBI had kept my role in the investigation secret, even from the boss himself. The *Affidavit in Support of Criminal Complaint, Arrest Warrant and Search Warrants* filed in the US District Court in *United States v. Robert Philip Hanssen* places a great deal of previously classified information into the public record; I relied on it heavily in writing this book. But the 103-page document only tangentially mentions my role when discussing the smoking gun that won the case: Hanssen's Palm IIIx.

The FBI denied my request to tell my story until July 6, 2001, after Hanssen pled guilty and I would no longer be required to testify at my old boss's trial. By then, a number of books about the Hanssen story, all of different flavors, were already in the hands of the big publishing houses. In February 2007 Universal Studios released *Breach* on the six-year anniversary of Hanssen's arrest. The movie is a thrilling dramatization of the investigation, but it fictionalized enough events to remind me that I still had a story to tell. The fame Universal Studios lent to me led to an enthusiastic public-speaking career. Over time, as I left the second biggest law firm in the world and started my own investigative group, accepted a position as general counsel with a humanitarian NGO, and ultimately became the national security strategist for the top global cybersecurity company, I formulated what would become O'Neill's law. My keynotes transitioned from speaking about the Hanssen story to tying Hanssen's lessons into my own life experiences and why we can't stop cyberattacks. I spoke about cyber spies and the world started to listen.

At a Charleston, South Carolina, Renaissance Weekend over New Year's 2016 I met my agent, Becky Sweren. Becky had just heard me deliver a keynote titled "Cybersecurity in the Age of Espionage" that connected the dots from Hanssen's espionage through the rise of Russia and why the majority of spies are now cyberattackers. She found me later and in a quiet moment encouraged me to write a book proposal. Becky met my skepticism head-on with words that sent my fingers to my keyboard on my flight home: "This is a story that needs to be told."

But I had plenty of help. To fact-check my recollections, I consulted the aforementioned *Affidavit in Support of Criminal Complaint*, written by Special Agent Stefan Pluta, along with publicly available documents related to Hanssen's indictment, plea agreement, and sentencing. I also leaned on the Office of the Inspector General's August 14, 2003, *Review of the FBI's Performance in Deterring, Detecting, and Investigating the Espionage Activities of Robert Philip Hanssen* to outline where the FBI made mistakes that allowed Hanssen to spy and how the FBI walked through the crucible of lessons learned to emerge stronger. Every investigator (and spy) knows that public records are his best friends. For background on the Hanjuan Jin, Gregory Allen Justice, and David Sheldon Boone cases, I scrutinized court filings and testimony.

Writing a narrative account seventeen years after the fact required a great deal of searching through my memories. I had journals and an ancient first draft for my conversations with Hanssen, but I reconstructed other conversations using my best recollection. For example, in chapter 4 I recall discussing the FBI's need to computerize into the modern era with Mr. Dies, but I cannot claim that the conversation is verbatim. In some cases I blended two separate conversations together to assist the pacing of the book. Most notably, in chapter 9, I blended two separate conversations with Kate (one that occurred in a restaurant with one that happened in a car) into a single scene across the Potomac. Neither Kate nor I can remember the name of the restaurant. In chapter 19 I moved the conversation with Hanssen about my mother's Parkinson's disease to the scene with Hanssen at church. Mom would have liked the Catholic Information Center setting more than a conversation across my desk in 9930. Also in chapter 19 I moved a conversation with Kate about Brian Kelley a bit earlier into the narrative. I was thinking a lot about the Kelley case then, and the conversation just fit better during the search of Hanssen's office. In chapter 22 I combined conversations that actually took place with Hanssen in two separate car trips into one trip to Invicta. Finally, the conversation with my father in chapter 24 over a glass of scotch at the beach house actually happened in their home in Maryland. I hope you'll agree that the nautical bar is a better setting.

Most of my FBI colleagues are no longer actively serving this many years after the case. I did not change anyone's name and enjoyed rekindling old friendships as I asked permission and ran through old stories. I did change the code names for the ghosts who show up in a few places; where I could not recall a person's name, I left it out.

I asked for permission to visit Hanssen in his cell at Supermax penitentiary, but I was denied. If I could visit him, I'd ask why he did it, even though I'm pretty sure I know.

I am indebted to my agent, Becky Sweren, who championed the book and inspired me to write it. To coax an old ghost out of the shadows is no small feat. My editor, Emma Berry, guided me when I might have rambled and reined in my propensity to sometimes overtell a story. Her editorial skills are reflected in all the pages of this book. My fortune in finding Becky and Emma reaffirms my belief in divine inspiration.

First drafts often miss a few signposts and get lost along the way. My friends Stephen "Kiwi" Roderick and Captain Christian Spain caught my most glaring mistakes and made me laugh in the way only close friends can with their many comments in the margins. Ryan "Murph" Murphy from Carbon Black tweaked some of the cybersecurity portions. Gene McClelland set me straight on a few facts that I misremembered and reminded me that Hanssen at one point sent the entire FBI on a wild-goose chase. Richard Garcia and I swapped stories from his side of the investigation. I never realized how much of a watchful eye he kept on me from his office down the hall. Kate Alleman shed light on my fuzziest recollections. Her laugh is as infectious now as it was back then.

Finally, I am grateful to my wife, Juliana, who stood by me during the worst of times so we could reach the best. We finally bought that piano she always wanted. When I watch her teach our daughter Hannah to play, I fall in love all over again. *Das ist wunderbar!*

*Eric O'Neill*
*Washington, DC*
*February 18, 2018*

## About the Author

**Eric O'Neill** is a cybersecurity expert and former FBI counterterrorism and counterintelligence operative. He is the founder of The Georgetown Group, a premier investigative and security services firm; serves as national security strategist for Carbon Black; and is the General Counsel for Global Communities, an international charity. He lectures internationally about espionage and national security, cybersecurity, hacking and fraud, and corporate diligence and defense, and has appeared as a national security expert on CNN and Fox. His writing has appeared in *The Boston Globe*, *The Hill*, *TechCrunch*, and *Mashable*. O'Neill is a graduate of Auburn University and the George Washington University School of Law.